High School Essays

High School Essays

N.C. Sinha

PRABHAT
PRAKASHAN

Published by
PRABHAT PRAKASHAN PVT. LTD.
4/19 Asaf Ali Road,
New Delhi-110 002 (INDIA)
e-mail: prabhatbooks@gmail.com

ISBN 978-93-5186-615-2
HIGH SCHOOL ESSAYS
by Shri N.C. Sinha

Edition
2025

Price
₹ 750.00 (Rupees Seven Hundred Fifty only)

Printed at
Narula Printers, Delhi

To My
Fond Memories of
Sankardev College, Shillong

Author's Note

Why should we write an essay?

Students cannot be blamed for asking such questions, especially when writing, as it might appear to them, has nearly been replaced by messaging through Internet communication system. They are more familiar with tweeting than writing; and for tweeting, they barely have space for 140 characters. It means they must make do with fewer than 140 letters for saying what they want to say. When they can make do with so little, why should they expend more words to write essays? Such questions will continue to nag them unless they know what exactly the essay wants to say; and why it is desirable for an essay to say what it wants to say and in the manner it wants to say. Finding answers to these questions will explain and define what an essay is and why it is necessary to write essays. An understanding of this will make them understand the necessity of writing of essays. The pleasure of writing can never be replaced by anything else, no matter what the level of electronic progress.

Essay is basically the act of 'trying out' or an act of attempting to accomplish something. It is also an analytic or interpretive literary composition. Essays, therefore, essentially reveal the personality of the writer besides giving his/her viewpoints on a specific subject matter. Essays help us express ourselves, our thoughts, our ideas and our perceptions about things we are associated with or about things we are impacted with or wish to have an impact on. Essays not only provide the required space and tool, they also let us leisurely saunter along. Tweeting or emailing cannot achieve this. This answers why we should write essays. We should write because we cannot always speak out minds coherently. Spoken words can be lost in translation, not the written words. That is the chief reason why we must write essays.

But writing essays requires some discipline. Since writing an essay means attempting to achieve something, it is necessary to follow certain methodologies and the writer of an essay must have the perseverance to undertake the job of writing. A systematically collected idea, facts and figures about any given topic should be presented elegantly and effectively to make it worth reading. Whatever the purpose of an essay, the basic structure of an essay remains the same irrespective of the topic.

Writing of an essay begins with the selection of the topic. It then becomes necessary to make an outline of the ideas that are expected to be covered. An essay must begin with an introduction. Introduction sets the tone. This is followed by writing of the body, which contains main points in support of the ideas. There may be sub-points which need to be elaborated. After all the points are covered, it is important to write the conclusion.

There is no fixed length of an essay. It could be written in just about 100 words or even in several thousand words. Generally speaking, essays are not very long. But they need not be too small either. On an average, an essay in one thousand words should be adequate. A range of 1,000 to 1,500 is generally accepted as ideal for competitive exams and that is the length of the majority of the essays in this book. The essays contained in this book are based on issues that are relevant and crucial for our understanding of the life around. Students will find in this book issues that concern them and their life. It is not simply a book of essays, but a book of issues as well. Students will find its usefulness not only in the topics but also in the data-related information it contains. The book may also be used for reference purposes. The contents are retrieved from archives and from authentic sources. The book does not contain any frivolous information that can be trifled with.

I sincerely hope that students will find this book radically different and quite useful as reference book as well. This book is different in content and treatment from the customary essay books available in the market.

—N.C. Sinha

Patna

Contents

Author's Note 7

1. India – The Land and its People 13
2. The President of India – Pranab Mukherjee 17
3. Prime Minister of India – Narendra Modi 20
4. Mohan Das Karam Chand Gandhi 30
5. Nelson Mandela 33
6. Subhash Chandra Bose 37
7. Sardar Vallabhbhai Patel 41
8. Lal Bahadur Shastri 45
9. Dr. A.P.J. Abdul Kalam 49
10. Atal Bihari Vajpayee 57
11. Chhatrapati Shivaji 63
12. Jhansi Ki Rani 68
13. Dr. Sarvapalli Radhakrishnan 72
14. Ashoka the Great 79
15. Festivals and Festivities in India 84
16. Durga Puja 88
17. Holi 91

18. Id-ul-Fitr 95
19. Diwali 98
20. Chhath Festival 102
21. Christmas 105
22. Republic Day 108
23. Independence Day 111
24. Teachers' Day 115
25. Visit to a Monument 119
26. Visit to a Hill Station 122
27. Visit to a Museum 127
28. Visit to a Book Fair 131
29. My Banker 135
30. Electronic Media—The News Channels 139
31. Internet—Way of Life 143
32. Newspaper 146
33. Population Explosion 150
34. Terrorism 153
35. Poverty 157
36. Corruption 161
37. Pollution 165
38. Global Warming 169
39. Internal Security 173
40. Uniform Civil Code 177
41. Reservation 181
42. How the Constitution has Worked 184

43. Health Services in India 189
44. Status of Higher Education in India 192
45. Pseudo Secularism 196
46. The Supreme Court of India 200
47. The High Court 204
48. Indian Languages 208
49. Women Empowerment 212
50. Inter-State Relations 217
51. The Public Services 221
52. The State of Jammu and Kashmir 226
53. The Malaise of Non-Governance 231
54. Importance of English in India 238
55. Practising Democracy in India 242
56. Fundamental Rights 246
57. Fundamental Duties 250
58. Central Bureau of Investigation 253
59. Globalisation 257
60. The Crumbling Institution of Marriage 261
61. How Should We Treat Our Elders? 266
62. Tenants and Landlords 270
63. Obscenity for Obscenity's Sake 273
64. Growing Population and Thinning Families 277
65. Euthanasia—Mercy Killing 280
66. Illiteracy—The Malaise that Afflicts India 285
67. History of the Origin of Indian Literature 289

68. Diabetes – A Sure Killer 294
69. The Indian National Flag 298
70. Poverty Alleviation 302
71. Bharat Ratna – The Highest Civilian Award 306
72. Human Rights 310
73. Sexual Harassment 314
74. Science Scenario in India 318
75. A Growing Environmental Challenge 322
76. Interlinking of Rivers 325
77. Pesticides in Food – The Silent Killers 329
78. Trends in Higher Education 333
79. Digital Evidence and Cyber Crime 337
80. Human Reproduction 341

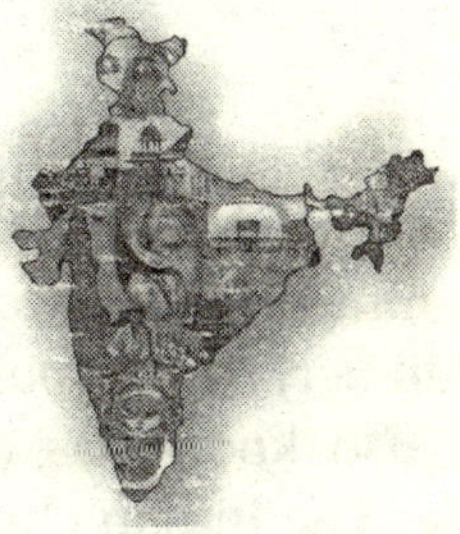

1
India—The Land and its People

India as one of the oldest civilisations of the world with a **kaleidoscopic** variety and rich cultural heritage has achieved multifaceted socio-economic progress during the last 66 years after independence. It has become self-sufficient in agricultural production and is today the tenth industrialised country in the world and the sixth nation to have gone into outer space orbit to conquer nature for the benefit of its people. India covers an area of 32,87,263 sq km, extending from the snow-covered Himalayan heights to the tropical rain forests in the south. As the seventh largest country of the world, it stands apart from the rest of Asia. Bounded by the Great Himalayas on the north, it stretches southwards and at the Tropic of Cancer, **tapers** off into the Indian Ocean between the Bay of Bengal on the east and the Arabian Sea on the west. The mainland comprises four regions, namely the great mountain zone, the Gangetic plains and the Indus, the desert region and the southern peninsula.

The river systems can be classified into (a) Himalayan Rivers, (b) Deccan Rivers, (c) Coastal Rivers, and (d) Rivers of the inland drainage basin. Since the Himalayan Rivers are formed by melting of snow and glaciers, they flow throughout the year, and receive heavy rainfall. The Deccan Rivers are rain-fed and fluctuate in volume. Many of these are non-perennial. The Coastal streams have limited catchment area and are usually of short duration. Most of them are non-perennial. The streams of the inland drainage basin of western Rajasthan are few and far apart and majority of them are of an **ephemeral** kind.

The climate of India is broadly described as tropical monsoon type with four clearly defined seasons: winter (January-February), summer (March-May), rainy south-western monsoon (June-September) and post-monsoon (October-December), which is also known as north-east monsoon in the southern peninsula. The Indian climate is affected by two seasonal winds: north-east monsoon, commonly known as winter monsoon, which blows from land to sea and south-west monsoon, also known as summer monsoon, which blows from sea to land after traversing through the Indian Ocean, the Arabian Sea and the Bay of Bengal. It is the south-west monsoon that brings most of the rainfall during the year.

India has rich and varied vegetation. India can be divided into eight distinct **florist** regions, namely the eastern and the western Himalayas, Assam, the Indus plain, the Gangetic plain, the Deccan, Malabar and the Andamans. India is rich in **flora**. According to the available data, India ranks tenth in the world and fourth in Asia in plant diversity. Having so far surveyed 70% of geographical area, the Botanical Survey of India has found over 46,000 **species** of plants. The **vascular** flora comprises 15,000 species. The Zoological Survey of India, which surveys the **faunal** resources of India, has identified a great variety of fauna numbering over 89,000 species.

India's population as on 1st March, 2011 stood at 1,210 million. India accounts for a **meagre** 2.4 per cent of the world surface area of 135.79 million sq km. Yet, it supports and sustains a whopping 16.7 per cent of the world population. The population density of India in 2011 was 272 per sq km. India is the second most populous state of the world after China. India ranks 11th in the list of 15 biggest economies of the world as on 31st March, 2011, but it does not figure in the list of 10 countries with the highest GDP per capita, nor for that matter does it figure in the list of the world's largest exporters. India does figure in the list of 10 largest importers having imported goods worth 488.60 billion dollars in 2011. However, India takes 'number one' position when it comes to inward remittances. It received remittances to the extent of 64 billion dollars in 2011.

India ranks second in sending its students abroad for higher studies. India is the third largest producer of coal, but it is nowhere when it comes to producing natural gas. Sadly, India also does not figure anywhere in the list of the countries with most heritage sites. Italy takes the first place with 47 heritage sites and South Korea occupies the last position with 10 sites. India is missing from this list.

A person aged seven and above, who can both read and write with understanding in any language is treated as literate in our country. A person who can only read but cannot write is not literate. The results of 2011 Census show that there has been an increase in literacy in India. Literacy rate in the country is 74.04%, 82.14% for males and 65.46% for females. Kerala continues to hold its premier position with its literacy rate of 93.91%, closely followed by Lakshadweep at 92.28%. Bihar with 63.82% ranks last in the country, preceded by Arunachal Pradesh at 66.95%.

Some of the contrasting facts of life revealed in Census 2011 are—while half of all Indians do not have a toilet at home, well over half own a mobile phone. Similarly, where millions have access to state-of-the-art technologies and consumer goods, they do not have a proper shelter over their head. Only 46.9% of the 246.6 million households have toilets. Of the rest, 3.2% make do with public toilets, and 49.8% **defecate** in the open. Lack of sanitary facilities continues to be a big concern for the country.

The Indian society is overwhelmingly made up of nuclear families. This is a drastic change from just a generation ago. They have more access to electricity and get their information from television than from radio. Less than a third of the population has access to treated drinking water. Two-thirds of households continue to use firewood, crop residue, cow-dung cakes or coal for cooking, thus putting their womenfolk to significant health hazards. Seventeen per cent still fetch drinking water from a source located more than 500 metres in rural areas or 100 metres in urban centres. For 45 per cent of population, bicycle continues to be the primary mode of transport. That in a **nutshell** is the overall picture of India.

Vocabulary

Kaleidoscopic—(adj.) continually shifting or rapidly changing. **Tapers**—(v) diminishes gradually. **Ephemeral**—(adj.) lasting a very short time, of temporary nature. **Florist**—(n) someone who grows and deals in flowers, a shop where flowers and ornamental plants are sold. **Flora**—(n) all the plant life in a particular region, a living organism lacking the power of locomotion. **Species**—(n) a specific kind of something, form or variety. **Vascular**—(adj.) of or relating to or having vessels that conduct and circulate fluids. **Faunal**—(adj.) Fauna is its noun form which means 'all the animal life in a particular region, a living organism characterised by voluntary movement'. **Meagre**—(adj.) deficient in amount, quality or extent, lacking excessive flesh. **Defecate**—(v) to have a bowel movement, to ease oneself. **Nutshell**—(n) the shell around the kernel of a nut.

□

2

The President of India—Pranab Mukherjee

Pranab Kumar Mukherjee became the 13th President of India on 25th July, 2012. He was born on 11th December, 1935 to a Bengali family in Birbhum District of West Bengal. His father Kamada Kinkar Mukherjee was active in India's freedom movement. He was also a member of West Bengal Legislative Council between 1952 and 1964 as a representative of the Indian National Congress. Rajlakshmi Mukherjee, Pranab's mother, was a quiet housewife.

Pranab Mukherjee attended Sri Vidyasagar College in Birbhum under the University of Calcutta. He did his MA in political science and history. He also completed L.L.B. from the Law Department of the University of Calcutta. He began his career as an Upper Division Clerk in Post and Telegraph Department. In 1963, he switched over to teaching. He taught political science at Vidyasagar College (in South 24 Parganas) and also worked as a journalist for a while for *Desher Dak* (Call of Motherland) before taking a plunge into politics.

His political career began in 1969 with the successful handling of the election campaign of V.K. Krishna Menon who was seeking election from Midnapore. The Prime Minister Indira Gandhi was quick to recognise his talent. She inducted him into her party and got him elected to Rajya Sabha in 1969. He continued to be re-elected to Rajya Sabha for four terms in 1975, '81, '93 and '99.

Shri Mukherjee soon became a loyalist of Indira Gandhi. He was often called 'man for all seasons'. He rapidly rose in stature. He was an active member of Indira Gandhi's Cabinet in the Emergency period. He was accused of exercising extra-constitutional powers for wrecking rules of governance. After Janata Party assumed in 1977, Shah Commission was appointed to probe excesses committed during the emergency. Pranab Mukherjee too was indicted by the Commission. However, Mukherjee came out unscathed as the Commission itself was discredited. He returned to Indira Gandhi's cabinet and rose to become Finance Minister from 1982 to 1984. He was noted for his work in improving the finances of the government that enabled Indira Gandhi to score a political point by returning the last instalment of India's first loan from International Monetary Fund (IMF). As Finance Minister, it was he who signed the letter appointing Dr. Manmohan Singh as Governor of Reserve Bank of India.

After the assassination of Indira Gandhi in 1984, he fell out of favour with Rajiv Gandhi. He thought he was more competent to become the prime minister than the inexperienced Rajiv Gandhi. On being sidelined by the Congress in Rajiv era, he formed his own party in 1986. His new party could not do much and he remained in political wilderness for some time. It was in 1991 that P.V. Narasimha Rao revived his political fortunes. Rao appointed him as the Deputy Chairman of the Planning Commission and subsequently made him a cabinet minister. He served as India's External Affairs Minister from 1995 to 1996 in Rao's Cabinet.

Shri Mukherjee always carried the **tag** of being loyalist of Gandhi-Nehru family and the principal architect of Sonia Gandhi's ascension to power in Congress. He was made General Secretary of AICC in 1998-99 when Sonia Gandhi was the president of the party. He became the leader of Lok Sabha for the first time in 2004 after winning Jangipur Lok Sabha seat from West Bengal. It was speculated that Sonia Gandhi would pick him for the job of prime minister when she herself declined it in 2004. However, she chose Dr. Manmohan Singh. Many thought it was because Sonia Gandhi considered him less pliable than Dr. Singh.

He held several important portfolios in Dr. Manmohan Singh's Government. Many found it ironical that the man who appointed Dr. Singh as Governor of RBI should have been serving under him. It needs to be said to the credit of Shri Mukherjee that he acquitted himself well in whatever responsibilities that were **entrusted** to him. He headed several GOMs (Group of Ministers) and he was invariably the one who was called upon to resolve crises the government faced from time to time. Many saw in him the best Prime Minister India never got.

In July 2012, he quit active politics to become the thirteenth President of India by comfortably securing 70% votes of the Electoral College.

Shri Mukherjee brought to the presidency the spirit of **expeditiousness** in disposal of files. Several pardon cases that were gathering dust during his predecessor's regime were cleared by him expeditiously resulting in death sentences to Afzal Guru and Kasab. If it were not for his pro-active approach, these would have continued to bother India.

Vocabulary

Tag—(n) a small piece of paper, cloth, plastic, etc. attached to something for identity, for marking or for giving information about something. **Entrust**—(v) to make somebody responsible for something or taking care of somebody. **Expeditiousness**—(n) the property of being prompt and efficient.

□

3

Prime Minister of India—Narendra Modi

Narendra Damodardas Modi is the 15th and present Prime Minister of India, in office since 26th May 2014. Modi, a leader of the Bharatiya Janata Party (BJP); was the CM of Gujarat from 2001 to 2014 and is the Member of Parliament (MP) from Varanasi. He led the BJP in 2014 general election, which gave the party a majority in the Lok Sabha - a first for any party since 1984 - and was credited for October 2014 BJP electoral victories in the states of Haryana and Maharashtra.

In the sacred land of Vadnagar, situated at a distance of 112 km from Ahmedabad and 34 km from Mahesana, is the oldest town of Gujarat. Narendra Modi spent his childhood and early youth in this historic place. He was the third child of six children born to Damodardas and Hira Ben. As a child Modi helped his father sell tea at the Vadnagar Railway station, and later ran a tea stall with his brother near a bus terminus. His early education took place in a government school and later he studied in B.N. High School in 1967.

During student life, Narendra Modi was a man of few words, but always spoke sensibly. His mind has always grasped the best. Since childhood he was always fond of books. He spent most of his time in the public library of Vadnagar as if this public library was his home. The people knew they would find him in the library if they wanted to meet him. He was more interested in reading the life histories of great men. It was here that he read the life histories of people like Vivekananda, Shivaji, etc.

Compassion for living beings and love of nature were Narendra Modi's second nature, from childhood. Even today he has implemented schemes such as animal hospital and animal health fair.

Rasbihari Maniar, the then teacher of Vadnagar B.N. High School, says about his student, "Narendra Modi was always been helpful and sensitive from early childhood. He took active interest in NCC work. Discipline, **compliance** and helping others was his **inherent** nature. Despite average financial condition at home, he always appeared self-confident. He also participated actively in school activities. Oratory skills, motivating speeches, brilliance and a sharp memory have been his identity. He instantly found solution to any problem".

He started helping his father in business and mother at home from early childhood. Whenever his mother fell ill, he would cook meals for the entire family and also wash clothes at the pond. He did not have more than two pairs of clothes at that time, but he always kept them neat and clean. He washed his clothes and before sleeping at night kept them under the pillow so that by morning they were pressed. Sometimes he would keep hot coals in a brass mug and iron his clothes.

Narendra Modi inherited moral principles of concern and **benevolence** from his parents. His mother Hira Ben had good knowledge of household medicines. It was a kind of God's blessing. She gave free medicines to the patients who came to their house. From 5 o'clock in the morning a crowd would assemble in their house. Narendra Modi would get up early, to help his mother and helped the patients waiting in the house. Narendra Modi himself tells, "My mother is not educated, but has been **bestowed** by God with the knowledge of medicines".

In 1942, the 'Quit India' movement was prevalent in the whole country, during this period work of Rashtriya Swayamsevak Sangh (RSS) started in Vadnagar. The task of cultivating patriotism and nationalism amongst children, teenagers and youth was initiated by RSS. Chandrakant Dave, the Hindi teacher of B.N. High School, used to organize the RSS activities in Vadnagar. It was at this time that Narendra Modi came in contact with RSS.

Communal Harmony and the 'Peelu Phool' Dramatic Experiment

Narendra Modi was a supporter of communal harmony from early childhood. **Eradication** of untouchability is a joint responsibility of the society. He highlighted this social problem by means of a school play titled, 'Peelu Phool' meaning 'yellow flower'. The play was unique in a sense because Narendra Modi was himself the writer, director and actor of this play. The theme of the play was connected with eradication of untouchability.the story revolves around a Dalit family. There is a Dalit family in the village. The Dalit woman has a son who falls ill. The mother takes her sick child to doctors, physicians, tantriks and many others. But no one was ready to treat the untouchable child. Someone suggested the woman that if she went to the village temple and touched the child with the yellow flowers offered to god, her child would get well. The Dalit mother runs to the temple, but she is not allowed to enter the temple. Finally, the Dalit woman literally begs the temple priest with open arms for her child's life. The priest's heart melts and he gives the yellow flowers to the woman. By the time the Dalit woman reaches home with the yellow flower her son had stopped breathing. Through this theatrical performance Narendra Modi, a student of eighth class at that time, gave the message—"Everyone has equal right over flowers offered to god".

Since early childhood Narendra Modi was fond of swimming. He is a good swimmer. During those days, he went to the Sharmishtha pond of Vadnagar. There were many crocodiles in the pond, but brave Narendra Modi was not afraid of them. Every year during monsoons, the villagers would take rafts and swim to the **canopy** in the middle of the pond and hoist a flag over it. Narendra Modi would also swim to the middle of the pond from the bank near the public library. During monsoons, the pond filled with water because of the rains therefore, it was quite risky to swim and hoist the flag. Moreover it was dangerous because of the crocodile. However, Narendra Modi would take any risk. Once he jumped into the pond with his friends, Mahindra and Bachu during one such occasion. The villagers played the drums to keep the crocodiles away from them. Narendra swam into the pond with his friends, changed the flag on the canopy and returned. Everybody in the village greeted them warmly.

Narendra Modi was an expert at fighting with crocodiles. One day Narendra Modi, along with a friend, went to the Sharmishtha pond and brought home a baby crocodile. His mother said to him lovingly, "Son, what you have done is not right. It is not good to separate a child from the mother. Won't you be sad if somebody separated you from your mother? Similarly, we should also not separate this child from its mother. Go instantly and leave this baby crocodile from where you have brought it". Narendra Modi immediately obeyed his mother and returned the baby crocodile to the pond.

Narendra Modi has inherited the qualities of social service and nation service from his family. He also participated wholeheartedly in the service of soldiers. In 1962, when there was war between India and China, a wave of patriotism flowed in the entire country. During that time, there was a large movement of Indian soldiers on Gujarat trains, which passed from the Mehsana railway line near Vadnagar. Narendra Modi was merely 12 years old at that time. Even at that small age, he had a strong desire to do something for the soldiers of his country's Army.

He saw many social service minded people going to Mehsana to serve the Indian soldiers at the railway station. Narendra Modi took permission from his parents and immediately went along with them. He enthusiastically joined the social workers in handing out food packets and tea and snacks to the soldiers of the Indian Army passing through the

Mehsana railway station. Filled with devotion for his country Narendra Modi, dedicated himself completely—ignoring time and sometimes his own hunger -- to serve the valiant soldiers. At times the train carrying the soldiers, passed the Mehsana railway station late at night. However, Narendra Modi in his fervour to serve stayed awake. Sometimes when he was extremely exhausted he would take a short nap in a corner of the station. Narendra Modi got immense satisfaction in serving the soldiers of the Army, who had left their homes to serve the country. Many other such incidents, displaying his concern and affection for his country, make him an extraordinary person.

At the age of 17, Narendra Modi forsaking studies and home left for the Himalayas to attain spiritual knowledge. Narendra Modi, after roaming about and meeting many sadhus and saints finally reached the Himalayas. He did not have a single paisa when he left home. He met many people and talking to them acquired good knowledge about human nature, but one day he realised he would not reach any destination by moving around like this. He had been roaming aimlessly for two years, therefore, he decided to return home. Narendra Modi says, "I wanted to do something, but I did not understand what I should do."

After two years, Narendra Modi returned to Vadnagar. Remembering that incident, his mother, tearfully says, "We did not get any news about him for two years. I was almost mad with grief. Suddenly, one day, he returned. He ate food and again went out. I opened his bag out of curiosity, and saw there was a kurta, a loin-cloth and my photo under his dhoti. I do not know from where he got my photograph. However, he remained in the house for one day and one night and then went away".

Narendra Modi, never returned to Vadnagar after he left it that day. Instead of his mother he considered his country to be the ultimate and dedicated his entire life to serve it and the society.

Narendra Modi came to Ahmedabad. He did not know where he had to go and what he wanted to do. There was no objective, no goal. He roamed around aimlessly. Sometimes he met his friends, sometimes went to his uncle's canteen while at other times, he would participate in social, religious and other activities taking place in Ahmedabad. Perhaps, he was in search of an aim. At this time, he again came into contact with the Sangh. He met Vakil Sahib and his disoriented life found a way.

After becoming a promoter, Narendra Modi got fully involved in the promotion and propagation of the Sangh. He was very popular amongst the voluntary workers. Despite being busy in social activities, he always remained spiritual at heart. During the time when he was the General Secretary of the BJP, he would spend one week in **solitude** in the Gir forest during Diwali. This was his routine every year, to come close to God and Nature. Narendra Modi says, "I am a Nature-lover and I enjoy being in the company of Nature."

For the last 40 years, Narendra Modi has been keeping fast twice a year during the Navaratras. During these nine days, he only drinks water. He worships Shakti and has travelled across India. He has visited all the 12 Jyotirlingas and in 1998, he also went to Marsarovar. As it is he is fond of nature and God. He likes to eat simple food. He had left his home at a young age and has always been a wanderer his whole life, therefore, he eats whatever he gets. He is not particular about taste, and has no preferences.

He has always used technology for the expansion of his work. Narendra Modi is always connected to the best technology in the world. He has a strong relationship with the social media. He is also one of the advanced leaders of the country who remains in touch with the social media. He has lakhs of followers, most of them being young people. One can listen to all his speeches on the YouTube. The youth of the country feel honoured to keep in contact with Narendra Modi. He tweets regularly and has more than 25 lakh followers. Narendra Modi is also the first politician of India to use digital technology for election campaign. He devotes himself completely to the task he undertakes, therefore perhaps he rarely has a full night's sleep. He goes to sleep by midnight and gets up at five in the morning, sleeping for only 4-5 hours.

Besides reading ideological literature, Narendra Modi also likes to write. He wrote his first book, "Sangharsh me Gujarat" at the age of 25 years within a period of one month. He also wrote a book titled "Setubandh" on the life of Vakil Sahib. A glimpse of the poet inside Narendra Modi can also be seen in his book of poems titled "Aankh aa dhanya chhe". He also wrote a book titled 'Jyotipunj' on the life of the workers and promoters of the Sangh. Besides, he has also translated many Marathi books into Gujarati. His resolve to protect the environment is evident in his book "Convenient Action", whereas social perceptions are visible in his book "Samajik Samrasta'. A book titled 'Shri Guruji' has been written by Modi on the life of Shri Guruji. Another book based on the letters of Shri Guruji titled, 'Patra Roop Guruji' has been edited by Narendra Modi. His love for words is apparent in his speeches. His tongue and fingers both seem to be blessed by Saraswati, the goddess of learning. He is not only a competent writer but also a vibrant orator, who can **mesmerize** millions of audiences.

If we look at some of the aspects of his personality, we would see that Narendra Modi is a **visionary** – it means that he has the potential to take each step to the final conclusion. Through this work, and principles, he has elicited the faith and trust of the people. Unique and quick decision taking, ability to play many roles simultaneously, complete dedication towards any work, the potential to devote himself completely to the fulfilment of a task without taking tension, the ability to priorities his work, faith in team spirit, strong conviction and belief on his own intelligence and the ability to face difficult circumstances and problems, the wisdom to take strong steps at the required time and behave politely, listen to a common man – the amalgamation of so many qualities has made Narendra Modi immensely successful. It is said that Management is doing things right, while Leadership is doing the right thing.

The secret of Narendra Modi's success lies in the fact that he always does what is right. This is the reason why the people of this country today have immense faith in him. It is this trust which has led to his becoming the Chief Minister of Gujarat three times amidst great popularity.

Narendra Modi, who has the image of a strict, disciplined and hard-working administrator, is extremely **generous** and kind and compassionate towards the poor and the deprived. His intention has always been to remove the problems of the society. What kind of a heart does a worker have? This is seen in the working style and behaviour of Narendra Modi .

One of his brothers, Somabhai, is a retired health officer who now runs an old age home in the city of Ahmedabad. Another of his borther Prahlad, an activist on behalf of fair price shop owners, has his own fair price shop in Ahmedabad. His third brother Pankaj is employed with the Information Department in Gandhi Nagar.

Before the 2014 General Elections, Prime Minister of India Narendra Modi had promised bringing foreign investment into India to create more job opportunities for the skilled and qualified Indian youth of India. Modi announced an innovative programme called 'Make in India' in his first independence day speech as the Indian Prime Minister on 15th August at the Red Fort.

Service and quick decision are inherent nature of Narendra Modi. Surat was flooded with water because of floods in Tapi River. The Chief Minister was himself on the job to ensure that the administration works efficiently. Narendra Modi reached Surat and personally supervised the work of cleanliness.

He was passing by a society. Suddenly a young man, who was angry, started shouting slogans with his friends against Narendra Modi. He saw all this happening from his car. Modi asked his driver to stop the car. His security guards were apprehensive the situation may turn ugly. Narendra Modi got down from the car and went straight to the young man and put his hand on his shoulder and asked, "Tell me son, what is the problem?" The furious man cooled down immediately and said, "Sir, our society is filled with slush. We have complained to the Corporation many times but since last 2 days nobody is cleaning the place. That's why I am angry".

On hearing this, the Chief Minster immediately called the officers and standing in the same place said, "The society should be completely clean by tonight". He kept standing there for 30 minutes and left the place only after the work started. People were happy and impressed with this action of Narendra Modi. Another secret behind Narendra Modi's success is that he believes in action; he does not delay or leave work for the next day. Narendra Modi's heart, which is filled with compassion and empathy, considers the pain of others as his own pain.

What is it which inspires Narendra Modi to serve the common man and think about public welfare? From early childhood, he was impressed with two great personalities—Swami Vivekananda and Modi's own mother Hira Ba. Inspired by these two in his childhood Narendra Modi learnt to serve people.

This spirit to serve the people and concern for their welfare is constantly flowing in the heart of Narendra Modi. As it is he has dedicated his entire life towards public welfare and to serve the country. Today, all around the country there is an atmosphere of frustration, despair and despondency. In these circumstances, the people of this country look upon Narendra Modi as a ray of hope and optimism.

Vocabulary

Compliance—(n) the action or fact of complying with a wish or command. **Inherent**—(adj) existing in something as a permanent, essential; or characteristic attribute. **Benevolence**—(n) kindness, kindheartedness, goodness, goodwill, charity, altruism, humanitarianism, compassion, philanthropy, generosity magnanimity, munificence, unselfishness, openhandedness, beneficence, bounty, bounteousness, etc. **Bestow**—(v) confer or present (an honour, right or gift).

Eradication—(n) the complete destruction of something. **Canopy**—(n) an ornamental cloth covering hung or held up over something, especially a throne or bed. **Solitude**—(n) the state or situation of being alone. **Mesmerize**—(v). magnesite, spell bound, bewitch, hypnotist etc. **Visionary**—(adj) (especially of a person) thinking about or planning the future with imagination or wisdom. **Generous**—(adj) (of a person) showing a readiness to give more of something, as money or time, than is strictly necessary or expected.

□

4

Mohan Das Karam Chand Gandhi

One of the most important dates of Indian history is 2nd October, 1869. On this day, a devout Hindu pious lady Putli Bai gave birth to a child, who was to become the darling of the nation and subsequently also the father of the nation. His father Karam Chand Gandhi was the Diwan of Rajkot in Gujarat.

Mohan Das went to school at the age of seven. Though he was an average student, he was regular and punctual in attending the classes. When still a child, he was married to Kasturba. After completion of matriculation and college studies, he went to England to study law. On becoming a barrister in England, he returned to India. He began his practice in law in Mumbai (then called Bombay). He was not successful in his practice. He then returned to Rajkot. But even there he could not excel as a lawyer. He always took up the cases that were genuine and true. He always stood for truth and **spurned** cases that were not truthful.

It was a chance that took him to South Africa. He went there to fight a law suit for his client based in South Africa. Circumstances made him stay there for over two decades. The pathetic condition of Indians living there moved him so much that he decided to fight for their cause. This brought him in direct conflict with the authorities. He was once thrown out of a train just because he was travelling in the first class, a facility that was denied to Indians. This did not put him off. Instead, it made him resolute to fight things out.

He acquired Tolstoy Farm there and created an Ashram, from where he launched his movement against the atrocities of the White on the Indians. He founded the Indian Congress. It was largely due to his efforts that the government was forced to pass Indian Relief Act in 1914 which improved the quality of Indians' life to a great extent.

After achieving success in South Africa, he returned to India in 1915, joined Congress Party and began to take active part in India's movement for freedom. The Satyagraha Movement was his brainchild. The mighty English empire became helpless against this movement based on the principle of non-violence. It was an unheard of thing. Non-violent movement coupled with non-cooperation almost crippled the British Empire. The Empire was at a loss. It simply did not have any clue on how to deal with this. Tackling a violent mob or violent movement is always easy and tried out methods are easily resorted to achieve desired results. But here was a movement where no one was resorting to any kind of violence. It was a new instrument and the English were not trained to tackle this. The historic Dandi March breaking the Salt Law unsettled the British Government. The Quit India Movement of 1942 proved almost decisive for the English. It fully dawned on the British Empire that it was no longer possible to rule India. Finally, in 1947, India secured its independence.

Even though India had achieved the objective of freeing it from the clutches of the English, Gandhi was not quite happy with the turn of events. First, he was firmly against division of the country on the basis of religion. He had even declared publicly that India could be divided only on his dead body. Second, he wanted the Congress to wind up as a political party. None of these two **pious** wishes was fulfilled. India was divided and caused **havoc** as Hindus and Muslims resorted to looting and killing. Gandhi was dismayed and hopelessly left alone to nurse his wound. The leaders who were with him in the struggle for independence were with the government and **relishing** the use of power and that went with it. Gandhi had clearly not bargained for it. There was no one to buy his suggestion to **disband** the

Congress. Thus disillusioned, he withdrew himself to **seclusion** and prayers. He had said that India could be divided only on his dead body. But he was forced by the circumstances to preside over the division of India. This angered some and he was done to death on 30th January, 1948. India celebrates this day as Martyr's Day.

Irrespective of what one might think of Gandhi after over six decades of India's journey post-independence, the fact remains that there has not been another personality in the world that has stirred up so much emotion of the question of non-violence. Gandhi continues to be one of the most celebrated personalities in the world who influenced the course of events not just in India but in other parts of the world as well. He is the 'Father of Nation' of India.

A Hollywood film made on him drew **acclaim** from all over the world and is one of the recipients of maximum number of awards. Even though times have changed and old values have taken a **tumble**, there is no denying the fact that Gandhi continues to be relevant and there is no **dearth** of people in any walk of life swearing by his name.

Vocabulary

Spurn – (v) to refuse or reject something or somebody in a proud manner. **Pious** – (adj.) having or showing a great respect for God or religion. **Havoc** – (n) mayhem, violent and needless disturbance. **Relishing** – (n) act of taking small amount of something into mouth to test its quality; (v) to derive or receive pleasure from, take pleasure in, get enjoyment from. **Disband** – (v) cause to break up or cease to function, to dissolve. **Seclusion** – (n) privacy, privateness; the quality of being secluded from the presence or view of others. **Acclaim** – (v) praise vociferously; to clap one's hands or shout after performances to show approval; (n) enthusiastic approval. **Tumble** – (v) to fall down as if collapsing, to roll over and over back and forth. **Dearth** – (n) paucity, shortage, an acute insufficiency.

□

5

Nelson Mandela

Nelson Mandela was born Rolihlahla Dalibhunga in a small village in the Eastern Cape on July 18, 1918. Madiba was his clan name. He was named Nelson by a teacher at school. He joined the African National Congress (ANC) in 1943 and, in 1952, started the first black law firm with his partner, Oliver Tambo. With South Africa then facing the prospects of a civil war because of the policy of **apartheid**, he sought reconciliation with the white minority that had kept him in prison for 27 long years to build a new democracy. He led the ANC to victory in the country's first election in 1994. Unlike other African liberation leaders who cling to power, Mandela voluntarily stepped down after one term. It was a **transcendent** act of forgiveness after spending 27 years in prison, which alone will ensure his place in history. He died on 7th December, 2013 at the age of 95.

When ANC was banned in 1960, Mandela had gone underground. But he resurfaced after the Sharpeville massacre, in which 69 black protestors were shot dead by police to lead an armed struggle. He was arrested and charged with sabotage and attempting to overthrow the government. He escaped the death penalty but was sentenced to life imprisonment. But as unrest grew and international pressure on the apartheid regime mounted, the ban on ANC was lifted and he was released from the prison in 1990 by the then South African President FW de Klark. The two shared the Nobel Peace Prize in 1993. India too honoured him by conferring its highest civilian award Bharat Ratna on him in 1990.

Many in South Africa, especially the whites, dismissed him as a terrorist and thought he was more useful in prison. What he did after coming out of the prison was the most extraordinary thing. He invited his white jailor as VIP guest to his inauguration as president, and he invited the prosecutor in the Rivonia trial to lunch. The concessions he made during the negotiations leading up to free and fair elections were amazing. He was more than keen to accommodate. Rugby was the white man's sport and Mandela's master stroke at the World Cup final was when he strode on to the turf wearing his Springbok jersey. The whole arena which was 99% white erupted into cries 'Nelson! Nelson!' And who could have believed that the South Africans would be celebrating a rugby victory? That was Mandela touch. People wonder if he could achieve so much in a few years in the government, what he could have achieved if those 27 years were not wasted. But many also believe that but for those 27 **mellowing** years in prison, Mandela would not have been what he actually became. Time in prison, they say, was crucial. Sufferings indeed embitter some people, but they also **ennoble** some people. Prison had ennobled Mandela.

In the long years, he spent in prison in the **inhospitable** Robben Island, Mandela's source of inspiration was William Ernest Henley's *Invictus,* especially the lines, "I am the master of my fate. I am the captain of my soul." Clint Eastwood turned it into a film that earned **plaudits** from all and sundry. Nelson never blamed others for his misfortune. He took responsibility for his own fate. He lived by the principle that bitterness and hate can achieve no lasting good. Despite the punishments heaped on him by a brutal apartheid regime, he did not seek revenge. He sought reconciliation and peace instead to lay foundations for a united South Africa. This is his **legacy**. It is not for nothing that he is placed alongside Gandhi, though he himself conceded he was not a saintly person like Gandhi. But like Gandhi, he believed that exclusionist politics could never work in a multicultural society like South Africa and he strived all his life to create an inclusive polity. And he largely succeeded.

Even his bitter critics could not help respecting and admiring him for his towering intellect and impeccable integrity.

Mandela never used his personal tragedies to score political points. His charm and wit saw him at ease with other heads of state, rock stars, activists and the people of South Africa's ghettos. Democracy may have failed in other parts of Africa, but not in South Africa thanks largely to the exemplary vision of Mandela. He faced tremendous **adversity** in his life—his personal life being in disarray—but not once did he seek to subvert the principles of democracy. Given his stature, people would have easily accepted any **diktat** from him. He was truly an inclusive and modern leader the likes of which the world will not get to see in any near time. The greatest tribute to him will be to adhere to the values he stood for. His departure from the scene has created a **cataclysmic** upheaval of sorrow all over the world, though it was known that the end was near. As Barack Obama said, "He no longer belongs to us. He belongs to the ages."

He was diagnosed with prostate cancer in 2001 and retired from public life. In June 2013, he was taken to hospital with a recurring lung infection but returned home where his bedroom was converted into an intensive care unit. He was last seen in public at the 2010 World Cup final in Johannesburg, a tournament he helped bring to South Africa for the first time.

Mandela was a charming and charismatic figure with a passion for boxing and an eye for women. He married thrice. He married Evelyn Mase in 1944, divorced her in 1957 and the following year he married Winnie Madikizela, who campaigned for his release and also became a key figure in the struggle. He married Graca Machel, a human rights activist, in 1998. He fathered six children and has twenty grandchildren. Mandela, one of the greatest men in the world, had a heartbreaking family life. His life of 95 years is a legacy. But it is also a story of loss and loneliness—separation from family for almost three decades, two broken marriages, and the death of three of his six children.

Vocabulary

Apartheid—(n) a social policy or racial segregation involving political, economic and legal discrimination against people who are not whites. **Transcendent**—(adj) exceeding or surpassing limits, especially in excellence. **Mellow**—(adj) unhurried and relaxed, laid-back. **Ennoble**—(v) to make noble, to confer dignity or honour upon. **Inhospitable**—(adj) unfavourable to life and growth, not hospitable. **Plaudits**—(n) enthusiastic approval. **Legacy**—(n) a gift of personal property by will; (adj) old or no longer in active use. **Adversity**—(n) a state of misfortune or affliction. **Diktat**—(n) an order given by the competent authority, often unpopular or harsh. **Cataclysmic**—(adj) severely destructive.

□

6

Subhash Chandra Bose

Few leaders of the world can claim of being as selfless as Subhash Chandra Bose, who was fondly called 'Netaji'. It is another matter that the word 'Netaji' no longer commands the respect it commanded with him. He was truly a leader of the highest quality and intellect. For him, only nation mattered; and he was willing and always ready to go to any extent to free India from the **yoke** of slavery. The air crash which is supposed to have killed him is indicative of the kind of risk he took to free India from the English control.

He was born with a fighting spirit. No matter what the **adversity**, he never **buckled** under pressure. He was a hot breed and a patriot to the hilt. Once at the Presidency College in Calcutta, the British principal made a **derogatory** remark about Indians in one of his lectures, Subhash Chandra Bose led an attack against him. He was expelled from the college. This only shows how passionate he was about his country.

He was one of the foremost leaders engaged in India's freedom movement. But he did not pursue the line of Gandhi and his non-violence. He was a hot breed and believed that English would not leave unless it was forced to. So, while Gandhi fought on the principle of non-violence, Subhash Chandra Bose prepared for the military **onslaught**. It was quite a Herculean task, but he formed Indian National Army called 'Azad Hind Fauj' and set on course to overthrow the British Government. He formed his army outside India and launched his forward march to Delhi. His famous call 'Dilli Chalo' even today **reverberates** through the minds of many elders.

Netaji was a Bengali born in Cuttack in Odisha on 23rd January, 1897, when India was under the yoke of the British Government. His father was a renowned lawyer and Subhash was the ninth child among fourteen **siblings**. He was a brilliant student and was influenced by the teachings of Swami Vivekananda. After graduating from Calcutta (now Kolkata), he went to England in 1919 to compete in Indian Civil Services. He duly qualified for it and joined apprenticeship, but soon left it and returned to India. The Jalianwala Bagh incident turned him against the British.

For a brief spell, he remained under the influence of Gandhi and remained in Congress. He joined Gandhi's non-cooperation movement in 1921. On the advice of Gandhi, he began to work under Deshbandhu (C.R. Das). He became a youth educator and later turned into a journalist to publish a Bengali weekly *Banglar Katha*. When Deshbandhu started a college, Subhash was made the principal of that college called National College. He also served the Calcutta Corporation as its Chief Executive Officer when Deshbandhu became mayor. He soon got **disenchanted** with Gandhi's pacifist policies and developed differences with Gandhi on several matters. On the question of complete independence, he differed with Gandhi. He formed Independence League, took part in civil disobedience and was jailed in 1930 and was released the following year following Gandhi-Irwin pact. Subhash was not amused. He lodged his protest and opposed discontinuation of civil disobedience movement as Bhagat Singh was hanged. He was soon to be arrested again under the draconian Bengal Regulation. He was released on medical grounds but also deported out of India. He used this period and opportunity to expand his contacts. He returned to India despite the ban being in place and was promptly arrested.

It was only after the elections of 1937 that he was released from jail. This was the most crucial period in his life as he became the president of the party and began to plan things in concrete terms. He set up National Planning Committee and chalked out various programmes. He was re-elected the president of the party by defeating Gandhi's handpicked man Pattabhi Sitarammiah. With the possibilities of the Second World War looming large, he put forth some tough conditions before the British government. The Government was asked to hand-over the reins of India to the Indians within six months or face a revolt. This tough **posturing** was opposed by some in the party. He resigned and formed his own group called Forward Block.

He started a mass movement against the British Government for seeking to utilise Indian resources to fight the war. Finding people responding favourably to his call, he was put under house arrest in Calcutta from where he escaped in 1941 despite strict **vigil** of the government. He went to Afghanistan and from there with the help of his well-wishers, he moved to Germany. He solicited the support of Germany and Japan. Germany offered him the opportunity of radio-broadcasting his appeal to the Indians settled all over the world. There was a tremendous response to his call for ousting the British. Rash Bihari Bose, who was running Indian Independence Movement in East India, made way for Netaji who formed 'Azad Hind Fauj' comprising primarily of the prisoners of war. Leading this army, he proceeded towards India in 1943. On the way back to India, his army liberated the Andaman and Nicobar Islands and his headquarters was shifted to Rangoon in 1944 and used it as his launching pad for liberating India. Soon his army crossed the Burma borders and moved into India in March 1944. This was the crucial moment for his army and for Netaji himself. The defeat of Germany and Japan in the war unsettled his scheme. He was forced to **retreat**. His objective of liberating of India could not be achieved.

It was about this time of August 1945 that details of life are **obscured**. There is no definite information whether it was Netaji who died in the air crash that occurred on the hills of Taipeh. It was August 18, 1945. Many believed Netaji died in that crash and still many others believed it was not Netaji who died in that air crash. Till date, no definite information is available about his death.

Indians all over the world celebrate his birth anniversary, not his death anniversary. No one knows when he died, or whether he died at all. Even though Netaji was not around to see India gaining independence, he had prescribed that for the initial ten years, India should be placed under benevolent dictatorship. Who knows India would have been a different India today if his advice was taken!

Vocabulary

Yoke—(n) an oppressive power, a pair of draft animals joined by a yoke. **Adversity**—(n) a difficult or unpleasant situation. **Buckle**—(v) fold or collapse, bend out of shape as under pressure or from heat, crumble or heave. **Derogatory**—(adj.) expressive of low opinion. **Onslaught**—(n) a sudden and severe onset of trouble, attack, bombardment, etc. **Reverberate**—(v) fill for a short time with sound and echoes, have a long or a continuing effect. **Siblings**—(n) brothers or sisters. **Disenchanted**—(v) no longer feeling enthused for something or somebody, not believing something is good or worth doing, disenchantment is its noun form. **Posturing**—(n) adopting a vain conceited posture, modelling, posing, etc. **Vigil**—(n) a period of sleeplessness, watch, a purposeful surveillance to guard or observe. **Retreat**—(v) pull back or move away, move back. **Obscured**—(v) made less visible or unclear, indistinct or blurred.

□

7
Sardar Vallabhbhai Patel

India is a country of jewels. Sardar Vallabhbhai Patel, also called the Iron Man of India (Lauh Purush), is one the most outstanding jewels of the country. Any Indian at any given point of time should take pride in him. If Gandhiji is credited to have crafted the independence of India, the credit of integrating India must go to Sardar alone. It was his foresightedness and **acumen** that ensured that some of the **fledgling** and splinter groups within the country were **wrought** together as part of India. Goa, Hyderabad and J&K are classic examples of how he single-handedly weaned them away from those trying to tear them away from India. India will ever remain indebted to him for this and many other services he rendered. Many believe that if Nehru had paid heed to what he had said about China, India would not have been humiliated in 1962 the way it was. He had forewarned Nehru about the designs of China. Many also believe that if he, not Nehru, were the prime minister, India would have been in a different league today.

Vallabhbhai and his elder brother Vithalbhai were sons of a peasant who was also bold and a patriot to the core. Their father Jhaverbhai Patel was part of the army of Jhansi Ki Rani that fought the British in its first war of independence of 1857. Both brothers were very enterprising and were known for their grit and determination. Both scaled great heights in academic field.

Vallabhbhai had his primary schooling in his village before moving on to Nadiad and Baroda to pursue his studies. In school days, he was known for his fearlessness, grit and determination.

He had a strong willpower. He was keen to go to England to study law and for the purpose he had saved some money. But on finding that his elder brother was keen to go, he stayed out; and only after his elder brother had completed his studies abroad, he went to England and returned after completing the course. He was a full-fledged barrister on returning to India. It was sheer hard work and his intelligence that brought him success and great fame as barrister. Besides, it was one of the objectives of his life to become a barrister. He achieved this objective despite earlier setbacks. Even the death of his wife did not come in his way to going to England for studies that would make a barrister. This speaks of his determination and strong will. It was this **trait** in his character that was going to stand him in good stead in the days ahead.

Meanwhile, Gandhiji had been making political news which drew the attention of Vallabhbhai. He was drawn towards Gandhi like an iron bar is drawn towards magnet. He joined politics in 1918. He began his political career as secretary of provincial political conference under the leadership of Gandhi. The quality of his work earned him **plaudits** and he became an instant success in the political arena. One of key elements of his works was to mobilise public opinion against what was called 'begaar'. It was because of his relentless pursuit of this issue with the commissioner that the issue was finally resolved with the closure of this practice. This reinforced his belief that what Gandhi was preaching was the right path and he whole-heartedly endorsed Gandhi's principle of non-violence. This brought him closer to Gandhi.

The principle of non-violence was put to severe test by him when he applied this in the district of Khera (also called Kaira) where revenue was forcibly being collected from the peasants, even though the crop had failed due to flood. He resorted to non-violent method of Gandhi and forced the government to return the land it had confiscated on account of non-payment of revenue. He carried forward this method again in 1928 when the government was forcing an unjust tax on the unwilling peasants in Bardoli. The farmers launched an agitation under his leadership. The government had seized peasants' land for their default. But Vallabhbhai did not **budge** from his stand. It was a long-drawn battle which came to an end only after his elder brother **brokered** a truce. Gandhiji was impressed with the spirit of Vallabhbhai and conferred on him the title of 'Sardar'. He was imprisoned for taking part in Salt Satyagraha.

He was now a full-fledged political worker. He had completely given up his profession of legal practice. He also advised his sons not to go to England for pursuing their higher studies. Vallabhbhai was also elected the President of the Indian National Congress in 1931. He displayed the same spirit in his fight against Rowlatt Act of 1919. This Act enabled the government to detain anyone without assigning any reason. The success of this movement overwhelmed the government.

His organisational skill was unmatched and he was able to feel the pulse of the people. Those associated with him believed in him and relied on his ability to lead them. It was precisely because of his popularity with the people and his organisational skill that he was elected the president of the party in 1931. The successful election campaign of 1937 bears testimony to his organisational skill. He was publicly applauded for this success. As a consequence of this, the Congress was able to form ministries in 7 out of 11 provinces. To keep a tab on the ministries thus formed, he was made the chairman of the parliamentary board.

He was arrested in 1942 for his participation in Quit India Movement and was kept in jail for three years. In 1945, when interim government was made, Vallabhbhai was made the Congress representative in the government after being released from the prison. Subsequently, in 1946, he became the deputy prime minister.

When India became free in 1947, he became the first Home Minister of India and he had to tackle certain issues on war footing. Muslim League launched direct action in several provinces which resulted in communal riots. There was total **chaos** all around. With the kind lawlessness that prevailed in several parts of the country, it required a man of grit and determination at the helm. He handled all of these with a great degree of tact and showed immense political acumen in dealing with the volatile situation. He differed with Nehru on several issues relating to Kashmir. Historians believe if Nehru had followed his advice, the Kashmir issue would not have gone to the UN, where it has remained unresolved till date. Kashmir continues to be a **vexing** issue for India. It was largely because of his political acumen that about six hundred princely states including Hyderabad were merged into India.

Vallabhbhai was the iron man of India and there is no dearth of people who still believe he would have proved to be a more successful prime minister than Nehru was and some of the burning issues that still plague India would not have raised their head. He died in 1950. Sardar Vallabhbhai Patel will ever remain **etched** in the minds of people and the pages of history.

Vocabulary

Acumen—(n) insightfulness, shrewdness shown by keen insight, a tapering point. **Fledgling**—(adj) young and inexperienced, newbie, newcomer, starter; the word refers to birds that have acquired their flying feathers. **Wrought**—(v) used only in past tense, the word means 'caused something to happen, especially a change'. **Trait**—(n) a particular quality in personality, a distinguishing feature of one's personal nature, attribute. **Plaudit**—(n) enthusiastic approval, acclaim. **Budge**—(v) move very slightly. **Brokered**—(v) negotiated, talked terms. **Chaos**—(n) a state of extreme confusion and disorder, bedlam, pandemonium. **Vexing**—(adj) extremely annoying or displeasing, causing irritation or annoyance. **Etched**—(v) cut or impressed into a surface, engraved, incised or inscribed.

□

8

Lal Bahadur Shastri

Jawaharlal Nehru was fading out in the minds of people after 1962 war **debacle.** Many thought it was Nehru's personal failure. India had begun to wonder as to who could replace Nehru. No visible leader was in sight. Nehru's was a towering personality. 'Who after Nehru' had become a national **refrain**. When Nehru died in 1964, the **mantle** fell on a short-statured man called Lal Bahadur Shastri, a man having no political profile whatsoever. The very idea seemed **ludicrous** to many. The man was born to be **dwarfed**. He was born on a date that is remembered as Gandhiji's birthday. On 2nd October, 1904, he was born in a non-descriptive family in Mughal Sarai of UP. He had a very difficult childhood. His father died when he was barely two years old. His mother did not stay at her in-law's place after her husband's death. Lal Bahadur somehow managed to complete his primary education from his native place. There were occasions when the young Lal Bahadur had to swim across a river to reach his school. It showed grit and determination of a young boy. It was this grit and determination that was to **steer** him when faced with the severest crisis of career. He moved to Varanasi to be under the guidance of his uncle. He was admitted to Harish Chandra High School. He at once proved his mettle at studies. He became darling of all for his qualities. Besides being brilliant in his studies, he also became known for his honesty.

It was during very period that Gandhi's movement was gaining ground and more and more people were getting drawn towards it. **Imbued** with the spirit of patriotism, he could not resist the temptation of joining the movement. He gave up his studies and plunged into the freedom movement. He was promptly arrested for taking part in civil disobedient movement. But he was released in view of his raw age and **diminutive** size.

He joined Kashi Vidyapeeth at Varanasi after completion of his high school education. The Vidyapeeth was quite far from his place of residence. As he could not afford to pay for transportation, he walked all the way to the Peeth and returned the same way after classes were over. This hardly left him any time for studies, but this did not come in his way to securing first division in the examination.

Lal Bahadur always wanted to serve people. So, after finishing his education, he engaged himself in a movement launched to rid society of the evil spirit of untouchability. He concurred with the view of Gandhi that it was a sin against humanity, God and godliness. His devotion to social cause, his hard work and honesty made him very popular with people. He entered into wedlock with Lalita Devi. It was a marriage without dowry. Lalita Devi gave him a charkha popularised by Gandhi as wedding gift and Lal Bahadur used this charkha for spinning yarn for his personal use.

Shastri was a well-read man. When free from movement activities or when in jail, he read Immanuel Kant, Harold Laski, Bertrand Russel, Hegel and many others. He faced many hardships during this period but nothing could dislodge him from his belief that non-violent movement launched by Gandhi was the right path. He was in it whole-heartedly.

In free India, he took up many responsibilities such as general secretary of the Congress Party and Railway Minister in the Union Government. He was so **conscientious** that he owned the responsibility of a railway accident and resigned his job. This has become a rarity in today's politics of India.

He became Prime Minister of India in 1964 and the very next year he had to face the war designs of Pakistan. The country was facing **innumerable** problems after the ignominious defeat at the hands of China in 1962. Indian economy was in shambles; it needed to stand up on its feet. But before any **tangible** steps can be taken, war was forced on the country. Shastri needed to **bolster** food production and also to tackle Pakistan across its borders. He needed kisan and jawan, farmers and soldiers: farmers to feed the nation and soldiers to defend the nation. He gave a call for **renouncing** food for a day every week and gave a slogan to the nation: Jai Jawan Jai Kisan. His appeal to renounce food for a day was lapped up by people and soldiers responded to his call by hitting Pakistan deep into its territory. Shastri's diminutive figure rose to be seen and acknowledged by one and all. He was no more a dwarf. He became a towering personality in the international arena.

Pakistan was forced to come to the negotiating table after suffering huge casualties and losses in the war. Russia offered to **mediate**. Tashkent Agreement was signed by the two countries. What followed shocked India. Shastri had a massive heart attack and he died in Tashkent. Not much is known about how and why this happened when the best possible medical facilities should have been made available to a visiting dignitary. He died on 11th January, 1966 just after one-and-a-half years in office. It was an **irreconcilable** loss for India. He was a true leader who put the cause above individual. It was precisely because of this trait of his that he is fondly remembered by the people of India who often wonder as to what would have been the shape of India if he had lived longer!

Vocabulary

Debacle—(n) a disastrous or embarrassing failure, a sound defeat, drubbing, whipping, etc. **Refrain**—(v) resist doing something, choose not to consume, abstain, desist or forbear. **Ludicrous**—(adj) resembling or extravagantly humorous, resembling farce, incongruous, inviting ridicule, ridiculous, absurd. **Mantle**—(n) the cloak as a symbol of authority. **Dwarfed**—(v) to make appear small by comparison, to check the growth of, to overshadow. **Imbued**—(v) diffused, hued, soaked, riddled, penetrated. **Diminutive**—(adj) very small, bantam, Lilliputian, tiny, midget. **Conscientious**—(adj) taking care to do things correctly and carefully, religiously, scrupulously. **Innumerable**—(adj) countless, infinite, myriad, numberless, too numerous to be counted. **Tangible**—(adj) that which can be touched and felt, that which is visible and seen to exist. **Bolster**—(v) to support and strengthen, to prop up with a pillow or bolster, to add padding to. **Renouncing**—(v) to give up, to leave voluntarily, to cast off, to turn away from. **Mediate**—(v) to act between parties with a view to reconciling differences, to arbitrate, to intermediate, to intercede, to liaise. **Irreconcilable**—(adj) impossible to reconcile, being unreconcilable.

□

9

Dr. A.P.J. Abdul Kalam

Regarded as an ideal Indian and a source of inspiration for the future generations, President Dr. A.P.J. Abdul Kalam was born on October 15, 1931 in an ordinary Tamil family of Rameshwaram in Tamil Nadu. His full name is Abul Pakir Jainulabedin Abdul Kalam. His father Jainulabedin and mother Aashiamma were a simple and religious-minded couple. They held an honourable place in the society and were regarded as an ideal couple. They lived in a joint family.

Kalam's father was a simple person. He never cared for luxuries and gave more importance to **rational** thoughts and human values. The senior-most priest of Rameshwaram temple, Pt. Lakshman Shastri was his dear friend. They used to have long **spiritual** discussions and Kalam as a boy listened attentively to those discussions. Although Kalam could not understand everything but his thinking has been largely influenced by it.

During his childhood, Abdul Kalam partook his meals with his mother sitting on the kitchen floor. His mother used to spread a banana leaf before him and serve him a simple meal of garnished rice, tasty sambhar, home made pickles and fresh coconut chutney.

Right from his childhood Dr. Kalam was honest, God fearing, labourious and simple, traits which he inherited from his parents.

Dr. Kalam's childhood was deeply influenced by his cousin Shamsuddin who was the sole distributor of newspapers in Rameshwaram. During those days there was great demand for Dinamani, a Tamil newspaper. Though Kalam had not yet learnt to read yet he satisfied himself by looking at the pictures, when Shamsuddin used to bring the newspaper.

When Second World War started in 1939, Kalam was only 8 years old. During those days, there was a sudden increase in demand for **tamarind** seeds in the market. Although Kalam did not know the reason, he started collecting tamarind seeds and selling them at grocery shops. This way he earned one anna everyday.

During that time emergency was announced in India because of the Second World War. As a result, the trains did not stop at Rameshwaram station. In that situation bundles of newspapers were thrown from the moving train between Rameshwaram and Dhanushkodi station. At that time Shamsuddin felt the need of an assistant who could assist him in picking up those bundles. Child Kalam was well prepared to help him and in this way he earned his first salary from his cousin Shamsuddin.

In his childhood, Kalam used to wear a **skull** cap, which is a symbol of being a Muslim. At that time Kalam was a student of class V in a primary school. Once a new teacher came to his class. Kalam was sitting in the front row with his friend Ramanand Shastri. The new teacher did not like a Hindu boy sitting next to a Muslim boy. So he ordered Kalam to sit at the last bench. Child Kalam did not like this. Ramanand Shastri too was very much grieved by this behaviour of the teacher.

When Lakshman Shastri, Ramanand Shastri's father came to know about it he called the teacher and reprimanded him, "You should not sow the seeds of religious **discrimination** in the hearts of innocent children."

The teacher apologized for his behaviour and eventually a great change came in his attitude.

Having completed the primary education, Kalam was admitted to Swartz High School in Ramanathapuram. He had to stay in the school hostel. While at Ramanathapuram he very often missed his parents, his home and especially the South Indian sweetmeat 'poli' prepared by his mother.

In spite of his great love for home, Kalam was fully dedicated to his studies because his parents and teachers had high expectations from him. He worked very hard to achieve his aim and nothing could deter him from his firm determination.

Once, during his school days, it so happened that the maths teacher Ramakrishna Aiyyar was teaching in another class. Unknowingly Kalam entered the class room. Seeing this, the teacher immediately caught hold off him by his neck and hit him with a rod before the entire class. Later, when Kalam secured the highest marks in mathematics, Ramakrishna Aiyyar narrated the **episode** at the time of morning prayer before everyone. He announced, "The boy whom I beat with a rod, will become a great man one day. Mark my words, this student is going to become the pride of his school and teachers."

Since childhood, Kalam developed a deep liking for the mysteries of the sky, and the flight of birds across the seas. He enjoyed the sight of cranes flying over the sea and long flights of birds. He decided that one day he too would go for long flights in the sky. Later he was the first person in Rameshwaram to fly in a plane.

When Kalam completed his schooling, he was brimming with **enthusiasm** and confidence. Without a second thought he entered Saint Joseph College, Tiruchirapalli, in 1950. During his college days he worked hard. He was a very disciplined student. When he was a final year student in the college he developed a great liking for English Literature. He read all the available books on English literature by great writers such as Tolstoy, Scott, Hardy, etc. Also when he was a student of the final year he developed a deep inclination towards Physics. He felt great pleasure in reading about the highest knowledge of **astronomy**, particularly our solar system.

To fulfil his dream, Kalam decided to study Engineering after his B.Sc. from Saint Joseph College. For this, he needed at least one thousand rupees, but his father did not have that much money. It was his elder sister Johra who came to his rescue. She mortgaged her gold bangles and necklace and got Kalam admitted to Madras Institute of Technology (MIT). At that time Kalam had a single ambition – to be a pilot.

Modesty is a good quality but Kalam had to face many difficulties at MIT because of it. Because of his humble nature, he was quite hesitant to ask questions or reply to them in front of everyone in the class. That is why, his fellow students used to make fun of him. Kalam was depressed about it. He lost his self-confidence. During those days, he used to remember his father's teachings and inspirational advices. His father often said: "One who understands others, learns; but a person is called wise when he understands himself. Learning without wisdom is nothing but crammed knowledge, it is of no use. Knowing oneself is much important." This thought brought self-confidence in him and he was recharged with enthusiasm for achieving his aim. During his studies in MIT, Kalam was inspired by three teachers - Prof. Spander, Prof. K.A. B. Panadalaiin and Prof. Narsingha Rao to give his thoughts a concrete form. Kalam was able to construct his work field with the joint assistance of these teachers which laid the foundation of his life.

After completing his third year from Madras Institute of Technology, he joined as a technical instructor at the Hindustan Aeronautics Ltd. After becoming an aeronautical engineer from Hindustan Aeronautics Ltd. he got two excellent job opportunities and both of which were enough to fulfil his childhood dreams. One was in the Indian Air Force and the other was in the Technical Development and Production Directorate, Ministry of Defence. Kalam prepared well with full dedication and hard labour. He was very much assured of his selection in the Indian Air Force.

But he was deeply disappointed when he came to know that out of 25 candidates, only 8 had been selected and he had stood ninth. It was a great setback. He was disappointed but he soon recovered from this. Another chance yet remained with him. Here he achieved success and was appointed as Technical Assistant in the Technical Development and Production Directorate, Ministry of Defence, Govt. of India.

In the 1960s, Dr. Kalam joined the Vikram Sarabhai Space Centre, Thumba (Kerala). There he played a key role in the development of the first **indigenous** satellite launcher. After that in 1982, he worked as Director of the Defence Research and the Development Organisation of India and was in charge of the Joint Controlled Launcher Development Programme. After that he worked as a Scientific Advisor to the Defence Minister and later as a Defence Advisor to the Prime Minister. He also played a major role in the 1998 nuclear experiments. Dr. Kalam was quite co-operative with his colleagues in the work front. He paid attention to their ideas. He never made an attempt to impose his ideas upon them. He tried to maintain discipline, faith and mutual understanding in his team. His behaviour was friendly with everyone. Because of these qualities, Kalam was a favourite among his colleagues. In spite of these, he has few friends in his private life. He has been totally dedicated to his work throughout his life and work has been his companion.

While serving the country in various ways, Dr. Kalam not only fulfilled the dreams of his parents and teachers but also his own. He put India in an equal position with advanced countries and thereby enhanced its honour and pride.

After retirement, Dr. Kalam taught at the Annamalai University in Tamil Nadu. He has been conferred with various prestigious awards. In 1981 he was awarded the 'Padma Bhushan'; in 1990, 'Padma Vibhushan', and in 1997, he was honoured with the 'Bharat Ratna', the highest civilian award. Besides this, he was awarded the Dr. Virender Roy Space Award, National Nehru Award and Arya Bhatt Award. Twenty-eight universities throughout the country awarded him the title of Doctor of Science.

Undoubtedly we can assume Dr. Kalam as a fortunate person after having received so many awards and honours but he did not get anything out of luck but as a result of sheer hard work and strong determination. He had to face obstacles throughout his life at every step. There was problem of economic scarcity, lack of will power, non-cooperation of colleagues, and bitterness, failures, ironical comments and many other things, but nothing could deter him from the path. On account of this, Dr. Kalam developed more modesty in his behaviour after every achievement.

Whether it was the assignment as a scientist or as a teacher, whatever work he was given, he accomplished it sincerely.

During his tenure as a teacher in Annamalai University, Dr. Kalam was nominated as the President of India. On 25th July 2002, he was elected the 12th President of India. He took oath as a president under Chief Justice B.N. Kripal.

As President, Dr. Kalam replied strictly to the criticism of those people who were protesting strongly against a scientist being appointed as President, who had the image of a 'missile man'. Dr. Kalam's heart is as soft as a child's although he has firm determination and will power in achieving his aim. He forgets himself in the company of children and becomes a part of them. He regards children as a seed in which the future tree is hidden. He is of the view that children are the future of India. He has not only hopes from the young generation, but also has full faith in them. He has the dream of educating each and every child of India and it is his message that we should nurture high dreams and at the same time create confidence in our heart to transform those dreams into reality, because this thought only can take our country towards path of progress.

Dr. Kalam believes that by 2020, our country will be able to become a developed country. To transform his ideas into a solid form, Dr. Kalam has many plans. These programmes can turn to a reality, but it is not possible only by the inspiration of a few selected Indians, for that, every Indian has to work together. He accepts that the role of the younger generation is of utmost importance in the development of a nation. Therefore he considers the Indian youth as the most powerful resource and inspires them to work unitedly. He opines that if you are a good man, then you can perform every job in the best manner. For example, if we take the instance of Dr. Kalam's personality then he is a capable scientist, an ideal teacher besides being a wonderful colleague and an excellent writer. He has not only a good knowledge of Indian classical music, but he is a perfect violin player too. He also has interest in gardening. He feels unlimited peace of mind and pleasure in the company of nature. He has a very busy work schedule, but even then he has kept a few regular habits such as morning walk, prayer, yoga, head massage with coconut oil before bath and drinking a glass of milk before retiring at night.

He always says that keep every moment busy and meaningful, but at the same time, always take out time to feel the **fragrance** of flowers or to watch the **myriad** colours of butterflies.

Dr. Kalam has this message for the young generation –

As a young citizen of India,
armed with technology, knowledge and love for my nation,
I realise, small aim is a crime.
I will work and sweat for a great vision,
the vision of transforming India into a developed nation
powered by economic strength with value system.
I am one of the citizens of a billion,
only the vision will ignite the billion souls.
It has entered into me,
the ignited souls compared to any resource,
is the most powerful resource
on the earth, above the earth and under the earth.
I will keep the lamp of knowledge burning
to achieve the vision – Developed India.

While delivering a lecture at the Indian Institute of Management Shillong, Kalam collapsed and died from an apparent cardiac arrest on 27 July 2015, aged 83. His death was mourned across the nation with thousands including national level dignitaries attending the funeral ceremony hold in his hometown of Rameshwaram, where he buried with full state honours.

Vocabulary

Rational – (adj) relating to, based on, or agreeable to reason or logic. **Spiritual** – (adj) things of a spiritual, ecclesiastical; or religious nature of, relating to, or affecting the human spirit or soul as opposed to material or physical things. **Tamarind** – (n) sticky brown acidic pulp from the pod of a tree of the pea family, widely used as a flavouring in Asian cooking. **Skull**—(n) a framework of bone or cartilage enclosing the brain of a vertebrate, the skeleton of a person's or animal's head. **Discrimination**—(n) the unjust or prejudicial treatment of different categories of people or things, especially on the grounds of race, age or sex. **Episode**—(n) An event or a group of events occurring as part of a larger sequence, an incident or period considered in isolation. **Ethusiasm**—(n) intense and eager enjoyment, interest, or approval. **Astronomy**—(n) the branch of science that deals with celestial objects, space, and the physical universe as a whole. **Modesty**—(n) The quality or state of being unassuming or moderate in the estimation of one's abilities. **Indigenous**—(adj) originating or occurring naturally in a particular place, native. **Myriad**—(adj) countless or extremely great in number. **Fragrance**—(n) a pleasant, sweet smell.

□

10

Atal Bihari Vajpayee

A product of Rashtriya Swayamsevak Sangh (RSS), Atal Bihari Vajpyee was born on 25th December, 1924 into a Brahmin family in Gwalior. His father Pt. Krishna Bihari Vajpayee was a school teacher and a well-known poet of his time; his grandfather was a renowned Sanskrit scholar. It could well be said that he was born in a scholarly environment and poetry was an in-born trait with him.

He became the tenth Prime Minister of India and occupied the office for three consecutive terms. The first time he had a very short stint of 13 days from May 16, 1996 to June 1, 1996. It was followed up by another stint of 13 months from March 1998 to April 1999 and the final full tenure lasted up to March 2004. He was closely associated with the process of making of Jan Sangh which later got re-christened as Bharatiya Janta Party. Vajpayee remained a parliamentarian for over four decades. He was elected to Lok Sabha nine times and two times to Rajya Sabha. He was the only parliamentarian to have been elected from four different states. The states he represented as a parliamentarian were Uttar Pradesh, Madhya Pradesh, Gujarat and Delhi. He won his first election from Balarampur and later moved to Lucknow in UP, a constituency he represented till 2009. He retired from active politics due to his ill-health. He no longer makes public appearances.

Vajpayee's first exposure to politics came about in 1942 when he along with his elder brother was arrested for taking part in Quit India Movement. In 1951, he was assigned the task of working for Jan Sangh, a newly formed right wing political party **espousing** the cause of Hinduism. He soon became an aide to the party leader Shyama Prasad Mookherjee. He was one of the founder members of this political outfit. In 1954, when Mookherjee went on fast-unto-death in Kashmir in protest against what he called ill-treatment meted out to non-Kashmiris in the valley, Vajpayee was with him through thick and thin. Mookherjee died in prison. In 1957, Vajpayee was elected to the Lok Sabha from Balrampur. His **oratory** in the Lok Sabha impressed Jawaharlal Nehru so much that he made a declaration that one day he would become the Prime Minister of India. How prophetic were those words!

His oratorical and organisation skills made him the face of Jan Sangh and after the death of Deen Dayal Upadhyay, the mantle of leadership of the party fell on Vajpayee's shoulders. He became the national president of the party in 1968 and together with Nanaji Deshmukh, Balraj Madhok and Lal Krishna Advani, he took the party to greater heights.

During 1975 to 1977, he along with many leaders was arrested and kept in jail following imposition of internal emergency by Indira Gandhi. **Heeding** the call of JP, who was then leading a movement against Indira's regime, he merged his Jan Sangh into Janta Party in 1977 and fought the election against Indira Gandhi. She was defeated and a new government led by Morarji Desai came to occupy power at the Centre. Vajpayee became the External Affairs Minister in this government. He made an immediate impact when he became the first External Affairs Minister to have made his speech in Hindi in the UN General Assembly. He had become established as an experienced statesman and a respected political leader by the time Janata Party dissolved in 1979. With the help of Bhairon Singh Shekhawat and Lal Krishna Advani, he formed BJP in 1980 with the backing of RSS. He launched a **vitriolic** attack on Indira regime and occupied the space of the main opposition party in the country.

The party opposed the growing Sikh militancy in Punjab and held Indira Gandhi responsible for this. He held her divisive and corrupt practices responsible for the **menace** of militancy in Punjab that was impacting the integrity of the country. The nation had to pay a huge price for this. BJP did not support Operation Blue Star launched by Indira Gandhi to flush out terrorists who had holed up in the Golden Temple of Amritsar. The party was also highly critical of the massacre of Sikhs that went on in Delhi and elsewhere following the assassination of Indira Gandhi in 1984. The party was equally critical of the reactions of some of the key Congress leaders including those of Rajiv Gandhi who seemed to justify the killing of Sikhs by saying that when a big tree fell, the earth was bound to feel tremors.

Even though BJP was left with only two members in the Lok Sabha in 1984, Vajpayee's towering personality stood out in the Parliament. His voice could neither be **subdued** nor be drowned in the **cacophonous din** of the House. Even the government heard him out. Vajpayee was a true nationalist. Nation was not just a piece of land for him. It was a living and kicking entity. He was a poet at heart. Circumstances made him a politician. He has himself stated it on a number of occasions that he wanted to spend his time in studies and musings. He never allowed the politician inside him to overtake the human side of his character. There is an interesting anecdote that will show the human side of his character. Rabri Devi was the Chief Minister of Bihar and Vajpayee the Prime Minister. Some of the key members of his party from Bihar urged Vajpayee to disallow Lalu entry into the residence of the Chief Minister who was his wife. There was no loss of love between BJP and Lalu. Yet, he did not accede to the request of his party men and said that Laloo was the husband of the chief minister and he had an inalienable right to stay with his wife. It was precisely because of such qualities that he was liked and respected by all irrespective of party affiliations.

BJP became the political voice of the Ram Janma Bhoomi Mandir Movement led by Vishwa Hindu Parishad and RSS. In the **ensuing** elections, BJP won in Gujarat and Maharashtra and also improved its tally in Karnataka. This gave a **fillip** to the party and, in 1996, Vajpayee was declared the prime ministerial candidate from the party. This was the beginning of the **ascendancy** of the party. In the ensuing elections in 1996, BJP emerged as the single largest party and was invited to form a government. This government lasted for 13 days. Till 1998, India had make-shift governments led by Deve Gowda and I.K. Gujaral. Elections were held in 1998 and BJP once again emerged as the single largest party. Vajpayee formed the government yet again with the help of several regional parties. However, after 13 months in power, AIADMK withdrew support to the government. Since no party was in a position to form the government on its own, Vajpayee continued as the caretaker government till elections. This time BJP returned to power in the shape of National Democratic Alliance (NDA) and continued till 2004. This period is regarded by many in India and elsewhere as the golden period.

The areas where Vajpayee seemed to have made positive impact were national highway projects, economic reforms and foreign policy initiatives. His quadrangular road projects were **immensely** successful and went a long way in improving linkage facilities, thus giving fillip to industrial growth. Push for economic reforms had a desired impact when many countries imposed sanctions against India on information, technologies and resources following successful conduct of five underground nuclear tests at Pokhran in Rajasthan in 1998. India successfully withstood the challenges and paved the way for further progress. Vajpayee's stature rose further not just domestically but also internationally. For the first time, it looked India was really poised for a big leap forward and become a superpower. National confidence was on a high plane. The nation had really become what Vajpayee called 'a living and kicking entity'.

He made serious and sincere efforts to normalise relations with Pakistan in 1998 and 1999. First, it was Nawaz Sharif and then it was General Musharraf with whom he made attempts to improve relations between the two countries. It was Vajpayee who started bus service between Delhi and Lahore. As a goodwill gesture, he himself travelled in the bus up to Wagha Border where he was received by the Prime Minister of Pakistan. But India's goodwill gesture was not **reciprocated** by Pakistan. What followed was Kargil war. Pakistan was soundly defeated.

Still Vajpayee did not lose his faith in dialogue and continued it with vigour in 1999 with Musharraf who had **usurped** power by throwing out Nawaz Sharif's Government. Not much success ensued as Pakistan did not reciprocate with sincerity.

Vajpayee also **mooted** the idea of inter-linking of rivers to meet the challenges of flood and drought. India really seemed to have been shining. But it seems the shine had not **percolated** down to every level of society which was perhaps why despite so much **trumpet** about it, NDA lost power in 2004.

This defeat shocked many and the party seemed to have failed to reconcile itself to the loss. But it has to be said to the credit of Vajpayee that even though the party lost power, Vajpayee did not lose **esteem** of the people. Even those politically opposed to him could not fault him. Vajpayee will go down in the history as a politician with a golden heart. His **benign** smiling face continues to endure. He was a politician with a difference. He was a poet at heart and it showed in his political dealings as well. A politician is required to make compromises to remain in power, not Vajpayee. He did not try out any **stratagem** to stay in power when his government lost the vote of confidence in 1998 by just one vote. This is unthinkable in today's political milieu when incumbents go to any length to stay in power and do not hesitate to resort to fair or foul means, with greater emphasis on foul means. Vajpayee set a high political standard which sadly no longer holds good. That precisely explains why politicians are so low in public esteem. The kind of respect and goodwill Vajpayee enjoyed even as the Leader of Opposition is unthinkable today. It was only Vajpayee who could speak about 'raj dharma'. The poet in him never allowed him to be a political hypocrite. He is sure to go down in the **annals** of history as a man love by one and all. Those who opposed him did so for political reasons. On personal counts, he was dear to all.

Vocabulary

Espouse—(v) adopt, embrace, follow. **Oratory**—(n) address, speech. **Heed**—(v) pay close attention to. **Vitriolic**—(adj) harsh or corrosive in tone, acerbic. **Menace**—(n) a source of danger, a threat or an act of threatening. **Subdue**—(v) to put down by force or intimidation, inhibit. **Cacophonous**—(adj) having an unpleasant sound, cacophonic. **Din**—(n) a loud harsh or strident noise, the act of making a noisy disturbance. **Ensue**—(v) issue or terminate, end, result. **Fillip**—(n) boost, encouragement. **Ascendancy**—(n) the state that exists when one person or group has power over another, control, dominance. **Immensely**—(adv) to an exceedingly great degree or extent, vastly, gigantically, colossally. **Reciprocate**—(v) act, feel or give mutually or in return. **Usurp**—(v) take over, arrogate, assume, seize. **Mooted**—(v) thought about carefully, weighed, considered, debated. **Percolate**—(v) permeate or penetrate gradually, spread gradually, sink in. **Trumpet**—(v) proclaim on or as if on a trumpet, play or blow on trumpet. **Benign**—(adj) pleasant and beneficial in nature or influence, kindness of disposition or manner. **Esteem**—(n) the condition of being honoured, respected. **Stratagem**—(n) contrivance, gambit, ploy, dodge. **Annals**—(n) chronological record.

□

11

Chhatrapati Shivaji

Shivaji Bhosle was a seventeenth-century Maratha warrior who was the first Chhatrapati of the Maratha Empire, which peaked in the eighteenth century and covered much of what we call the Indian sub-continent today. He was born on 19th February, 1627 at a place called Shivneri. He married Putalibai in 1653. He had two sons Sambaji, Rajaram and four daughters. He died in 1680 at Raigad fort near Pune in Maharashtra. Even as his acts of bravery, gallantry, chivalry and heroism remained generally restricted to the Maratha region, he is mainly known as the saviour of Hindus and the defender of Hinduism. He has left an everlasting imprint on the pages of Indian history. He was one of the most towering personalities of his time who took on the might of the Mughal. Born in the family of Shahji, a small landlord, he showed the promises of **prodigious** proportions right from his early childhood. His mother Jija Bai was both religious and intelligent. Shivaji grew under her direct care and supervision. She took great pains to imbibe the spirit of love for the motherland. She groomed him like a shining star. She imparted all kinds of training to him so that he could face to the **rigours** of life. Shivaji was fearless, brave and adventurous. At the same time, he was a very **magnanimous** human being.

Right from the childhood, Shivaji was a **shrewd** strategist. He was intelligent and very promising from the very childhood. Patriotism was **steeped** into his blood and psyche. He would not hesitate to take any step to serve the cause of his motherland or to defend the faith that his mother practised. It was his mother

Jija Bai who instilled these traits in him so that he became trained in warfare tactics and a fearless fighter. He could not stand the oppression heaped by the Muslim rulers on the hapless Hindus. What once looked like an impossible mission, he made it possible in a very short span of time. To put an end to the oppressive Muslim regime, he brought together the landlords, chieftains and others to form a formidable fighting force in order to **stem** the influence of the Muslim rulers who were **wreaking havoc** on his countrymen. He swiftly conquered the state of Bijapur and other territories under the control of the Mughal even as he seemed to be negotiating peace with Aurangzeb.

Shivaji carved out an independent Maratha state in the territories north and south of Konkan. Shivaji urged the emperor to recognise his rule over Bijapuri district of north Konkan, but the emperor sent his most experienced noble Shaista Khan to crush Shivaji instead. After a ceaseless military campaign lasting for over two years, Shivaji in a daring move attacked the camp of Shaista Khan in April 1663 and cut off his thumb. Being an astute strategist, he proved equal to the tactics of Aurangzeb. In fact, he proved he was more than a match for Aurangzeb. The emperor tried to weaken his spirit, but he failed in this mission. A compromise treaty was signed in June 1665.

Pledging his loyalty to the emperor, Shivaji agreed to visit him at Agra. But the treatment he received at the imperial court did not go down well with him and Shivaji refused to compromise. Aurangzeb placed him under house arrest. Before the emperor could take any further action, Shivaji escaped to the Deccan on 28th August, 1666. After returning to the Deccan, there were no further **skirmishes** with the Mughal and Shivaji concentrated his energy on streamlining and devising laws for the Maratha government as he expanded and consolidated his power. Shivaji crowned himself king in his Raigarh fort on 17th June, 1674 assuming the title Chhatrapati (Lord of the Umbrella or King of Kings).

Shivaji amassed huge wealth in the course of battles he fought with his **foes,** but he did not amass it for his own use. He equitably distributed the collected wealth amongst the poor and improved their lot. One of the great qualities of Shivaji was to treat his enemies with respect and dignity they deserved. He never tried to belittle or **denigrate** them. His sense of decency never deserted him even while he was dealing with his enemies. He held a very high moral standard and it was always visible in his dealings with others, especially with the **vanquished**. He saw to it that children, women, the old and **infirm** were not harassed. As a matter of fact, he provided them protection and comfort whenever warranted necessary. This endeared him even to those he defeated and conquered. His secular **credentials** were unquestionable. His generosity was equally **unimpeachable**. Even his enemies praised him for this quality of his. Khafti Khan, a court historian of Aurangzeb, while describing him as 'a hellish dog', credited him with possessing qualities. He described him as 'most secular and generous'. Coming as it does from the mouth of an enemy's historian, it certainly is a great certification for Shivaji. A French envoy, Mauser Germaine, at his time also paid rich tributes to the secular credentials and humanitarianism of Shivaji.

Shivaji was a great administrator and, like his contemporaries, a **despotic** ruler with a noble face. His central and provincial governments were based on the systems of the Deccani sultans and Vijaynagara. He imposed a military tax called *chauth* in 1672 on his Mughal subjects. This was done to meet the expenses towards their defence. His army drew its main supplies from the neighbouring kingdoms. His army rested from July to September and went on a war and **plunder spree** from the time of Dussera. He had also developed a very strong navy. He was perceived as the protector of Brahmans and cows and as the architect of Hindu self-rule and as the defender of Hindu religion and culture. Distinguished Hindu saints blessed him and asked their disciples to support him. The Maratha **terrain** enabled Shivaji to train his soldiers and guerilla tactics and on the ways and means of surrounding and killing the enemies. Many regard him as the founder of Hindu empire and regret that he did not live long enough to give stability to the Hindu empire.

Shivaji died without nominating a successor which led to **internecine** war between various groups for supremacy leading to disintegration of the kingdom Shivaji had carved out. So long as he remained on the scene, he was able to keep all small chieftains and landlords together to serve the larger cause of protecting Hindus from the marauding Mughal. If it were not for him, Aurangzeb would have run through Hindu bastions. It was his resoluteness that not only **thwarted** the attempts of Aurangzeb to overtake Maratha region, but also succeeded in keeping him and his **rampaging** troops at bay. His healing touches to the defeated chieftains also helped keep them together under his leadership. But what he had so **painstakingly** fused and integrated began to fall apart the moment he died in 1680 of some mysterious ailment.

Vocabulary

Prodigious – (adj) very large or powerful and causing surprise or admiration, colossal. **Rigours** – (n)the quality of being hard to endure. **Magnanimous** – (adj) kind, generous and forgiving, especially towards an enemy or rival. **Shrewd** – (adj) marked by practical hard-headed intelligence, astute, sharp, savvy, calculating. **Steeped** – (v) devoted fully to, absorbed, engrossed. **Stem** – (v) to stop something that is flowing or increasing. **Wreak** – (v) cause to happen or to occur as a consequence. **Havoc** – (n) violent and needless disturbance. **Skirmishes** – (n) a minor short-term fight. **Foes** – (n) enemies, adversaries. **Denigrate** – (v) cause to seem less serious, play down, belittle, asperse, derogate, defame, smear; **Vanquish** – (v) come out better in a race, competition or conflict, beat, defeat. **Infirm** – (adj) lacking bodily or muscular strength or vitality. **Credentials** – (n) documents attesting to the truth of certain stated facts, certificates, bona fides; **Unimpeachable** – (adj) that which cannot be doubted or questioned, beyond doubt or reproach, free of guilt, not subject to blame, blameless. **Despotic** – (adj) characteristic of an absolute ruler or absolute rule having absolute sovereignty, authoritarian, dictatorial. **Plunder** – (v) steal goods, take as spoils, loot. **Spree** – (n) a brief indulgence of one's impulses; (v) engage without restraint in an activity and indulge as while shopping, fling. **Terrain** – (n) reference to an area of land while describing its natural features. **Internecine** – (adj) of conflict within a group or organisation, bloody, internal. **Thwart** – (v) hinder or prevent. **Rampaging** – (v) a sudden act of wild and violent behaviour often causing damage and destruction. **Painstakingly** – (adv) done with a lot of care and attention to details.

□

12
Jhansi Ki Rani

She was born not to play a **subservient** role to her male counterparts. She was not the one to remain tied down to household activities, oblivious of what was obtaining outside. It was, therefore, not a matter of great surprise that she should plunge into what was essentially perceived to be in the domain of men. A woman fighting for the cause of the nation and taking up arms to defend motherland was unthinkable. Jhansi ki Rani, as Lakshmi Bai was popularly known, did exactly that. It would not be an **exaggeration** to call her the greatest woman warrior of India, nor will it be improper to say that she was the first to have started real fight for liberating India from the clutches of the British Rule. She lived for the country and died fighting for the country. She has gone down in the history of India as one of the most illustrious individuals who sacrificed her life for the country and its people.

She was Manu (Mannikarnika) as a child. Born on 13th November, 1835 in the Brahmin family of Moropanth and Bhagirathi, she showed her inclinations of being illustrious and courageous right from the very early stage of her life. At the age of four, she lost her mother and the responsibility of grooming her fell on the shoulders of her father. While completing her education, she took special lessons on horse riding, sword fighting, shooting and other martial arts. This kept her bodily and mentally agile, which was to serve her in good stead at the later stage of her life.

Early marriage was a tradition those days and Manu too was married off at an early age. She was married to Raja Gangadhar Rao, the Maharaja of Jhansi. Consequently, she became the queen, Jhansi ki Rani. A formal name of Lakshmi Bai was bestowed on her. Her marriage was solemnised in a temple in the city of Jhansi. She gave birth to a male child, who unfortunately died within four months of his birth. There was no further birth in the family. She adopted Damodar Rao as her son. Having a heir for the throne was necessary those days as Lord Dalhousie had promulgated a law called Doctrine of Lapse, whereby an Indian estate having no legal heir would merge into British Empire.

Gangadhar was not keeping well. It was, therefore, thought expedient to adopt a child and pronounce him as the legal heir to the throne. But Lord Dalhousie did not recognise Damodar as the legal heir to the throne since the child was not their own. An adopted child cannot be conferred the right of being legal heir was his interpretation of the law. Dalhousie tried to **annex** the estate of Jhansi on this plea because Gangadhar had expired in the meantime. Finding her alone and **desolate**, he thought he was going to have a cake-walk over her estate. Lakshmi Bai had no such intent of handing over her estate to the British on a **platter**. In fact, Dalhousie was using this as a **ploy** to expand British Empire in India.

Jhansi ki Rani was offered a life pension of ₹ 60,000 and was permitted to use the city palace. When she was communicated the decision to annex her estate, she was reported to have retorted that she would not **relinquish** control of Jhansi. However, no resistance was actually offered when the bid to take over was made. But this attempt to bulldoze occupation of Jhansi backfired because it hurt the sentiments of Indians. There were other reasons also for the **disenchantment** of people. The cow slaughter was banned in the estate. But with the takeover, British allowed this practice to resume. This deeply hurt the sentiments of people. The British also refused to release money for the celebration of her son's sacred thread ceremony. All these added to the discomfiture of the people as also to the personal discomfiture of Lakshmi Bai. The people of Jhansi saw these moves as an insult to their queen.

This kind of humiliation heaped on her made her more resolute and determined to fight for her rights. She decided she was not going to yield. She was going to defend Jhansi at all costs. She had become a symbol of patriotism and self-respect. She strengthened the defence of Jhansi and cobbled up an army of the rebels to fight the English. Women too were enlisted in the army and they were **imparted** extensive training in warfare. Some of the illustrious names that came to her support were Khuda Baksh, Ghulam Ghaus Khan, Moti Bai, Lala Bhau Baksh and several others. They and many more drawn from both communities of Hindus and Muslims came under one umbrella of Lakshmi Bai top launch a **blistering** fight for the cause of their independence and to protect the dignity of their queen. But then there were a few traitors as well. There was one Naya Khan and the other Dinkar Rao.

The British attacked her **bastion** in March 1858. Instead of surrendering to the British force, she chose to meet the challenge. The fight continued for nearly two weeks. Though it was known that she should not be able to sustain her fight for long, yet she and her warriors did not surrender before the might of the British Empire. She personally led the fight back and fought on bravely as long as she could. The British army was amazed to see her speed and agility. But it was too good to last. The British army broke the defence and entered the city of Jhansi. When it became obvious that she was not going to hold out, she along with some of warriors left Jhansi and moved to Kalpi. Rebels from other places also joined her there. Tatya Tope of Kalpi was also there. From there she moved to Gwalior. Another battle ensued and she fought on bravely as though she was possessed. On the second day of the resumed fight, when she was barely twenty-two, she achieved martyrdom. 18th June, 1858 was the day when she laid down her life for the cause Independence. In a male-dominated society, Lakshmi Bai, a woman of substance, showed her **mettle** in the battlefield. She had no formal training of any kind except her sense of self-respect, dignity and yet she took on the might of the British Empire and sowed the seeds of struggle for India's independence.

It could well be said that it was Lakshmi Bai who had launched the first war of independence which India lost but sowed the seeds for independence with her heroic act of bravery.

Vocabulary

Subservient—(adj) too willing to obey other people. **Exaggeration**—(n) a statement or description that makes something seem larger, better or worse than it actually is. **Annex**—(v) to take control of a country or region, etc. usually by force. **Desolate**—(adj) [of a place] empty and without people making one sad or frightened; very lonely and unhappy; **Platter**—(n) a large plate that is used for serving food. **Ploy**—(n) words or actions that are carefully planned to get advantage over somebody. **Relinquish**—(v) to stop having something, especially when that happens unwillingly. **Disenchantment**—(n) no longer feeling enthusiasm for something. **Impart**—(v) to pass information, knowledge to other people. **Blistering**—(adj) done very fast or with great energy, extremely hot in a way that is uncomfortable. **Bastion**—(n) a group of people or a system that protects a way of life or a belief when it seems it will disappear, a stronghold where people can take refuge when in distress or take shelter during a battle, citadel. **Mettle**—(n) the ability and determination to something successfully even when in adverse conditions.

□

13

Dr. Sarvapalli Radhakrishnan

Dr. Sarvapalli Radhakrishnan, the second President of India, was a devout Hindu and a great **philosopher**. He was born on 5th September, 1888 in Tirutani village of Tamil Nadu. His parents, Sarvapalli Veeraswami and Sitamma were a deeply religious couple.

Radhakrishnan was the second child of his parents. He was brought up with great love and care. Sri Veeraswami was a priest who also worked as a teacher. As a result, the atmosphere of religion as well as education prevailed in the family.

Radhakrishnan obtained his primary education in Tirutani and secondary education from Bellore College. After passing the B.A. examination from Bellore College, he took admission in Madras Christian College for higher education. Madras Christian College was a reputed college during those days.

By getting educated in missionary institutions, Radhakrishnan acquired a good command over the English language. He also had an opportunity to think about the Hindu religion and Indian culture. Christian **missionaries** were critical of the Hindu religion and Indian traditions. They used to instigate the poor and helpless Hindus to conversion by pointing that Christianity was superior and Hinduism was an inferior religion. Radhakrishnan used to often think about it when he was alone. Slowly and gradually he began to feel proud of Hindu religion and culture. He used to get hurt by the propaganda against Hinduism and the missionary activities of conversion.

From the Christian College, Radhakrishnan took admission in M.A. (Philosophy) in the same college. It was during the same period the Indian youth were developing an attitude of self-respect because of the motivating speeches of Swami Vivekananda.

Radhakrishnan's family was neither poor nor rich. They were not rich enough to bear the burden of college education. In order to continue his education smoothly, Radhakrishnan began taking tuitions.

Radhakrishnan was specialised in Philosophy and Logic. He studied in depth the *Upanishads, Gita, Brahmasutra,* and original Buddhist and Jain texts. He also studied the works of western philosophers like Plato, Platinus, Kant, Shakespeare, Wordsworth, Dante etc.

He was appointed as a Professor of Philosophy at Presidency College, Madras in 1909 after acquiring his M.A. degree from Madras Christian College. Thereafter, Radhakrishnan climbed steadily on the path of progress.

While teaching at Presidency College, Madras, Radhakrishnan delivered lectures in several institutions and also wrote scholarly essays in several national and international journals.

Radhakrishnan taught in Presidency College, Madras till 1917. By then, he was considered a reputed scholar nationally as well as internationally. Those days, Dr. Vishweshwaraiyya was the Diwan of the State of Mysore. He was a **meritorious** person. He invited selected scholars from all over India from all fields for the all-round development of Mysore. Highly impressed with the learning of Radhakrishnan, Dr. Vishweshwaraiyya appointed Radhakrishnan as a Professor of Philosophy in the Maharaja College of Mysore.

Those days well-known and reputed scholars like

Dr. Radhakumud Mukherjee, Prof. Shah and Prof. Wadia were teaching in the Maharaja College. Soon, Radhakrishnan too gained popularity due to his erudite lectures and learned speeches. Students from Madras University often came to attend his lectures.

Several universities of the world honoured him with honorary degrees for his scholarship. More than a hundred universities honoured him with doctorate degrees, amongst which 'Doctor of Law' offered by Harvard University and Overlin College need to be mentioned.

Dr. Radhakrishnan used to dress in a dhoti, a long high-necked coat and a turban. He had such good grasp over philosophy that he never used prepared notes to solve philosophical issues. When he solved philosophical **complexities** in fluent English, dressed **impeccably** in white, it appeared as if some religious-incarnate was speaking. Students and teachers of the college held him in high esteem for his extraordinary learning.

Dr. Radhakrishnan taught for three years in Maharaja College of Mysore. In this short span of three years, he won the hearts of all the students.

Those days, Dr. Ashutosh Mukherjee was the Chancellor of Calcutta University. He had appointed highly meritorious scholars like Dr. C.V. Raman, Dr. Saha etc., in the Calcutta University. Having been highly impressed by his learning, he appointed Dr. Radhakrishnan as the Head of the Department of Philosophy in Post-Graduate department of the university.

Calcutta University was reckoned amongst the best universities of India. Even the British Government used to recognise the merit of an individual passing from that university.

While teaching in Calcutta University, Dr. Radhakrishnan's popularity began spreading abroad too. It was from here that he was sent as a representative to the International Philosophical Congress held in America. He left a lasting impact, due to his impressive and scholarly speeches to the general audience.

Dr. Radhakrishnan was highly praised for his **oratorical** skills. Different nations of the world invited him to speak on Indian and western philosophy. His speech had a mesmerising effect on the audience. The actual significance of his speeches lay in his genius, which is beyond description. It was this spiritual force in him which drew everyone towards him, lifting them to the higher realms of freedom from the narrow mental confines.

In 1926, the Andhra University was established. Five years later, in 1931, Dr. Radhakrishnan was appointed as its Chancellor. In a very short span of time he completely transformed the university. By dint of his hard work, he ensured the construction of laboratories, hostels, library and the university block. He used to get every work executed quickly and efficiently taking his colleagues by surprise.

While at Calcutta, Dr. Radhakrishnan was appointed as Professor of Oriental Philosophy in Oxford University. Sometimes later, when Pandit Madan Mohan Malviya, the founder of Banaras Hindu University, became ill, he appointed Dr. Radhakrishnan as the Chancellor of that university.

Dr. Radhakrishnan refused to accept salary as the Chancellor of Banaras Hindu University. He held that it was a national institute and he wanted to serve the nation selflessly.

Dr. Radhakrishnan had a quick and logical sense of **repartee**. Once he went to England to deliver a lecture on Indian philosophy. The audience there had gathered in huge numbers to listen to him. A Britisher amongst the audience asked Radhakrishnan - "Is there a society called Hindu? Do they have a common culture? You are so diverse. You don't have the same colour - some are white, some are black, some wear dhoti, some lungi, some kurta, and some wear shirt. Look, we Britishers are the same - same colour and same dress." To this, Dr. Radhakrishnan gave a very apt reply - "Horses are of different colours, but donkeys are alike. Different colours and diversities are signs of progress."

Dr. Radhakrishnan was supervising the work of Calcutta, Banaras and Oxford Universities at the same time. He executed his job well due to his scholarship, administrative skills and extraordinary common sense.

In 1938, Dr. Radhakrishnan met Gandhiji at Sevagram. Those days Gandhiji used to advise people against drinking cow's milk. He considered cow's milk as an extension of cow's flesh. While conversing with Dr. Radhakrishnan, Gandhiji said the same to Radhakrishnan. Dr. Radhakrishnan replied, "In that case we should not drink mother's milk also."

Dr. Radhakrishnan was a devout Hindu who was thoroughly steeped in the Indian culture. At the same time, he had great regard for other religions too. He was humble and patient by nature. He listened with respect and patience to all, even those who held difference of opinion with him.

Dr. Radhakrishnan was a great philosopher, writer and a nationalist. He has authored several works on philosophy and culture, important among them being – The Philosophy of the *Upanishads, Bhagwad Gita,* Eastern Religion and Western Thought, Indian Philosophy, and Hindu View of Life.

Dr. Radhakrishnan, without earning a foreign degree presented a comparative viewpoint of the Indian Philosophy and gained reputation in the foreign lands, which portrayed a bright picture of India all over the world.

Although Dr. Radhakrishnan was basically a teacher, he gained more popularity as a writer and a professor of Philosophy. He also excelled in his capacity as a teacher and later as founder and chancellor of academic institutions, executed all these tasks successfully. While on the one hand, he had a complete command over his subject as a professor, on the other hand he had a wonderful capacity to present his subject matter effectively.

The contribution of Dr. Radhakrishnan as a teacher is unparalleled. He served several universities at the same time. He deserved the honour bestowed on him by the students in India and abroad.

The session of the second Asian Educational Conference was held in 1937-38 at Lucknow. Dr. Radhakrishnan chaired this session. Besides, he led Indian delegation to several international conferences.

Maulana Abul Kalam Azad, the first education minister of free India, constituted a commission to organise higher education in independent India. Dr. Radhakrishnan was made the chairman of this commission. It was on the recommendation of this commission that the University Grants Commission was constituted.

In 1949, Dr. Radhakrishnan was appointed as India's first ambassador to the Soviet Union. Those days, the world feared the might of Marshal Stalin of the Soviet Union. The Russian leader knew well about Dr. Radhakrishnan that he never went to jail during the freedom struggle, and that from the Russian point of view, he was progressive. But he also knew well that this man was a pure Indian and was highly reputed internationally.

During a meeting with Marshal Stalin, Dr. Radhakrishnan explained about Ashoka the Great. He said that in our country there was a great king. He was a great warrior who had conquered several kingdoms for his empire. But after a deadly war, he felt revulsion towards violence and became a monk. You too have arrived at the seat of power through violence, therefore, you too need to renounce violence and adopt the approach of that great monarch.

Dr. Radhakrishnan performed his duties as ambassador of India to Russia very efficiently. The beginning of Indo-Russian friendship is in fact his contribution.

After the promulgation of the Constitution, the first elections in India were held in 1952. Dr. Radhakrishnan was unanimously elected as India's first Vice-President. While holding the important position of the Vice-President of India, he also became the Chancellor of Delhi University and the vice-chairman of the Sahitya Akademi. In 1954, he was honoured with 'Bharat-Ratna'.

The Vice-President is also the Chairman of the Rajya Sabha in India. As Chairman of the Rajya Sabha, Dr. Radhakrishnan was directly associated with Indian politics. His lectures on political issues used to be fresh and novel in its interpretation.

Although Dr. Radhakrishnan had held the post of President of India in 1961 due to the illness of Dr. Rajendra Prasad, but on that occassion he neither accepted the salary of President nor did he change his residence. In 1962, he was elected as the second President of India after Dr. Rajendra Prasad. The 1962 Indo-China and the 1965 Indo-Pak war were fought during his tenure as President. Dr. Radhakrishnan played an appreciable role in building up the morale of Indian soldiers through his profound speeches.

Dr. Radhakrishnan held the positions of Vice-President from 1952 to 1962 and of President from 1962 to 1967, with great dignity. On being elected as the President, he took only Rs 2500 as his salary, whereas the actual salary of the President of India was Rs. 10,000.

Dr. Radhakrishnan regarded time as definitely precious, but truth as even more precious. He held that man's transformation into a demon was his defeat, man's turning into superman was his miracle and man's becoming a man was his victory.

The role of Dr. Radhakrishnan as the President of India was praiseworthy. After completing his tenure as the President of India in 1967, he spent the rest of his life at his home in Madras leading a complete and dignified life. He passed away at the ripe age of 87 on 16th April, 1975.

Vocabulary

Philosopher—(n) a person engaged or learned in philosophy, expecially as an academic discipline. **Missionary**—(adj) of, relating to, or characteristic of a missionary or a religious mission. **Missionary**—(n) a person sent on a religious mission, expecially one sent to promote christianity in a foreign country. **Meritorious**—(adj) deserving reward or praise. **Complexity**—(n) the states or quality of being intricate or complicated. **Impeccable**—(adj) (of behaviour, performance, or appearance) in propriety, faultless. **Oratorical**—(adj) relating to the art or practice of public speaking.

□

14
Ashoka the Great

Indian history is **replete** with great personalities who shaped the destiny of the nation as also of the world. This can very well be said of Ashok the Great. He was the last major emperor in the **lineage** of the Mauryan dynasty. He could at once be placed alongside Alexander the Great as both had set out to **conquer** the world. Ashoka the Great had set on the course to becoming Digvijayee, but ended up being Dharmavijayee. In the year 259 BC, Ashoka converted to Buddhism.

Not much is known about his family except that Ashoka was the son of the Mauryan King Bindusara. Ashoka is believed to have usurped the throne, killed all possible rivals, and began his reign as a tyrant. This story is not borne out by his own **inscriptions** which are the oldest surviving Indian written documents of any historical significance. No record is found about his death as well. According to some Tibetan accounts, it is learnt that he died in Taxila. He had two grandsons who succeeded him and divided the empire to suit their requirements. Not much is talked about his sons and daughters. Within fifty years of his death, the sprawling empire that he had built disintegrated.

His **coronation** as king was held in 269 BC, four years after he **ascended** the throne in 273 BC. Some Buddhist records reveal that this coronation was delayed because he forcibly occupied the throne by killing his **siblings** numbering ninety-nine. Although no support evidence is available, it is generally believed to be true account of Ashoka's life. That he was ruthless in his pursuit of power is hard to disbelieve especially after getting to know about the Kalinga war. He was a great warrior who wanted to conquer all. He brooked of no resistance and did not mind razing to ground any opposition that raised its head against him. Kalinga is the result of the same spirit. Incidentally, it was this war of Kalinga that changed him. Kalinga was a powerful state on the East coast of the Bay of Bengal. Ashoka wanted Kalinga annexed to his state and in the thirteenth year of his reign, he **decimated** Kalinga after a bloody war on the bank of the river Daya, also called Kalinga. The water of this river had literally turned red with the blood that flowed into it. The sight **unnerved** Ashoka. The sheer scale of blood bath shook his conscience and filled his heart with a sense of **remorse** and **contrition**. He wanted to expiate; he wanted to atone for this sin of killing so many human beings with whom he had personal enmity. It forced him to embrace *Dharma*. It transformed him into a different being altogether. He became a symbol of compassion. Morality and **piety** dictated the course of his life henceforth. He began to preach *Dharma* and conducted his own life accordingly. He became known as Dharmashoka. He sent his sons Mahendra and daughter Sanghmitra to Sri Lanka as his religious mascot and representative.

Nearer home, he created 'Officers of Righteousness' (*dharma-mahamatra*) to **propagate** and implement his policies. These officers were directed to look after the well-being of the people and their sufferings. They were especially assigned the task of provide succour to women and the sick and those distressed in any manner. They were instructed to bring to his direct notice the matters relating to welfare of people. He made hospitals, not just for humans but also for animals. To provide relief to passengers, trees were planted on the highways, rest-rooms were erected at places and wells were dug for making **potable** water available to the thirsty passengers. He also created a special cell in his government to dole out charity to the poor. In short, Ashoka made all possible provisions for improving the quality of life of the people in his regime. Through Buddhism he wanted to spread the message of righteousness in the world. Moral values of honesty, compassion, benevolence and tolerance of all became the mainstay of his life. To achieve that end, he sent emissaries to Egypt, Macedonia and Syria, besides sending his children to Sri Lanka as permanent envoy to that country. Buddhism became an important religion of the world under his rule.

The keynote of Ashoka's reform was humanity in internal administration and the abandonment of aggressive war. In place of the traditional policy of territorial expansion, he substituted conquest by Righteousness and he claimed to have won many victories by this method. Ashoka believed that by setting an example of enlightened government, he might convince his neighbours of the merits of this new policy and thus gain the moral leadership of the whole civilised world. By no means, he gave up his imperial ambitions, but modified them in accordance with the humanitarian ethics of Buddhism. In domestic affairs, the new policy was felt in general relaxation of the stern justice of earlier times. He declared that all citizens were his children, and more than once reproved his local governors for failing to apply this precept thoroughly. He strongly supported the principle of *ahimsa* (non-injury to men and animals), banned animal sacrifices. His regime was largely responsible for the growth of vegetarianism in India.

For Ashoka, Buddhism seems to have been a system of morals which led to peace and fellowship in this world and heaven in the next. A streak of Puritanism in the emperor is to be inferred from the edict banning rowdy popular fairs and allowing religious gatherings only. Ashoka's Buddhism, though enthusiastic, was not exclusive. He showed respect to all sects. Salient features of the religion were inscribed at various places and **engravings** were made on rocks and pillars. One can see such engravings and inscriptions at Sarnath temple at Varanasi and at several other places all over the country and elsewhere. The pillar with four faces of lions at Sarnath is now the symbol of India's national emblem and the Ashoka wheel is at the centre of the Indian flag. A reading of inscriptions on the ROCK EDICTS and PILLAR EDICTS reveals the kind of works the emperor had done in his reign. These inscriptions also give an insight into his thought process his actions and his philosophy. One of the edicts reads like this: "Happiness in this world and in other world is difficult to secure without great love of morality, careful examination, great obedience, and great fear of sin and great energy." These readings give a clear indication about the essential character of the man the Ashoka and the king that he was.

He built several *stupas,* dome-shaped shrines. He also built several monasteries and pillars. Monasteries were built to facilitate meditation by the monks lodged there. Pillars were essentially meant for inscriptions and these inscriptions were used by the emperor for directly communicating with people. The memorials that still survive show his intent of what he tried to do for the people and what he actually achieved with regard to providing justice to people he ruled. Ashoka improved communications by planting fruit trees along the roads to provide shade and food, dug well at intervals, and setting up rest-houses for weary travellers. He developed the cultivation of medicinal herbs supplied to men and animals alike.

Ashoka did not differentiate between his own son and those of others and treated them equally. It seldom happens that a king puts his own children and those of others on the same pedestal. It is a rare quality, especially in an emperor. It was characteristic of Ashoka to practise what he preached, and to preach what he practised.

This has to be said to the credit of Ashoka that the rise of Buddhism began when he embraced it and took it upon himself to propagate it not only in India but also in foreign countries. Under him the Buddhism grew rapidly and spread to far flung areas. At this point of time, the Buddhism had lost much of its sheen in India largely because the various sects quarrelled amongst themselves. Also, due to heavy donations received, Bhikshus had begun to lead a life of luxury that led to their moral **degradation**. It was Ashoka who altered all this. Ashoka, according to a scholar of the 19th century, was 'half monster and half idiot'. But the king of the rock and pillar inscriptions comes alive as a real man and a man far ahead of his time. "He was by no means an other-worldly dreamer, but every inch a king, a little naïve, often rather self-righteous and **pompous**, but **indefatigable**, strong-willed and imperious. It is with good reason that the Indian Republic has adopted for the device of its state seal the capital of an Asokan column', observed Al Basham, a historian of a very high standing, in his book *The Wonder That Was India*. To the modern student, Ashoka towers above the other kings of ancient India.

Vocabulary

Replete – (adj) filled with something, with a full supply of something. **Lineage** – (n) the series of families that somebody comes from, ancestry. **Conquer** – (v) to put down with force or authority. **Inscriptions** – (n) words written in the front of a book or cut in metal or stone. **Coronation** – (n) a ceremony at which a crown is formally placed on the head of a new king or queen. **Ascend** – (v) to rise, to go up, to climb. **Decimate** – (v) to kill in large numbers, to annihilate. **Unnerve** – (v) to make somebody feel nervous, frightened or lose confidence. **Remorse** – (n) the feeling of being extremely for some wrong done. **Contrition** – (n) the state of being very sorry for some wrong done. **Piety** – (n) the state of being pious, the state of having or showing deep respect, especially for god and religion. **Propagate** – (v) to spread an idea, belief or a piece of information amongst people. **Potable** – (adj) water safe for drinking, fit to drink. **Engravings** – (n) a picture made by cutting design on a piece of metal and then printing it on a piece of paper. **Degradation** – (n) changing to a lower state, abasement. **Pompous** – (adj) puffed up with vanity, ceremonious, grandiloquent, overblown, pontifical. **Indefatigable** – (adj) showing sustained enthusiastic action with unflagging vitality, tireless, unwearying.

□

15
Festivals and Festivities in India

It would not be an exaggeration to say that India is a country of festivals and festivities. Being a country of different communities belonging to different religions, it is no surprise that almost throughout the year, one festival or the other is celebrated in some parts of the country without let or hindrance. The nation, it would seem, is always in a celebratory frame. And strangely enough, these festivals and festivities are so well **ingrained** in the lives of individuals that they are celebrated with the same degree of **gaiety** and enthusiasm throughout the year. Festivals and festivities add to the charm of our life. Life without these festivities would become **drab** and dry. Therefore, these are essential **ingredients** of India. Indian culture is centred around these festivals and festivities. They make our life delightful, colourful and charming. Not all festivities or festivals are religious in nature. Though religious festivals are the major cause of festivities, there are seasonal festivals that are of great significance. For instance, Lohri, Makar Sankranti, Onam, Pongal and Bihu are seasonal festivals. In India, the arrival of new crop is celebrated with gusto and with religious fervour. Holi, Baisakhi and Basant Panchami are important seasonal festivals. Holi is a festival of colours. This festival is said to soothe frayed tempers of enemies too as they sink their differences and get immersed in the colour of love and friendship. This marks the end of the winter season. Baisakhi is celebrated with **gusto** by Sikhs. It is essentially a Punjabi festival and it is celebrated at the end of the harvesting season. It's sheer joy to watch them celebrate this festival. Basant Panchami heralds the advent of spring and it also provides an opportunity to celebrate Saraswati Puja. Saraswati is the Goddess of learning. So, students consider this to be their exclusive **prerogative** to celebrate it.

Then there are festivals of national importance; they are celebrated with gay abandon. In short, there is hardly a day in India that passes by without some kind of festival being celebrated. For once we can say that the much-touted observation of Shakespeare that 'if all the days of the year were festivals, the days would be as tedious as any' would not apply to India. In India, everyday is a day of festivities and yet they are not tedious. National festivals are not necessarily religious or cultural in nature. Independence Day and Republic Day are celebrated as national duties. By celebrating these days as national festivals, we rededicate ourselves to the cause of nation. With these celebrations, we often associate some cultural programmes. We also take this opportunity to recall and remember those who rendered yeoman's service to the cause of nation and often use this opportunity to honour those who have excelled in walks of life bringing glory to the nation. Nature of celebration is the same throughout the country. These celebrations show that despite so much diversity, India is one as a nation. Besides, Gandhi Jayanti is also celebrated as national festival. By doing this, the nation records its gratitude to the Father of the Nation without whose sacrifices India may not have got her independence so easily. If his birthday is celebrated as Gandhi Jayanti, the day he died is celebrated as Martyr's Day. Likewise, we celebrate Valmiki Jayanti on 18th October every year to show our appreciation of Valmiki having given us the epic *Ramayana*. In the same manner but with religious fervour, we celebrate Guru Nanak Jayanti. Incidentally, this day is also celebrated as Kartik Purnima. This is a winter festival. On this occasion, grand cattle fair—biggest in Asia— is organised at Sonepur in Bihar where people from far-flung places including from foreign countries come, congregate and buy cattle of their choice. Foreign tourists usually flock to this place to watch the spectacle. In the process, they earn foreign exchange for India. So, it can very well be said that festivals and festivities are not mere celebrations for the sake of celebration. They also have economic significance. India shows its gratitude to Dr. Ambedkar for giving her the Constitution of India. His birthday on 14th April is celebrated as Ambedkar Jayanti. Not just that, India also celebrates Guru Ravidas Jayanti on 25th February besides celebrating Mahavir Jayanti on 23rd April. Indian calendar is never short on celebrations.

Indian religious festivals are Id-ul-Fitr, Dussera, Diwali, Christmas Day, Id-ul-Zuha. These festivals are celebrated all over the country with extreme religious fervour and gaiety. Ganesh Chaturthi too has acquired the status of national festival as it is now being celebrated all over the country with the same fanfare and enthusiasm. There are some festivals that are place-centric, being regional in nature. But people from all walks of life take part in these festivals as well. Festivals are a great source of uniting people by promoting communal harmony. Festivals help bring people emotionally and physically closer and they add a lot of colour and interest to life. They make life much more interesting and colourful. Festivals fulfill a certain need in human beings. Celebrating festivals is a great way of reviving and renewing social contacts and friendships. Even frozen contacts are revived in times of festivities.

No wonder then that India is called a nation of festivals and festivities. These festivals and festivities not only provide opportunities for letting out some of the steam accumulated over a period of time in individuals, they also provide business opportunities and these national festivals are eagerly awaited by corporate houses and individual consumers. Festivals also make economic sense besides cementing cultural ties.

Vocabulary

Ingrained—(v) a habit or an attitude that has existed for a long time and, therefore, difficult to change. **Gaiety**—(n) the state of being cheerful and full of fun. **Drab**—(adj) without interest or colour, dull and boring. **Ingredients**—(n) one of the things from which something is made, especially one of the foods that are used together to make particular dish. **Gusto**—(n) enthusiasm and energy in doing something. **Prerogative**—(n) a right or advantage belong to a particular person or to a group because of their importance or social standing.

□

16
Durga Puja

Durga Puja is one of the most important religious festivals of Hindus. Dussera is the culmination of Durga Puja festival. As a matter of fact, Dussera and Durga Puja are two different celebrations with some similarities and some dissimilarities. Durga Puja is essentially the worship of mother goddess Durga, the mythical daughter of Himalaya and Menaka and the wife of Lord Shiva. Durga is a transition of sati, i.e., change of form from one state to another. In Bengal, the celebration goes on for nine days. On the tenth day, the idol is immersed in water and with that the festivities come to an end. It begins with the hymn of mother goddess. The hymn is called Mahisasurmardini. This is sung in the early hours of the morning.

Dussera, on the other hand, is celebrated as a mark of victory of Rama over Ravana who had kidnapped the wife of Rama. It is said that Rama invoked mother Durga by worshipping her to secure power to kill the demon across the sea. Thus empowered, he attacked the demon in Lanka and secured release of his wife. It is this victory of Rama over Ravana that is celebrated as victory of good over evil. This is Dussera. This is generally celebrated in northern parts of India.

The word 'Durga' in Sanskrit means fort, or a place which is difficult to break into. Another meaning ascribed to the word is that it is 'durgatinasini' meaning 'destroyer of miseries or sufferings'. Thus, Hindus believe that Durga protects her devotees from the forces of misery and sufferings. There are many incarnations of Durga according to religious beliefs.

She is Kali; she is Bhagwati, Bhavani, Ambika, Lalita, Gouri, Kandalini, Java, etc. She has one hundred and eight names. She is believed to have incarnated with the divine powers of all divine beings. These divine beings offered her the required physical **prowess** and weapons to slay the **demon** 'mahisasur'. Her nine appellations are Skondomata, Kusumonda, Shalloputri, Kaartrati, Brahmacharini, Maha Gouri, Katyani, Chandraghanta and Siddharthi. Durga is depicted as having got eight or ten arms. These arms represent eight quadrants or ten directions of Hinduism. This is suggestive of the belief that she protects her devotees from evils **emanating** from all directions. Like Lord Shiva, Goddess Durga is also referred to as 'Triambake', meaning three-eyed Goddess. While the left eye represents desire (the moon), the right eye represents action (the sun) and the central eye is representative of knowledge (fire).

Lion which she rides on represents power, will and determination. Durga riding the lion becomes the symbol of her mastery over all of the above qualities. The sword held aloft by her in one hand symbolises knowledge. Knowledge must be as sharp as sword. Her trident symbolises three traits: *Satwa* (inactivity), *Raja* (activity) and *Tamas* (non-activity). She is destroyer of all three types of misery—physical, mental and spiritual. Durga stands on the lion in a fearless pose of 'abhay mudra' which signifies freedom from fear. In the idol that we see during puja, Durga is shown escorted by her two daughters Lakshmi and Saraswati and two sons Kartik and Ganesh. In the idol, we also see Lord Shiva besides Mahish and Asur.

Durga Puja is the favourite festival of eastern India, especially that of Bengal. It is said that Durga Puja was first celebrated by those on the banks of the river Rarhi in Bengal. They were very progressive and richly endowed people of Bengal. They were the ones who took the tradition of celebrating Durga Puja to other places outside Bengal. They not only carried traditions with them, but also brought the idol makers and drum beaters from Bengal. Dhak, Dhol and Dhunuchi dance are their gift that whole of India relishes today.

Goddess Durga is worshipped in almost every Hindu household with great enthusiasm and with religious fervour.

The belief is that it not only **alleviates** the devotees of their misery but also dispels darkness from their life and brings all-round happiness and good fortune. Majority of the offices, institutions and workplaces remain shut for days during the festivities. This period is used for common rejoicing. Religious rites are performed by almost all Hindus irrespective of their social standing. People visit places of worship and pandals. In cities, the rejoicing is more pronounced as people move in drove at night and enjoy decorations and cultural programmes. Both married and unmarried girls undertake fast and offer special prayers called 'Anjali'. They appear in their best possible attire. People wear new dress and every household relishes sweet.

The puja usually lasts for three days. The ritual of sacrificing goats, buffaloes and rams are still carried out at certain places. Earlier, it was a regular ritual performed almost at all puja venues. But these days, these sacrifices are few and far between. The progressives amongst the Hindus felt these sacrifices were uncalled for. Hence, this practice has nearly come to an end except for some places that still follow the age old tradition of sacrifices.

The tenth day is celebrated as Bijoya Dashami when people greet and meet each other. This is done after the idol is immersed with fanfare. The scene brings tears to the eyes of the grieving devotees. People visit one another's house and **partake** of sweet. At most of the places, a formal Bijoya Sammelini is held at the puja pandals.

Vocabulary

Prowess – (n) great skill at doing something. **Demon** – (n) an evil spirit. **Emanate** – (v) to produce or show something. **Alleviate** – (v) to make something less severe; to relieve pain or suffering. **Partake** – (v) to eat or drink something that is offered. have, give or receive a share of; to consume.

□

17
Holi

This is one festival which is celebrated in a manner that gives joy to everyone irrespective of age. It's a festival of colours. It's a festival of immense joy. This is one of the most interesting and important festivals of the Hindus. It's called Phagua or Fagua and is held in the month of Fagun and that is the month of March. With the onset of Holi, the winter is finally out. Most of the Hindu festivals have a mythical background and the festival of colours is no exception to that rule.

The story about the origin of Holi festival goes like this. Hiranyakashipu had a son named Prahlad, who was a devotee of Lord Vishnu. Hiranyakashipu did not approve of this as he did not like Vishnu. He rather hated Vishnu and his son was a devotee. He tried his best to dissuade his son from that, but Prahlad would not relent. When persuasions did not work, Hiranyakashipu decided to punish Prahlad. He decided to kill him, but no matter how many times he tried to kill him, he did not succeed in his attempt to do so. It puzzled him no ends and finally he decided to take the help of his sister Holika. The myth has it that her body was fireproof. She could enter any fire-pit and yet remain **unscathed.** Hiranyakashipu asked her to take Prahlad into her lap and sit in the fire. She did exactly that. But as the luck would have it, Prahlad came out of it unhurt and Holika was reduced to ashes. This festival of Holi is celebrated to honour that event. The festival begins with the burning of bonfire called Holikadahan. The joy that goes with the festival is symptomatic of joy derived from Prahlad's escape and Holika's death, thus defeating the design of Hiranyakashipu.

There is another theory that goes with the celebration of this festival. It is said that Holi is the beginning of the harvesting season. When crop is ready for harvesting, the heart of the farmers is filled with joy and this joy finds expression in this festival of colours. By **smearing** one another with colour, people share the joy of one another. As a ritualistic gesture, the new ears of corn are roasted on the Holi fire and distributed amongst friends and relatives as *prasad*. They embrace each other and sink all differences they may have had. So, this festival is for celebrating new hope. New leaves **sprout** on the trees; beautiful flowers appear all around as greenery rules the roost.

On the eve of the festival, a huge fire is made at a central place where people of the area or the locality can easily **congregate**. Heaps of wood, dung, thorns and other things are collected from all over the places and burnt. Long preparations go into the making of this a success. Sometimes people steal articles of furniture from the neighbourhood or from those houses which are not properly looked after and burn them in this bonfire. Therefore, during this period of time, people zealously guard their wooden furniture or things made of wood, lest they are stolen and burnt away as *Holika Dahan*. This kind of thing needs to be discouraged and condemned. It is for this reason that some people think about this festival of Holi as the festival of the hooligans, by the hooligans and, for the hooligans, and, therefore, many people avoid it. Otherwise, it's a festival of joy and of **camaraderie**.

Holi is also one of the most boisterous festivals of all. It really requires physical strength to live up to its boisterousness as those taking part in this festival of colours sometimes go berserk and use force to smear colours on the unwilling. This is one of the seamy sides of this festival. If celebrated with restraint, the festival is immensely pleasing as people jostle and bustle with sprinklers. The day usually begins with people singing and dancing in groups. Groups of men and women generally separately move out in streets, in the neighbourhood with sprinklers filled with coloured water and sprinkle colours on their friends and relatives and often on strangers too. Usually, no one minds as they all understand the significance of this. Those who move out into streets and roads know that they have to face such scenes and are mentally prepared for the same.

It is important to remember the spirit of the festival and not get carried away by the boisterousness side of it. The underlying spirit is to enjoy the festival as it celebrates decimation of evil represented by Hiranyakashipu in the form of Holika. The festival is celebrated to mark the escape of Prahlad from the evil design of his father who hated godliness represented by Vishnu. So, the festival is actually the celebration of God and godliness. This, therefore, must be the centre of our focus while celebrating the festival. When we sprinkle colours on others, we share the joy. But that cannot be said when mud or garbage is thrown on a passerby or on a stranger. This gives it an ugly colour which must be shunned at all times.

This festival of Holi is celebrated with great fanfare and religious fervour in Gokul and Barsane and parts of U.P. Efforts are made to re-live the Radha and Krishna episode. Holi is romanticised in our films too.

Holi is celebrated by different people in different manner in different parts of the country. But the underlying spirit is the same everywhere except at some places where we get to see its ugly form. Ordinarily, it is celebrated in measured **sobriety** at majority of places. People go out, sprinkle colours on one another and indulge in merry-making. After day-long activity, they return to their homes and wash themselves clean. It usually takes days for the colours to go. In the evening, again they become busy playing with colours, but this time, it is with dry colours called *abir*. **Diurnal** boisterousness makes way for quieter evenings when they meet one another, apply *abir* and partake of sweets.

Vocabulary

Unscathed—(adj) not hurt, unharmed (not to be used before noun). **Smearing**—(n & v) the act of staining or daubing with a dirty substance, a slanderous defamation act. **Sprout**—(v) to start to grow, to produce new leaves. **Congregate**—(v) to come together in a group, to assemble. **Camaraderie**—(n) a feeling of friendship and trust. **Sobriety**—(n) a state of being sober, a state of being not drunk. **Diurnal**—(adj) relating to day as opposed to night.

□

18
Id-ul-Fitr

It would not be any exaggeration if it is said that Id-ul-Fitr is one of the most taxing festivals of all. Taxing because during the entire month of fasting in the month of Ramazan, nothing, not even water, is consumed in the day-light of the sun. Only after the sun has set in, food can be eaten and the process of eating has to be completed before the sun rises in the morning. The kind of **ordeal** that Muslims are required to undergo during the month is difficult to find in any other festival. This is a fundamental religious duty enjoined upon all Muslims through the Quran and *hadis* where law and religion exist side by side. According to the edict of the religious laws of Muslims, fasting in the month of Ramazan is **mandatory**. This is mandatory in order that the soul of every Muslim is purified. So, Id-ul-Fitr is a process of purification or a process of bodily **ablution**.

After the month-long fasting, the Id prayer is offered once the moon is sighted. It is unthinkable that this prayer can ever be stopped. And yet, once in 1342, this prayer was stopped by Md. Bin Tughlaq.

In the holy month of Ramazan, all Muslims, some of their children, undertake the fast for the whole month. They eat food in the evening and in the unearthly hours of morning before the sun rises. They eat nothing the entire day. They do not even drink water during this period, come what may. This is nothing short of an ordeal. But they undergo this ordeal with great enthusiasm. On the last day of the month, they eagerly await the appearance of the moon on the horizon. Once the moon is sighted, they erupt in joy. The following day is celebrated as Id-ul-Fitr. They take holy bath the following morning, get dressed in the best possible attire, and congregate to offer their prayer. After this prayer, they **embrace** each other and say 'Id Mubarak'. In the afternoon, they partake of the best possible food, and in the evening, they receive friends and relatives and treat them to quality food that their ladies prepare.

In this month of Ramazan, Muslims take special care to see that they do not cross the line of decency as **ordained** by law. They lead a life of purity during this holy month. They do nothing that could cause grief and discomfort to any. During this month, they offer their prayers five times a day and give alms and food to the beggars and *faqirs*.

This is a very important festival of the Muslims and they make elaborate preparations for this festival. Preparations begin well before the start of the fasting month. Every aspect is taken care of before they plunge into the fasting feat. All people, young and old, rich and poor, able and not-so-able, get for themselves the best clothes they can buy or procure. They get new skull caps and new shoes for their feet. It's their day for rejoicing after month-long fasting and prayers. They put on their best attire after a ceremonial bath and prayers offered in a congregation. Children are the happiest lot as they put on their colourful clothes. Sweets and fruits are consumed and offered. Their faces glow as they happily meet and greet one another.

The method of celebration is rather simple and uncomplicated. There is a pattern that is followed by one and all. At a specified time, they all gather at a designated place, and from there they proceed to an *Idgah* for prayer. All of them stand together and read the prayer together. After the prayer is over, they embrace each other and congratulate one another for having successfully undergone the fasting. 'Id Mubarak' is on everyone's lips. This is such a moment when everyone is treated as equal. There is no distinction between small and big, rich and poor or young and old. Each one of them is equal in esteem and status. This is a unique festival. This is a festival of camaraderie. All are treated as brothers. Many of them return straightaway to their homes from the *Idgah* while some make it to the graveyard of their near and dear ones and place flowers or wreaths on them.

This is the way Id is celebrated and enjoyed by the Muslims all over the world. This festival teaches brotherhood and **instils** a feeling of togetherness. This also affords Muslims a chance to purify themselves once every year so that they understand the importance of this purity and imbibe this spirit forever.

Vocabulary

Ordeal – a difficult or unpleasant experience. **Mandatory** – (adj) required by law. **Ablution** – (n) a ritual washing of a priest's hands or of sacred vessels, convenience, public toilet or lavatory. **Embrace** – (v) to hug, to cover, to put one's arms around somebody expressing love and friendship. **Ordained** – (v) fixed or established especially by an order or command, decreed, enacted. **Instil** – (v) to enter drop by drop, to gradually make somebody feel, think or behave in a particular way over a period of time.

□

19
Diwali

This festival of lights is one of the most important festivals of the Hindus. Though essentially a Hindu festival, in the past as also in the present times, the festival has been imitated by many other religious groups. The celebrations of Shab-i-Barat, for instance, in the fourteenth century India, clearly showed the imprint of Diwali. Fireworks were let off and lighted lamps were placed on the newly white-washed graves in an obvious imitation of the Hindu Diwali. This was regarded as **blatant** disregard of the shari'a and such customs were not found in Ghazni, Iran, or Arabia (*Source:* Rizvi, *History of Sufism*). Today Deepawali or Diwali is celebrated all over the world, not just by Hindus but by others too. It is being celebrated in the White House as well since 2003.

For the Hindus, it is a festival that occurs on *Amavasya* (the dark fortnight) in the month of Kartik. The crop of rice is ready for harvest. Farmers are jubilant. Extensive cleansing programme is undertaken by all households. This is the time to clean up. It is difficult to find a Hindu household that is not cleaned up or white-washed on this occasion. Cleanliness is the other name of this festival. Dung and earth are used for smearing *kachcha* walls and courtyards.

As we all know, most of the Hindu festivals originate from some myth. In this case, the myth has it that when Lord Rama returned to Ayodhya with Sita after defeating Ravana and after fourteen long years, the people of Ayodhya could not contain their happiness. They were overjoyed at the sight of their beloved lord and they expressed their happiness by lighting up the entire kingdom to welcome the victorious Rama. Then on, this festival is celebrated in the memory of Lord Rama. It has continued till this date and will continue till eternity. From hygienic point of view too, this festival is very important. Due to the preceding rain, dirt and insects cause disease and unease. This necessitates cleaning up. Houses are repaired and white-washed. This helps drive away insects, mosquitoes being the most deadly of them all. First by white-washing and then by lighting up, these mosquitoes and insects are driven away. This drives away diseases as well. The unease is thus dispelled.

Diwali is celebrated as Kali Puja by the Bengalis while Vaishyas celebrate it as Lakshmi Puja. It is a sacred festival. It symbolises victory of good over evil. It symbolises dispelling of darkness with the illumination through lights. Even though it is essentially a Hindu festival, it is celebrated by all religious groups in India. Muslims also take part with their Hindu friends and neighbours. Sikhs also celebrate because it was on this day that their sixth Guru Sri Hargobindji was released from jail by Jahangir.

On this occasion, market-places are lit up beautifully. The whole city wears a bridal look. Shops and houses are done up **aesthetically**. Sweet shops do brisk business on this day as there is great demand for sweets. People queue up for buying crackers and candles. At night, the houses are illuminated with earthen lamps and candles. These days electric bulbs are extensively used for lighting up premises. When seen from the roof-tops, it presents a beautiful spectacle. Children are the ones who enjoy it the most. They burst crackers and enjoy the fun of it all. Cities and towns are drowned in the glitter of light and in the sound of crackers and fireworks. These sounds keep reverberating almost throughout the night. Apart from individual houses, offices and corporate buildings are also lit up adequately and this provides a picturesque look.

A great number of Hindus worship Goddess Lakshmi, the Goddess of wealth on this day. By doing that, they try to invoke the Goddess to deliver wealth to them as wealth means prosperity. Diwali is a festival that is celebrated all over the country, rather in every street of the country. And they celebrate it together to convey a message of unity in diversity. This festival of lights is loved and lapped up by all without exception.

It is, however, important to remember that anything that is overdone creates unsolicited problems. Excessive bursting of crackers disturbs the peace and pollutes the atmosphere. Sometimes, these also cause accidents. People are beginning to realise that some **moderation** in the use of crackers is desirable. Excessive bursting of crackers leads to noise pollution and this affects human lives. This often leads to **lacerating** of ear-drums and that contributes to hearing impairment. To offset this impact of crackers, many concerned people have started a campaign against bursting of crackers. Young ones are told about the **seamy** side of this and people are gradually waking up to this reality.

Equally disturbing is the phenomenon of the grown-ups squandering away their hard-earned money by gambling and drinking excessively on this day. This occasionally leads to skirmishes which cause damage to their person and property. When such things happen in large scale, they become spoilers and go against the spirit of Diwali. The festival is meant to bring happiness and prosperity to all. Instead, if it brings misery and unhappiness to some, it means the festival is not celebrated in the prescribed manner. Moderation is required here too. People should understand festivals are meant to break the **monotony** of life and to add spice to life, not to destroy it. Excessive indulgence in gambling and drinking is bad from every angle and must be avoided. The day is important in several other ways as well. A new calendar comes into operation on this. Some business outfits begin new accounts book on this day.

It is heartening that the day is celebrated in the desired manner by the majority of people. It is equally heartening to see people from different communities mingle freely, greet one another and partake of sweets. That is Diwali in its truest spirit.

Vocabulary

Blatant—(adj) something done in an obvious and open way without caring if people are shocked, flagrant. **Aesthetically**—(adv) in a tasteful way, something done beauteously and artistically. **Moderation**—(n) the quality of being reasonable and not being extreme. **Lacerate**—(v) to cut skin or flesh with something sharp, mangled, torn. **Seamy**—(adj) morally degraded, unpleasant and offensive, slovenly, seedy, sleazy, sordid, squalid. **Monotony**—(n) the quality of wearisome constancy, routine and lack of variety.

□

20
Chhath Festival

Worship of sun god is one of the oldest forms of worship. Sun being the energy supplier of the universe, it has commanded unrestrained veneration by people since time immemorial. The festival Chhath is the only festival of its kind in India where direct obeisance is paid to the sun, first while setting in the West and then while rising in the East. This is the most important festival of the inhabitants of Bihar, Jharkhand and Nepal. They celebrate it not only in their provinces and countries but in all parts of the country and large parts of the world as they have settled in every corner of the earth.

Chhath, also called Dala Chhath, is an ancient Hindu festival and it is the only Vedic festival that is dedicated to the sun god of the Hindus. This puja is performed to thank Surya for sustaining life on the earth and urging the sun god to continue to shower **benevolence** on the mankind by granting certain wishes. Sun worship is believed to cure a variety of diseases including leprosy and also helps ensure longevity and prosperity of the family and that of the elders.

Usually, the world bows before the rising sun. These are perhaps the only people in the world who pay **obeisance** first to the setting sun and then to the rising sun. Symbolically speaking, it means that they first pay respect to what is past and only thereafter open up to the future or to what is to come later. It's a tribute to the great character of the worshippers of *chhath* that in this world of commercial considerations they pay respect to what is past when majority of the people tend to look up to what **beckons** them. Offering of *arghya* first to the setting sun and then to the rising sun is actually the celebration of a glory that the cycle of birth starts with death. This is seen as the most glorious form of sun worship.

If Id-ul-Zuha is one of the most difficult of all festivals because of the rigours through which a devotee or worshipper has to pass, *Chhath* is another festival that entails almost the same degree of rigours, though for shorter period. Everything used for this puja has to be absolutely pure and stigma-free. Arrangements have to be impeccable and free from all kinds of blemishes. Places have to be cleaned up with the sprinkle of holy waters and have to be guarded zealously against any kind of dirt or impurities.

The rituals of the festival are rigorous and observed over a period of four days. These include holy bathing, fasting; and during this period, the worshipper abstains from drinking water too. This is called *vrata*. The entire process of worship is usually spearheaded by women who are called *parvaitin*. Men also join them these days. She acquires the status of a deity. *Parvaitins* pray for the well-being of their family and for the prosperity of their offspring. If a family starts this puja, it cannot be stopped unless some death occurs in the family. *Parvaitin* stands in the water for long period of time and offers *arghya* to the sun god. Those offering *arghya* are supposed to adorn unstitched clothes. The process begins with what is called *nahay-khai* or *kaddu-bhat*. Those offering puja bathe in the holy river of Ganga and eat rice and plain gourd (*kaddu*) and this is prepared in a specifically made *chulha* with the help of twigs and branches of tree. Some devotees spend all of those days at the river bank itself to ensure absolute purity. The first *arghya* is offered on the third day when the sun sets in the West and the process is completed on the fourth day by repeating the rituals in the early hours of morning when the sun rises in the horizon. After this, she offers *prasada* to all. Special care is taken while consuming *prasada* so that not even a **remnant** of it falls off here and there. Purity is maintained at all times during the puja. Even roads leading to the river bank or the pond where *arghya* is offered are cleaned up thoroughly.

Chhath puja is celebrated on the sixth day of the month of Kartik, Shukla Shashthi, which usually occurs in October-November in the Gregorian calendar. It is also celebrated in the summer called *Chaitra Shashthi* and this according to Gregorian calendar happens in the month of March-April.

According to a popular belief, the *Shakya Dwipi* Brahmins who were **adept** in the methodologies of the sun worship, were invited by the local kings for doing this puja for them. It was these Brahmins also known as *Maga Purohits* who started this puja. Today this festival is observed mostly in those places where these Brahmins are found. Chhath rituals find mention even in *Rigveda* and in *Mahabharata* epic Draupadi is shown to be observing these very rituals. So, it can be said that Chhath is more ancient than it is actually thought to be. In the epic, it is shown that the rulers of Hastinapur celebrated this festival on the advice of Dhaumya, the noble sage. With the performance of this puja, not only Draupadi successfully overcame her personal problems, but also Pandavas got back their lost kingdom. It is also said that this festival of Chhath was started by Karna, the sun of Surya. He was then the king of Angadesh, now comprising Bhagalpur district in Bihar. He was a great warrior and played a pivotal part in the battle of Mahabharata.

Chhath is a festival of bathing and worshipping followed by a period of abstinence and segregation of the worshipper from the main household for four days. During this period, the worshipper observes purity and sleeps on the floor on a single blanket. This is the only festival where priests do not play any part. *Prasada* offerings include *kheer, thekua* and fruits, and the offerings are carried in winnows made of bamboo.

Vocabulary

Benevolence—(n) quality of being kind, helpful and generous. **Obeisance**—(n) bending the head or body or knee as a sign of reverence or submission. **Beckon**—(v) to give somebody a signal by moving finger or hand or nod, wave, appear inviting. **Remnant**—(n) a part of something that is left after the other parts have been used, removed or destroyed. **Adept**—(adj) having or showing knowledge, skill and aptitude, expert.

□

21
Christmas

Christmas is the greatest festival of the Christians. This festival is celebrated with the same degree of fervour as Muslims celebrate Id-ul-Zuha and Hindus celebrate Diwali, Holi and other festivals. It is celebrated on 25th December every year and is celebrated almost all over the world. Jesus Christ was believed to have been born on this day. Celebrations of Christmas may well be likened to Krishna Janmashtami that Hindus celebrate. However, the degree of pomp and gaiety is greater in Christmas as it is celebrated all over the world, especially in the European countries and in the countries where Christians abound in number.

The birth of Christ was not officially celebrated until the middle of the 4th century. It gradually evolved into a Christian festival. Christ's birth was celebrated first in Rome in Antioch and in the East. How exactly it came to England is not known. But it is known that St. Augustine brought it into England as Christmas Day in the year 598 with the baptising of ten thousand English converts.

X'mas is a great occasion for all Christians. They prepare for this festival very extensively over a long period of time. On the evening of Christmas or X'mas, Christians go to church in large numbers for Midnight Mass. They put on their best attire. They sing **carols** along with special prayers. Besides these special prayers, they are very punctual about their **vespers** and **matins**.

After the church ceremony, they greet each other and visit each other the following day. Special delicacies are prepared that day. They distribute cake and cookies to their relatives, friends and neighbours. Guests are treated to wine and cake on this day and this is carried through to nights as well as almost throughout the week.

Christmas trees laden with gifts and sparklers are a common sight together with **cribs** at each household. Santa Claus distributing gifts and sweets is another common sight. Children too often pose as Santa Claus. Sweet shops do brisk business on these days and most of the Christians throng to shops to buy sweets for the occasion. Christmas shopping is a big event all over the world. Special thrust is given on decoration and beautification of shops and houses to make them as attractive and eye-catching as possible. They are decorated with pictures, buntings and flowers. Window shopping too becomes an important ingredient of this festival as people go out to watch shops that are so expensively and aesthetically decorated on the occasion. In short, they leave no stone unturned to make it as enjoyable as possible.

Special effort goes in making of Christmas tree. They bring branch of a tree and place it in a corner of the house. This tree is then decorated with tiny bulbs, sparklers and flowers. At night, it presents a great spectacle. The members of the house then sit together and sing prayers praising Jesus. They are also joined by friends and relatives who are presented gifts and sweets. Greeting cards are also sent to friends and relatives and, in this way, they share the joy with one another. The festival brightens up every face.

Christmas is also a festival of feast and dance. Holding a feast is one of the most common features of this festival. The lady of the house is the most active person on the occasion as she proudly moves about in the best possible dress she can afford. It's a matter of pride for her to make a demonstration of quality things in the household including plates, cutleries, articles of furniture and clothes. After the feast, they often take to dancing and singing. It is a very common sight in large cities and in foreign countries. Dancing in pairs with quiet but soulful music is quite common. Children too take to dancing and singing. In this way, the Christians enjoy this, festival of Christmas. The celebrations come to an end late at night. After this, they gather in a church where they offer prayers.

This festival is celebrated in order to recall what Jesus, the son of God, did in order to make the life of people better. It is a celebration of the belief that God had sent Jesus to deliver people of their sins and miseries for which he himself suffered **crucifixion**. He suffered this death on the cross in order to save the mankind. The underlying message is that those who have faith in him will be saved. The essence of the festival lies in leading a life of nobility, of prayer, love and sacrifice.

Christmas instils a feeling of togetherness and happiness in each participant's heart by bringing together the distantly placed members of the family, and friends of all shades of religion and culture of the world. This is a moment of joy for all. Therefore, the festival is celebrated with great enthusiasm, pomp and show.

Vocabulary

Carols—(n) joyful religious song celebrating the birth of Christ. **Vespers**—(n) a late afternoon or evening worship service usually in a church. **Matins**—(n) the first canonical hour of the daybreak, Morning Prayer. **Cribs**—(n) a bin or granary for storing grains. **Crucifixion**—(n) the act of executing by a method widespread in the ancient world, the victim's hands and feet are bound or nailed to a cross.

□

22
Republic Day

Republic Day is the red letter day in India's history. India became a republic on 26th January, 1950 with the adoption of the Constitution. Prior to this date, India was an independent state, but not a republic. A state becomes republic only when its head of state is elected. In the case of our country, President is the head of the state, although a titular head. There was no head of the state in the country prior to adoption of the constitution. Dr. Rajendra Prasad was the first elected President of India. Hence, India came to be known as republic with the adoption of the Constitution of India on 26th January, 1950. This day is celebrated as the Republic Day. This could well be called the beginning of a new era for India. Every individual, who had attained the age of 21 years, was conferred the right to elect his/her representative for Parliament and for the legislative assemblies. Every year the Republic Day is celebrated with great pomp and show. Though the celebrations are held at all state headquarters, the show that happens at New Delhi draws the attention of the whole world.

The President in his capacity as the Supreme Commander of the Armed Forces takes the salute at India Gate at New Delhi. The national tricolour is unfurled by the President and the national anthem is played out. There is a grand march past lasting for hours. Dignitaries from various countries and from within our own country are extended invitation to the occasion, to witness the Republic Day parade. Through this **gala** parade, India showcases its achievements and military prowess. At the end of it, there is an air display in which air force displays its skills in the air. Through these drills and parade, a strong message of solidarity is conveyed to the people of the country as also to the people of the world. Not just military prowess, but also industrial **strides** and economic progress made by the country are displayed. Also on display are those cultural events that record India's unity despite diversity.

Preparation for the event starts well in advance. Elaborate arrangements are made to accommodate as many people as possible. The parade begins in the early hours of the morning. It begins with the laying of wreath by the Prime Minister at the Amar Jawan Jyoti at India Gate. This is paying homage to those martyrs who laid down their life for the nation. Those willing to witness the parade and the procession gather there well before that in the winter morning. The President being the Supreme Commander is ceremonially received by the Prime Minister and his entire cabinet together with all three chiefs of army, navy and air force. The President is ceremoniously conducted to the saluting base. He arrives there in a coach driven by five horses. He is usually accompanied by a foreign dignitary invited to the occasion as chief guest.

A big procession follows. Leading the procession is a column of the heroes of the past. These are war medal winners led by the Param Vir Chakra winners. Thereafter, the soldiers from army, navy and air force march past to martial tunes. Platoons from every region take part in the march past. These are followed by pageants of various states displaying their specialities. Therafter, Delhi school children put up their show of well-rehearsed drills. Folk dances and cultural troupes take their turn and display their skill. Delhi police also show their prowess. While all this goes on below, rose petals are showered from above. Running commentary is given of the goings-on. These are broadcast by AIR and Doordarshan. It's a spectacle worth watching and most of the news channels telecast the programme live for the benefit of viewers distantly placed. The procession passes through different parts of the city before terminating at the Red Fort. Rashtrapati Bhawan and India Gate are illuminated at night and this presents a delightful sight to the viewers. The entire process of the Republic Day parade culminates two days later with the Beating Retreat.

What happens in New Delhi is the central event. Republic Day parade and processions are also held at the provincial capitals with the Governor taking salute. Flag hoisting is done with great fanfare. This is the most important national festival of India and it is celebrated everywhere, in every institution, in every office and almost in every establishment. District magistrates hoist the national flag at their district headquarters. This ensures participation at all levels.

Republic Day is a national holiday. People go out in their best attire and spend happy times together and pledge their commitment to serve the country to the best of their abilities. In defence establishments, parade is held in grand military style followed by *Bara Khana*. This is a special event for the soldiers who re-dedicate themselves to the service of the nation.

Vocabulary

Gala – (adj) a special public celebration or entertainment.
Stride – (n) one long step, distance covered by a step.

□

23
Independence Day

India became independent on 15th August, 1947 after over two hundred years of slavery under the British. The day is celebrated as Independence Day. A nation's independence is the most coveted thing for its people. India had long remained under the rule of the British. Prior to that, India had been enslaved by the Mughals. India's freedom came after a long struggle, which took lives of so many. It was on this day that the British finally left the Indian shore **for good**. It was made to hand-over power to the Indian leaders. This is the most cherished day for all of us as we celebrate the day of independence achieved through the sacrifices of our elders. India's freedom struggle provides an insight into the much talked about philosophy of non-violence of Mahatma Gandhi. India's freedom was secured not through guns and military prowess, but through the weapon of non-violence. This weapon of Gandhi was something that the English were not trained to tackle.

Although there were some violent activities as well, they were not the prime reason for India securing freedom. India achieved freedom, but not the kind of freedom it had sought. The English divided India on the basis of religion. The regions with Muslim domination became Pakistan and the regions with Hindu majority remained India or Hindustan or Bharat.

Hoisting the national flag from the ramparts of the Red Fort, Nehru delivered the famous speech of 'tryst with destiny' on 15th August, 1947 from the ramparts of the Red Fort. He went on to become the first Prime Minister of India with Sardar Vallabhbhai Patel as his deputy.

The main event for the Independence Day is celebrated in Delhi being the capital of India. It is celebrated with gaiety and enthusiasm in every part of the country. In Delhi, the celebrations begin with the unfurling of the national flag at the Red Fort by the Prime Minister of the country. Massive seating arrangements are made for the people gathered there for watching the spectacle and for hearing the speech of the Prime Minister. Foolproof security arrangements are also made lest some untoward incidents occur to scuttle the celebration. Separate enclosures for VIPs and common people are made to ensure security of all and to avoid any chaotic situation.

On reaching the Red Fort, the Prime Minister greets the people as the slogan 'Bharat Mata ki Jai' **rants** the air. He then proceeds to unfurl the national flag and as he does that, the national anthem is sung by a select group of people comprising students and others. This is followed by twenty-one gun salutes.

The Prime Minister then delivers his speech from the **rampart** of the Red Fort from where Jawaharlal Nehru had delivered his first speech for independent India. In his speech, he highlights the achievements and progress made by the country in various fields and puts for the programme that the nation is to pursue to improve the quality of life of the people. He dwells at length on all matters of concern and presents a blue-print which the nation intends to follow to bring about the economic development in the country. His speech also touches upon those areas that are a matter of concern. In short, he touches upon all aspects of nation-building and suggests ways and means of re-building the nation. His speech concludes with the rant of Jai Hind three times. People who gather there repeat this with the Prime Minister. This is followed by national anthem sung by the school children who are specifically brought for the purpose.

Independence Day is celebrated at all places throughout the country. The chief ministers of respective provinces unfurl the national flag at their state headquarters. Likewise district magistrates do it at district headquarters and in the same manner the other officials according to hierarchy do this at their designated places. All institutions and establishments, whatever their size and shape, do it at their respective places. Sweets are distributed on the occasion in schools and at other institutions and offices across the country. The day usually starts with the playing of national and patriotic songs on public address system. These songs charge up the atmosphere and people by and large take pride in being what they are.

Independence Day is celebrated with great fervour in military units. After attractive parade following the flag hoisting by the commanding officers of such units, a *Bara Khana* is organised. *Bara Khana* is a special occasion in military installations. Eminent people including ex-military personnel are invited to this event. All of them relish this and happily take part in this *Bara Khana.* This is special lunch.

Independence Day is celebrated in other countries as well. Not only the members of Indian community celebrate it in their own ways in foreign countries, the Indian embassies celebrate it in a big way. They invite prominent people from all walks of life. Special displays and shows are made acquaint the people of the host country about India the nation. Such celebrations provide an excellent opportunity to our embassies to show-case the achievements and progresses made by India in various fields.

People in general celebrate this national festival in the manner that befits them or suits them. Since this happens to be a national holiday, youth and children often take to flying kites and playing games. Colourful balloons are also released in the sky and often visit places. In short, they enjoy the day in every possible manner. Everybody is touched by the spirit of the day.

This is a national festival, therefore, a national holiday.

Vocabulary

For good – (adv) for a long time without essential change, permanently. **Rant** – (v) to speak or complain about something in a loud and angry way. **Rampart** – (n) a high and wide wall of stone or earth with a path of top built around a castle, town, etc. to defend it, bulwark, wall.

□

24
Teachers' Day

This day is celebrated as Teachers' Day because on this day of 5th September in the year 1888 was born one of the greatest teachers of our times: Dr. Sarvapalli Radhakrishnan, who went on to become the President of India in 1962. The day is celebrated to express our respect and gratitude to a person who brought so many laurels to the country. By celebrating this day as Teachers' Day, India remembers one of its illustrious sons of all times. By celebrating this day, this same respect is extended to all teachers as they are all expected to impart those very values and standards that Dr. Radhakrishnan stood for.

India celebrates its Teachers' Day where students across the country participate in certain programmes that are exclusively meant for their teachers. They make their teachers feel special as they **bestow** flowers and bouquets to them. India has a tradition of holding teachers in high esteem. There are innumerable examples of how students or disciples of teachers have out of their way shown respect to their teachers. Eklavya had merely taken Dronacharya as his teacher and yet he did not hesitate to pay his fee when demanded by the teacher. The teacher demanded his thumb and the taught gave it without batting an eyelid. This simply shows the kind of esteem that can be shown to a teacher. This need not be emulated by others.

A good teacher according to Dr. Radhakrishnan "must know how to arouse the interest of the pupil in the field of education for which he is responsible. He must himself be a master in the field of education and be in touch with the latest developments in the subjects; he must himself be a fellow traveller in the exciting pursuit of knowledge". He not only believed in what he said, he practised it himself. He did not have a great time in his young days. In fact, he came from a very poor family and making both ends meet was a difficult thing for him. After doing his masters in philosophy, he took to teaching. His wonderful and famous ways of teaching endeared him to one and all. Pupils began to flock to him and this smoothened his economic crisis. It was this style of teaching which made learning a lively exercise with him and it was this way of teaching that took him to places as a man of **erudition**.

Teachers, one fondly hopes, should be able to imbibe some of those qualities that Dr. Radhakrishnan was known for. Teachers should have the ability to face up to any situation known or unknown through sheer intelligence and through **alacrity** of mind. The teachers we see today do not quite inspire the same confidence in us that the teachers of the past did. This is not to say that the teachers of our times are not up to the mark. But yes, they are not up to the mark of Dr. Radhakrishnan.

Speaking about Teachers' Day is speaking about Dr. Radhakrishnan. It will be interesting to know that when Dr. Radhakrishnan was appointed Ambassador to the USSR in 1949, few had expected him to be able to deliver anything positive. Most thought that his grounding in idealist philosophy would not stand him in good stead with Joseph Stalin, an **ardent** communist perceived by many as monstrous. But the teacher in him took control of the situation even when face to face with Stalin. With the help of an interpreter, he told Stalin that he came from a country where an emperor **renounced** war after securing a bloody victory and went on to become a monk. He was obviously referring to Ashoka the Great. He then added, "You have **waded** your way to power through force. Who knows that might happen to you also?" Stalin smiled and said, "Yes, miracles do happen." Stalin then revealed that he had spent five years in a theological seminary. This meant he did not rule out the possibility of that miracle. Before leaving for India, Radhakrishnan paid Stalin a courtesy call. Stalin was not keeping well. Dr. Radhakrishnan patted him on the cheek and on the back. Stalin said that he was the first person to have treated Stalin as a human being and not as a monster. Stalin was touched by this gesture of Dr. Radhakrishnan and felt sad that he was leaving. He knew he was not going to live long but wished Dr. Radhakrishnan to live long. Stalin died within six months. It was this quality in him that endeared him to such a person as Stalin who was known for his ruthlessness.

It is the teacher who makes or unmakes a life. A good teacher can transform the life of his/her pupils. Even though we cannot have another Dr. Radhakrishnan in our midst, there is no dearth of quality teachers either in our society. For instance, Anand Kumar of Super 30 at Patna is an internationally-acclaimed teacher. His methods are creating waves and are making lives of so many pupils drawn from the lowest rung of society. Year after year he has been shaping up the life and career of so many who would not have been able to see the light of the day on their own. Likewise, there are others at different places of the country quietly shaping the life and career of so many and in the process are contributing to the nation-building.

There is no **gainsaying** the fact that teachers play a **pivotal** role in determining the destiny of a nation by imparting quality education to children. Quality, however, should not remain restricted to the lessons for examinations, but it should refer to those aspects that contribute to making of character. A nation, no matter how well endowed with technological skill and economic well-being, cannot enrich itself if it did not have citizenry of character. A teacher's job is to build character as also to build society and nation by imparting quality education to his/her pupils in the manner Dr. Radhakrishnan did. The central idea behind the celebration of Teachers' Day is to achieve this end. And once that is achieved, that would be the true celebration of Teachers' Day.

Vocabulary

Bestow—(v) grant a qualification, title, right, possession, etc., give as a gift. **Erudition**—(n) great academic knowledge;

Alacrity – (n) great willingness or enthusiasm, liveliness and eagerness, briskness, smartness. **Ardent** – (adj) very enthusiastic and show strong feelings for something/somebody. **Wade** – (v) to walk with an effort especially through mud or water. **Gainsay** – (v) question the truth or validity of, take exception to, challenge, dispute. **Pivotal** – (adj) of great importance because other things depend on it.

□

25
Visit to a Monument

Monument is a structure erected to commemorate persons or to capture events of historical importance. It could be a burial vault for a famous person or an important site marked and preserved as public property. A monument is a lasting reminder of something of exceptional quality or significance. India is full of such monuments which people from all over the world flock to see time and again.

Taj Mahal is one such monument which is regarded as one of the wonders of the world. Monuments are also called historical buildings; and historical buildings remind us of our history. People visit these buildings or monuments not only to view and to marvel at their excellence, but also to gather information about the incidents or history leading to building of such monuments. These monuments are a storehouse of information. They satisfy our quest for knowledge about our surroundings and our history.

Sheer beauty of Taj Mahal is something that is never lost on any visitor. If it is watched on a full moonlit night, the watcher is left spellbound. Its magic casts spell on all without exception. That a monument of this quality and excellence could have been built some four hundred years ago beats our imagination. Engineers of our own times claim to have mastered the art and science of raising of structures simply because they have developed machineries that make constructions of all kinds so very easy. But the masons and labourers who worked day and night to build Taj had no such facilities, nor did they have structures that they could copy or emulate. They had no past experience or expertise to fall back on. And yet, what they created in that distant past is nothing but magical. If our engineers set out to create another Taj Mahal today, they will, in all probability, fail to match the excellence of the one that stands at Agra.

Rising on the high red sandstone base topped by a huge terrace of white marble on which rests the famous and eye-catching dome flanked by four pillars tapering minarets, Taj Mahal is an example of engineering marvel. Its beauty is beyond description, especially when seen on a moonlit night. The stones sparkle brightly. The sheer beauty of this monument is enough to instil life even into a **sedate** person. Visitors keep steaming in from far and wide to let sink in its beauty into their psyche. **Sublime** is the word that can describe Taj.

This monument, the recorded history says, was built by Shahjahan in the fond memory of his wife Mumtaz Mahal. Contrary to what is popularly believed, Taj Mahal, according to PN Oak, a well-known historian, is not an Islamic mausoleum but an ancient Hindu Shiva temple known as Tejo Mahalaya. But the popular belief, as propounded by most of the historians, is that it was built by Shahjahan to **perpetuate** the memory of his wife whom he loved so much. The monument, one can say without any hitch, is a dream in marble. The surroundings add to the charm of this dream. The high and majestic towers at four corners, the expansive lawns, the towering and majestically swinging cypress trees, and the bristling fountains add to the beauty and excellence of the monument. Magnificence of the monument drew an observation that it has been 'designed by giants and finished by jewellers'. This shows the monument has the size of magnificence and the delicacy and **subtlety** of an artist. Magnificence and artistry are a rare combination. But that rare combination is found in this monument.

The central dome is the repository of romance and beauty that immediately strikes any visitor, no matter how prosaic he or she is. There is a broad circular gallery around the building. The carvings on the marble and **filigree** work are exemplary works of fine art. One cannot help admiring these carvings and filigree works. In the centre of the main dome, there are two tombs supposed to be those of Shahjahan and his queen. But they are not the real tombs. The real ones are downstairs. Both are identical in shape and size. On the tomb of the queen are inscribed the verses from the Holy Quran. The excellence in mosaic work could strike anyone as something from another world. They are so difficult to describe in words. They are **astoundingly** beautiful. That they are preserved to this date in this majestic manner is another wonder of our times when it is a general complaint that we are not good at maintaining and preserving things. The upkeep and maintenance of some of the monuments certainly are an exception to this rule. Hope this zeal of maintaining such monuments does not die out. We are indebted to the apex court of the country that it disallowed an attempt to **usurp** the surrounding areas of Taj Mahal for some political projects. This would certainly have done massive damage to the monument. Any such attempts must be **deprecated** and discouraged. Taj Mahal is a world heritage and no one has any business or authority to damage our heritage.

Visiting Taj Mahal is an experience of a life time. We are fortunate that we have such a monument in our own country. Every Indian must have the privilege of visiting this monument. This is not only **enthralling** to eyes and mind, but also highly educative. That beauty could be so enduring can be believed only when one sees Taj Mahal with one's own eyes.

Vocabulary

Sedate—(adj) characterized by dignity and sobriety, calm, sombre. **Sublime**—(adj) inspiring awe, worthy of adoration and reverence, of very high quality and causing great admiration. **Perpetuate**—(v) cause to continue or prevail. **Subtlety**—(n) a subtle difference in meaning, opinion or attitude, the quality of being difficult to detect and analyse. **Filigree**—(n) delicate decoration made from gold or silver wire. **Astoundingly**—(adv) so surprising as if difficult to believe. **Deprecate**—(v) to feel and express strong disapproval of something. **Enthral**—(v) hold spellbound.

□

26
Visit to a Hill Station

A visit to a hill station is always a pleasure and an exciting experience. By visiting a hill station, the visitor tends to put self into the lap of nature. It looks as though one has come in direct communion with nature. Nature in its pure and divine form greets the visitor with open and extended arms and the visitor is **willy-nilly** drawn into them. That in essence is the beauty of a hill station.

There is no death of hill stations in India. Being a huge country, it has a large number of hill stations where one can relax and enjoy for a while before once again returning to the **drudgery** of real life that the real world presents.

India is basically a hot country. Indian plains remain terribly hot during the months of April, May and June. They remain moderately hot during the remaining months almost till October. Hill resorts during these months remain hot favourites for those seeking physical and mental quietude. From October to February, there is an unusual rush for hill stations.

Of the many hill places that I have seen, my fascination for Shillong is a non-abating fascination. I visited this hill station on a number of occasions primarily because this is not a hill station in the ordinary sense of the term as Darjeeling or Shimla or Nainital or Ooty or other most sought-after hill stations are. Besides being the capital of Meghalaya, the station presents a life that is both routine and unique. This station remains lively and full of normal existential activities throughout the year. Flow of life in this hill station is constant and regular. This element is largely missing in places mentioned above as also in Mussoorie and Manali. These stations **bubble** with life only and primarily during those months when tourists flock to those places. On the remaining months called slack season, life takes a back-seat as they await the arrival of tourists. Shillong does not wholly depend on the arrival of tourists to enjoy the hub and activities of life. Shillong has a life of its own and is hardly ever influenced by the arrival or departure of tourists.

As the name Meghalaya suggests, it is the abode of clouds. With regard to rains, it can be said to be **fickle**. It can rain any time, any moment without any warning whatsoever. Rains in Shillong or especially in Cherrapunjee area are a spectacle worth watching.

Although the best time to visit Shillong is the months of September-October and April to June, one can enjoy Shillong at all times. Reaching Shillong from the plains is not difficult. One could go to Guwahati by railways, roadways or airways. From Guwahati, one may go by road or by rail. There is no rail link to Shillong. Helicopter services are available from Guwahati. Buses ply between Guwahati and Shillong Outer Agency. This is by way of an arrangement with the Indian Railways. Railways issue tickets right up to Shillong. All a passenger has to do is to have it recorded at the Outer Agency office just outside the Guwahati Railway Station.

Luxury taxis are also available. It takes nearly three hours to cover the distance of 103 kilometers of circuitous road. Those not accustomed to travelling on hill tracts may face the problem of vomiting. Most of those who undertake this kind of journey keep some medicine with them. It requires special skill to drive on such roads. After crossing the Barapani Lake, one begins to feel the cool breeze blowing across. Guwahati is hot, Shillong is cold. This transition from hot to cold is soothing.

Outer Agency is right in the heart of the city. Hotels and lodges abound the area. All important offices and institutions are closeby. The main business centre is also closeby. The first thing a first timer is asked to see or visit is the botanical garden-cum-city garden, which is within the walking distance from the Outer Agency. Police Bazar and Burra Bazar are the hubs of the business centre at Shillong. City buses are available for all local points. City buses of Shillong are small in size. The local inhabitants of Shillong are tiny in size. Their buses suit them and their requirement. Those from the plains find it a little difficult initially.

There are several beautiful locations in and around Shillong. One can have pleasant time in the city garden which is so close to the main centre. There are boats for boating. It's a beautiful garden in the middle of the city. For longer boating rides, one can go to Bara Pani at some distance. Tourists like to go there. It's a whole-day programme. Quality eateries are available in the place. Seven-Sisters Falls is an important tourist destination in Shillong and so is the Elephant Falls near air-force base in Upper Shillong. Mawphlong and Tura are equally important tourist destinations. But the most attractive destination is Cherrapunjee which records the highest rainfall in the country. Dalhousie in Himachal Pradesh is another hill station which is credited to receive maximum rainfall. Cherrapunjee and Dalhousie are the two hill stations that receive maximum rainfall. Beauty of Cherrapunjee rainfall lies in its being so **sonorous** and musical and the viewer gets to see the plain **tracts** of Bangladesh below. Its beauty is simply incredible. To fully enjoy the sight and to have a real mental and physical peace, one should stay there for a few days and feel the pulse of the nature in its purest form.

Shillong presents a unique cultural scenario inasmuch as all local shops are manned by ladies and men usually do domestic **chore** or attend to other outward activities. Ladies are the virtual guardians. Meghalaya has Matriarchy as social system. Under this system, girls bring in their husbands after marriage. Girls inherit the property of their mother. Khasis, Jaintias and Garos are the local tribes of the state. Bengalis form an important section of the local population besides Nepalese.

It's great to watch these tribal women run their business while their men assist them. *Didi* and *Mama* are common modes of address. Interacting with them is a joy. They are well-informed people who read newspapers regularly. They write their language in Roman script. Most of them speak good English and Hindi. Therefore, communicating with them poses not much of a problem.

Visiting Shillong during the puja season is an unforgettable experience. Shillong is seen in its most colourful outfit during the festive seasons of Durga Puja, Diwali and Christmas. Since there is huge Bengali population, Durga Puja is celebrated with great pomp and show and with religious fervour. During three days of Saptami, Ashtami and Navami, the environment of Shillong reverberates with the rant of Mahishasurmardini. Idol immersion which is carried out near Golf Links is worth watching. Thousands of people line up the road right up to the Golf Links. Come Diwali and the entire stretch of Shillong appear to have been **woven** in one thread running through. And come X'mas, the locals in their best and traditional attire present a spectacle that cannot be forgotten.

It is so refreshing and **rejuvenating** to visit any hill station, but it is hugely rewarding and educating to visit Shillong which is also called "Switzerland of India" or some even call it "Scotland of the East". Much of the sheen of the place has been lost because of excessive felling of trees and illegal mining. One hopes there is a check on this.

Vocabulary

Willy-nilly – (adv) willing or not willing, whether or not wanted to. **Drudgery** – (n) hard boring work. **Bubble** – (n) a ball of air or gas in a liquid, or a ball of air inside a solid substance as glass. **Fickle** – (adj) liable to sudden unpredictable change, mercurial, volatile, erratic; **Sonorous** – (adj) having a pleasant full deep sound. **Tract** – (n) an area of land, especially a large one; **Chore** – (n) a task done regularly, job, task. **Woven** – (adj) this is the past participle of verb 'weave' and 'woven' is its adjectival form meaning 'made by interlacing threads or strips of material or other elements into a whole'. **Rejuvenate** – (v) to make somebody/something feel or look younger or more lively. □

27
Visit to a Museum

Visit to a museum is a must for all those who wish to learn and know about the history and civilisation of their country or of the world. Museums are a place where invaluable antique pieces related to art, culture and civilisation are kept for viewing and for studying. They are repositories of the past. The antiques kept in museums are a window to what our ancestors did and the way they lived. As a matter of fact, museums are great historical, anthropological and archeological monuments that tell a tale of the ancient world. But for them we would not know how our civilisation progressed to bring us to the present state. The objects kept in museums are a matter of great interest for those who are keen to explore history. Every country treasures things of the past and they are treasured in a place called museum. Usually, every city has a museum where it showcases things that are of prime importance. Museums are, therefore, a necessary element in our life and we all should spend some time exploring the antiques in museums.

Like many I too had an opportunity to go to a local museum in the town. Though it could not be equated with the size of museums that we see in metropolises or in big cities, it is nevertheless a worth visiting place. I went there with my family, my children. My children are very **inquisitive** by nature. They kept **nagging** me with questions and that **impelled** me to keep questioning those stationed there to explain things. The hall we entered into was a massive hall where exhibits were arranged neatly in a systematic way. The collections were made up of objects collected from various parts of the country.

The museum we visited is a local chapter of the national museum situated in the town. The hall we entered into had a section of the species now extinct. It was quite revealing to see the models of various species of dinosaurs. Data relating to their extinction were presented through charts and diagrams. I had to do lot of explaining to my children, who marvelled at the sight of dinosaurs' carcass. There was that piece of rock which Neil Armstrong had brought from the surface of the moon. Everybody was curious to touch it, but the rock was kept at a distance behind glass and visitors were strictly warned against touching anything. There were coins of the distant past, of the dynasties now only part of history. Some of these coins were of gold, some of silver and some others of copper and nickel. Some of these coins had some spark left in them while quite a few of them had got rusted. We were told these were kept in the same state in which they were found.

There were several household items and utensils such as spoons, ladles, plates, saucers, cups, cauldrons, griddles and host of other things like toys and models of animals, such as those of dogs, cats, rats, cows, buffaloes, goats, horses, oxen and many others that we could not easily identify. There were some clay models of birds as well. These included parrots, pigeons, sparrows, crows, hawks, eagles, vultures and so on and so forth. There were models of human beings as well in an adjoining room. This included toys of men, women, children—boys and girls—the new-born in the laps of mothers, or held in the arms of mothers. Men and women wore dresses of different kinds, shapes and sizes that spoke about the prevalent fashion and style in the relevant period. It was obvious that they represented different times and different cultures and periods of civilisation. Much of it all was inscribed on the models and what was not easily understood was explained by the guide who accompanied us. **Curator** was also at hand to explain other details.

We revisited the room where rocks of various shapes and sizes were kept. It was the very room in which we had seen the rock brought by Neil Armstrong. We revisited this room because we had missed out on other rocks kept there. There were several beautiful specimens of rocks in this room. There were also ores of various metals, both in original forms and in the finished states. There were old **relics**, old dresses worn by warriors at different stages of time. Weapons of various kinds also drew our attention. These were the ones used by our ancestors to deal with their enemies or to hunt down their prey. The weapons we saw included spears, swords, lances, shields and armour. They looked very heavy, large and strong which threw an insight into the kind of personality and the physical strength those warriors possessed in the distant past.

There was yet another hall which had the collections brought from different sites. These included potteries, bangles, statues, metal instruments and various kinds of objects that were used by our ancestors. These, we were told, were dug out of the earth where they were buried. They were relics of the buried townships of the past. Some of such articles are still in use in our own times. These objects throw ample light on the kind of life and culture the people of the distant past pursued.

Specimens of handicraft and **artefacts** collected from all over the world were also on display in the museum. These tell a story of how these crafts developed in different parts of the world and how they were put to use. There were plenty of other and interesting things that we saw in the museum. We were particularly overjoyed to see that our children were **evincing** interest in the objects they were seeing.

It is always a pleasure to take a peep into the past as it is the past that helps us move forward into the future. And what could be a better way of peeping into the past if not by visiting museums that bring us in direct contact with the past? A visit to museum should be an important curricular in every school as it helps the young minds to know the past, for without having adequate knowledge of the past, it is not possible to make long strides for the future.

Vocabulary

Inquisitive—(adj) showing curiosity, inquiring or appearing to inquire. **Nag**—(v) to bother persistently with trivial complaints, to query and harry constantly. **Impel**—(v) urge or force a person into an action, cause to move forward with force, to force, to propel. **Curator**—(n) the custodian of a collection (in a museum or library), conservator. **Relic**—(n) an object, a tradition, a system to have survived from the past. **Artefact**—(n) an object that is made by a person, especially something of historical or cultural interest. **Evince**—(v) give expression to, to show clearly one has feeling or quality.

□

28

Visit to a Book Fair

Book fair is a regular annual event at Gandhi Maidan. It is held every year in the month of November after the festivities come to an end. As a matter of fact, book fair is an extension of the festivities for the people of the state capital. There is no dearth of book lovers at Patna. Therefore, for those who organise this fair every year, end up with sizeable profit. Book lovers too end up being the beneficiaries because they get to buy the books they always wanted to buy. Book fair is a great opportunity for book lovers.

Book fair also provides an opportunity to see some of the renowned writers who descend to the fair to promote their books or to give a talk on what is trending in this arena. Reading sessions occasionally resorted to by the writers give an opportunity to students and **budding** writers to interact with writers. It's a pleasant exercise both for the readers and the writers. If readers find pleasure in having a question-answer session with writers, writers too find it worthwhile discussing and knowing the mind of prospective readers. The exercise is mutually beneficial. This exercise also helps the publishers who are able to promote their product.

As students, we get free access to the fair. Most of us like to visit the fair on at least two occasions. We first visit it on the inaugural day. This day is always an important day as several writers come to witness the inaugural session and then inauguration is done with a great deal of fanfare. Usually it is inaugurated by some high dignitary like Chief Minister or Governor. In short, it's a big event and we do not like to miss out on such opportunities. Important announcements are made on the inaugural day and often we end up being the beneficiaries of those announcements. Normally, we do not buy any book on this day. We just loaf around and see for ourselves the kind of publishers that have come. We also take a look at those books that tend to help us professionally or ready us for future competitions. We also look for new authors, who may have come up with something really worthwhile. Generally speaking, inputs about new authors and their works are made available by various readers and publishers. Sometimes they are done through talks and sometimes through pamphlets and occasionally through public address (PA) system at the venue itself. After going through all counters and outlets, we generally make up our mind on what to buy.

We revisit the fair on another day. This day we buy what we had made up our mind on. By this time, competition also becomes stiff amongst publishers. They offer competing rebates and this suits us because we do not like to tax our guardians much. They are already much taxed and harried because of the rising cost of education. Besides, if we could save something, we could spend on eateries. Book fair does not mean there are only books to buy. There are good eateries where one could spend some valuable time: reading and eating while someone keeps reading aloud some parts of the new releases. Book fair is nothing short of a fair. It has all the frills and thrills of a regular fair, books or no books.

The book fair was a great spectacle to watch. There were hoardings of various kinds inviting readers from all hue to read and **explore** the world of knowledge. There were books of all kinds: books for the grown-ups, books for children, books for adults, books for students, books for professionals, books for housewives and books for gardeners. Books of all descriptions were on display. There were several stalls managed by various publishing houses. If there were local publishers, there were national and international publishers with various kinds of books, periodicals, audio-visual teaching aids and materials.

There were books on computer hardware and software, books on how to improve spoken English, and so on and so forth. It really made us very happy to see the variety. The sheer reach of these books was mind-boggling. There was so much to choose from. No doubt, sometimes we were in dilemma as we faced the problem of plenty. But this did not pose much of a problem as we had been attending to these book fairs for many years now and we had come to understand the **intricacies** of it all.

Books on wide range of disciplines were available at competitive price. Nothing could have been more satisfying than this. Books on engineering, information technology, computer science were a special draw for us. I was also drawn towards the books on literature. Even though a student of science, I was fascinated by literature. These books were displayed on the stalls of almost all publishers. Books on performing arts, sports, finance and management were also on display. On display were also books on anatomy and medicine together with books on law and banking. There were university books; there were sponsored books. There were books on all shades of life. One only had to decide which shade to take on and whether one had enough money to buy them, for books are expensive these days despite rebates. Dictionaries drew attention of many. I always wanted to have a quality dictionary. I bought one. I also bought books on computer science and physics. I also bought a new book *Jingling Coins Rusted Coins*, a memoir of an unknown banker by J.J. Jadway. I had heard a great deal about this book. It recorded the evolution of Indian banking system and threw some light on the workings of Indian Air Force. It proved to be a beneficial read.

The book fair drew a large number of readers from all over the state. Some readers came from distant districts to buy books. Students from various schools flocked to the venue in great numbers and went away happy after buying some books they had not been able to get from shops. Book fair provides a unique opportunity to readers from various walks of life to get hold of books they generally do come across at small towns or in small shops. Children also come in great numbers because they get to buy book of their choice. Besides enjoying the event with their parents, they also end up buying some pictorial and colourful books.

Books, it is said, are the best friends. If you have no one to turn to, turn to your books. They will provide you the joy you have not known. We are happy that we get to have book fair every year without fail. Mere presence of these fairs stimulates us to read. There is no substitute to books and there is no better way of learning than by reading. As Lord Bacon said, "reading **maketh** a perfect man".

Vocabulary

Budding—(adj) beginning to develop. **Explore**—(v) inquire into, travel to or penetrate into, examine minutely, dig into, search, research. **Intricacies**—(n) marked by elaborately complex details. **Maketh**—(v) 'makes' is its modern form.

□

29

My Banker

Banking in India has never been the same as it was prior to 1969. It was in this year that 14 major banks were nationalised followed by another dose of nationalisation of eight banks in 1980. Besides, these banks that were nationalised in instalments, State Bank with its seven associate banks provides a strong banking platform from where a customer can pick his banker. In addition to these, there are quite a few large private and some foreign banks that cater to the banking needs of their customers. Banking is an essential part of our economic life. Quality banking system is essential for any economy to sustain itself in today's globalised economy. India is no exception. In fact, India is in the forefront of banking arena. A customer has plethora of choices before him. Gone are the days when he was forced to shuttle between one or two banks. From nationalisation in 1969 to liberalisation and globalisation in the nineties, banking in India has come full circle. From class banking in the pre-nationalisation era to mass banking in the post-nationalisation era to class and mass banking combine in the globalised and liberalised era is the story of Indian banking.

While there are many banks to choose from, I chose Punjab National Bank (PNB) as my banker precisely for two reasons: its extensive reach and its quality customer service. This is not to say that other banks do not offer these. A few I have tried out have failed to give me the satisfaction PNB has given me. Besides, the bank has a chequered history.

PNB began its journey from Anarkali Gali of Lahore in Pakistan on 12th April, 1895. In its onward journey, it created many milestones. One such was created when after partition in 1947, the bank flung open its strong room to anyone and everyone returning from Pakistan if only he or she could produce any piece of paper that could barely suggest he or she had an account with the bank, notwithstanding the status of the account—a banking feat never repeated anywhere by any bank. The bank has earned respect and trust of its customers and done nothing to lose this respect and trust ever since. Majority of the branches of this bank had remained in Pakistan and very few thought this bank could survive this. The bank not only survived this, it became a stable bank after this banking feat.

My association with the bank dates back to the eighties when out of sheer frustration with the largest bank of the country for its lack of service, I shifted my account to a branch of PNB and ever since I have done business with this bank. Even when I had occasional differences and concerns, they were at once addressed by the concerned authorities. I never had any serious issues with the bank or with the quality of services rendered. I have had the opportunity of dealing with several nationalised and private banks, but the element of satisfaction I derived at PNB was nowhere to be found. Maybe, this is because of my long association with the bank. Whatever the reason, my banker is PNB.

Even though in terms of size and number of branches, PNB does not match up to those of State Bank, a comparison with State Bank will not be out of place here. Being inquisitive by nature, I delved a little deep to see what the banking scenario was after the nationalisation of major banks in the sixties and the eighties. The overall banking scenario was—the banks were expanding thick and fast. Number of offices of the public sector banks in India as on June 1969 stood at 8,262. This shot up to 55,410 offices as on June 1988 which records a rapid growth. From 55,410 offices as on June 1988 it grew to 60519 offices as on 1991. It would be interesting to see the position of PNB in comparison with SBI.

Distribution of Offices in India

	June 1969	*March 1991*	*March 2001*	*March 2009*	*March 2010*
State Bank	1,569	8,513	N/A	11,450	12,638
PN Bank	570	3,014	3,853	4,430	4,997

What is most pleasing about PNB is that its employees are not **overweening**. They do not covey a feeling that they know everything and that the customer should accept his/her words as final. A customer dislikes nothing more than this attitude. Sadly, a large number of employees of the public sector banks suffer from this **malaise**, State Bank being the worst offender. Needless to say, this drives away many self-respecting customers. PNB employees are largely accommodative on this aspect and they allow the customers to have their say. This one positive quality endears them to customers.

There were occasions when I had to get drafts made at break-neck speed. PNB rarely disappointed me. On occasions, they went out of their way to meet my request. This was the first bank to treat its customers as bank customer instead of branch customer when Centralised Banking System or Core Banking System came into force. This facility of operating my account from anywhere went a long way in solving some of the pressing problems I would have faced if this facility was not in place. Remittance of fund to children studying at different centres was made so easy and **hassle**-free by the bank with the introduction of this facility. I am aware of the fact that this facility has been withdrawn lately because of fraudulent abuse of the facility. But I really had to suffer no such problem. I am still allowed access to my account from various places. Maybe, it's a case of mutual trust.

PNB is a big bank with big dreams and schemes. Its branches are available in remote rural areas and in most of the semi-urban centres in addition to being available in big cities and metropolises. It makes it easy and convenient to do banking business with this kind of bank. I had the opportunity of recommending some of my friends and relatives to this bank.

None of them ever reported any lack of **cordiality** from the bank or deficiency of service. I can, therefore, say I am in the hands of a bank that cares for me and for my banking needs.

Vocabulary

Overweening—(adj) showing too much confidence or pride. **Malaise**—(n) physical discomfort (as mild sickness or depression, unease). **Hassle**—(n) an annoying situation as it involves doing something difficult or complicated requiring lots of efforts. **Cordiality**—(n) pleasant and friendly.

□

30

Electronic Media—The News Channels

There was a time when getting news was not an easy thing. Getting correct and authentic news in time was a tall order. When Indira Gandhi was assassinated in 1984, we did not get to know about it from our news channels at first. It was Radio Moscow that reported it first and we heard it on BBC. It was long after that All India Radio broadcast the news and by the time it was aired by India news media, the whole world had come to know about it.

But that is no longer the situation now. No sooner a thing happens than it is flashed in the electronic media. This is thanks to the number of news channels we have today. Nothing goes amiss; nothing goes unreported. With the **advent** of 24-hour news channels, there is a mad rush for breaking news. Every channel claims to provide this or that breaking news. And when news does not happen on its own, these channels create news of their own. If that also does not help, then these news channels serve what is not news.

The **mushrooming** growth of news channels has put electronic media under pressure to keep its clientele base intact. It is not an easy task to keep news listeners **glued** to TV. It is equally not easy to keep viewers engaged to any particular news channel as the viewer has remote in his/her hand. To keep the viewer interested, the news channels have to tailor their news to suit the taste or requirement of viewers. More the viewer, greater the target rating points (TRP). TRPs quantify the gross rating points achieved by an advertisement or a campaign among targeted individuals within a larger population. It is this TRP which sustains a news channel and to improve this rating, news channels go to any extent to manufacture news to keep the targeted individuals glued to TV watching a particular channel. This also gives rise to the **menace** of 'paid news'. About 'paid news', it can well be said that it is **scandalous** phenomenon in India media in which mainstream media barring a few exceptions were found to be systematically engaged in publishing favourable articles in exchange for payment. It applies to both electronic and print media. It would be no exaggeration to say that paid news is rotting Indian democracy.

A highly disturbing phenomenon these days is that certain news channels overdo things. If something catches their imagination, they repeat that something so relentlessly that they begin to sap the energy of viewers. If something happens somewhere that has news value, all channels devote their entire energy on that particular event as if there is nothing else to talk about, nothing else to report. The viewer is left with no choice but to switch off the TV set if he she does not want to be overfed on that particular thing. The latest news that is being overfed is the news about Asaram. The same obsession is seen in the dream of a certain sage that led to digging for gold. Likewise, there was a time when a child by the name of prince had fallen into a hole. For days together, there was nothing but this. All channels vied with one another to devote their energy on this single episode. During the period, there was a spate of news on children falling in holes. Suddenly, children seemed to be falling in pits or holes as though with a design. For days together, there was no other important news but this. Possibly, this was actually happening and the media was doing its duty by highlighting these incidents. But is it not strange that no such incident is being reported now? Have all holes been covered or have children stopped falling into them? Likewise, after the ghastly incident of 16th December, 2012, rape on the electronic media seems to have become the national topic.

This kind of mad rush eats into the credibility of electronic media, especially the news channels who are otherwise doing a great job. It goes to the credit of the electronic media that the ills that plague our society are getting exposure so fast and quick. It would seem that such things did not happen in the past. Nothing can be farther from truth. Things did happen in the past as well. Only we did not have this kind of media coverage then. Today wrong doers are **wary** of media. In the past, they were not because this kind of news channels did not exist. With the help of technology, electronic media today can produce and reproduce anything. This is the positive of it. We need to zealously guard this positive.

News channels need to exercise self-restraint and must stay within their limit. They should not indulge in what has come to be known as media trial. Courts have repeatedly cautioned media to exercise restraint while reporting. Media must report as things happen. It is for the people to take informed decision on what is reported. But that would be an ideal situation. Whether our news channels will attain to that ideal situation remains to be seen.

But despite what many may say about the over-**intrusive** news channels, the fact of the matter is—if we did not have an alert media, many dark spots of our society would remain **obfuscated**. In the process of exposing them, media may appear over-intrusive. But we must prefer this to complete blackout as we had in the past when we had to depend on BBC for authentic and reliable news.

Vocabulary

Advent—(n) the coming of an important event, person, invention, etc. **Mushroom**—(n) fleshy body of any of numerous edible fungi. **Glued**—(adj) affixed or as if affixed with glue or paste; **Menace**—(n) a person or thing that causes, or may cause, serious damage, harm or danger. **Scandalous**—(adj) shocking and unacceptable, giving offence to moral sensibilities and injurious to reputation, disgraceful, shameful. **Wary** – (adj) marked by keen caution and watchful prudence, openly distrustful and unwilling to confide. **Intrusive** – (adj) encroaching, invasive, meddlesome, officious. **Obfuscate** – (v) to make something less clear and more difficult to understand, often deliberately, to make obscure.

□

31
Internet—Way of Life

Science and technology have revolutionalised human life. The changes wrought about have changed our perception about things around. Internet is one of the latest technological advances made by humans. The moment we talk about Internet, various images flash through our minds. Computers of all shapes and sizes and computer networks come to our mind. Through these computers and computer networks, we get connected with people round the globe. In no time, we move from one end of globe to the other end. It is all thanks to Internet. If we wish to **elicit** some information – authentic ones at that – we at once get them through Internet.

Internet has brought us in contact with the entire world. Nothing is anymore away from us; nothing is anymore beyond our reach. India got the exposure to Internet in August 1995. Initially, it remained under the control of the government, but in 1998, the facility was opened up for all. Private parties were allowed to provide this service to people. Earlier, it was the **prerogative** of Bharat Sanchar Nigam Limited (BSNL). With the arrival of the private parties, service became more easily accessible and people began to reap benefits of the facility. It benefited mainly the business corporate houses, professionals, scientists, teachers and students. Internet has everything for all.

Internet has changed the quality and pace of life. What took days, months and sometimes ages to reach specified destinations, Internet made it possible to reach them in a **jiffy**. In almost no time, one could transmit information from one end to another, no matter what the location. Instead of writing a post-card or an inland letter to a friend or a relative, the desired communication can be completed through e-mail in absolutely no time. This is the magic of Internet. The world has been squeezed into a small ball that can be handled even by an infant.

Internet is useful for just anyone. It is very useful for common people. The banking face of India has radically altered with the advent of Internet. Internet banking is now an absolute need of our times. Reaching out physically to those living in villages – there are six lakh villages in India – will not be possible without Internet. Dr. K.C. Chakraborthy, the former CMD of PNB, went to the extent of suggesting that 'Internet banking is required by the poor, not the rich' as he said, 'transaction costs are so much less'. If banking is one sector, there are other sectors that have switched over to Internet for their day-to-day functioning. Some of the private corporate houses encourage their executives to function through internet. Indian Railways have taken to Internet in a big way indeed. Internet has become a way of life.

Shopping through Internet has become a routine matter. Instead of visiting shops in person, it is comparatively easy to view things on shopping sites and place orders. Things are delivered in no time at the doorstep. Payments too can be made through Internet. Electricity bills and host of other bills can be paid through Internet. For getting gas now, it is no longer necessary to stand in queue. Even for routine purchases, it is no longer necessary to carry cash. Payments can be made through credit cards and debit cards. It is all because of Internet.

Internet is very useful for students and teachers. Many students instead of buying books take to reading e-books to acquire knowledge. Materials of various kinds are easily available on Internet. Service providers like Google make things so easy by providing ready information on almost any matter or subject. Teachers also often impart online tuition to their students irrespective of where they are placed.

Internet is often abused too. Everything has a bright and a dark side. It is not the fault of Internet that some people use it for evil purposes. It is the user who is to blame for this. It is these users who have given rise to cyber crime. This is one of the worst uses of Internet and every civilised society has a role to play insofar as containing of this menace is concerned. Those who wish to take the benefit of Internet to enrich the quality of their life make proper use of Internet. But those who are criminally inclined abuse this facility. It is always the user not the facility that is to be credited or discredited.

Vocabulary

Elicit—(v) to get information or reaction from somebody often with difficulty, call forth, derive by reason. **Prerogative**—(n) a right or advantage belonging to a person or to a group of persons because of their importance and social position. **Jiffy**—(n) a moment, blink of an eye, instant.

□

32
Newspaper

The origin of newspapers in India dates back to the 18th century. The first in this **genre** was published in English in Calcutta in 1790 by James Augustus Hicky. His *Bengal Gazette* was the first English newspaper and also the first printed newspaper in the sub-continent. This was followed by *Bombay Herald* in 1789 followed by *Bombay Courier* the following year. This paper finally merged with the *Times of India* in 1861. But the first newspaper published in any of the native Indian languages was in 1818 with the publication of *Samachar Darpan* in Bengali, and the first Hindi newspaper *Samachar Sudha Varshan* began its circulation in 1854. Prior to that a newspaper in Kannada language *Mangalooru Samachara* was published in 1843 and the first Malayalam newspaper *Rajyasamacharam* started circulation in 1847. The first Marathi newspaper was *Dyanprakash* and the first Tamil newspaper was *Swadesamitran*.

According to the data made available by the Registrar of Newspapers for India (RNI) for the year 2010-11, the number of newspapers and periodicals published in India was 82,222. This included 10,205 dailies, 394 bi-tri-weeklies, 27,321 weeklies, 10,422 fortnightlies, 25,072 monthlies, 5,208 quarterlies, 719 annuals and 2,881 others. These newspapers were published in as many as 152 languages and dialects during the year 2010-11. The largest number of these (32,793) was published in Hindi followed by 11,478 in English. There were 5,643 bilingual newspapers. Except for Kashmiri language, the daily newspapers were brought out in all the principal languages of the country and they were published from all states and union territories.

The state ranking number one in this respect is Uttar Pradesh with the publication of 13,065 newspapers. The state ranked number one even in the matters of dailies with 1,909 newspapers. The oldest existing newspaper is *Bombay Samachar,* a Gujarati newspaper published from Bombay since 1822.

The office of the Registrar of Newspapers for India (RNI) came into existence on 1st July, 1956, on the recommendation of the first Press Commission in 1953 and by amending the Press and Registration of Books Act, 1867. The functions of RNI are both statutory and non-statutory. Statutory functions include **compilation** and maintenance of a register of newspapers containing particulars are all the newspapers published in the country. It also includes issuance of certificates of registration to the newspapers published under valid declarations. It scrutinises and analyses annual statements sent by the publishers of newspapers every year. The RNI informs the district magistrates about availability of titles to the intending publishers for filing declarations and it ensures that newspapers are published in accordance with the provisions of the Press and Registration of Books Acts.

Non-statutory functions include the **formulation** of newsprint allocation policy with guidelines and on competence to issue eligibility certificates to the newspapers enabling them to procure **indigenous** newsprint. The RNI assesses the requirements and needs of newspaper establishments to import printing and composing machinery and allied materials before certifying the same. The national readership survey (NRS) initiated in 1974 was aimed at providing data as basis for buying and selling advertising space in the press medium. It also provides data on comparative exposure levels to other major mass media like television, cinema and radio. To **wriggle** out of the monopoly of the NRS, some media got together to form Indian readership survey (IRS) in 1994 primarily to offer the members a readership and market study to rival the NRS. IRS is a continuous readership study with a sample of over 2,50,000 and data is collected and released every six months to **mitigate** any seasonal biases. Both NRS and IRS subsequently merged into what came to be known as Readership Studies Council of India (RSCI).

It was soon felt necessary to lay down a standard and uniform procedure by which a member publisher should compare its net paid sales. Audit Bureau of Circulation (ABC) came into being to address this issue. This is done by having the circulation figure checked and certified by a firm of chartered accountants approved by the Bureau. It issues ABC certificates every six months to those publishers whose circulation figures conform to the rules and regulations set out by the Bureau. Press Information Bureau (PIB) is a nodal agency entrusted with the task of **disseminating** information to print and electronic media on government policies, programme initiatives and achievements. This is done by press releases, press notes, feature articles, background papers, press briefings, photographs, press conferences, interviews, database available on Bureau's website, press tours, etc.

Then there are news agencies like Press Trust of India (PTI), United News of India (UNI), and Press Council of India that provide efficient and unbiased news to all subscribers. The Press Council of India functions under the Press Council of India Act, 1978. It is a statutory, quasi-judicial body, acting as a watchdog of the press. It **adjudicates** the complaints, if any, against the press for violation of **ethics** and for violation of the freedom of the press, respectively. Prasar Bharati is the largest public broadcaster in India. It is an autonomous body that comprises Doordarshan (DD) television and All India Radio (AIR) networks. These were earlier tagged with the Ministry of Information & Broadcasting, GOI.

One would be tempted to conclude that with the **mushrooming** of television news channels, the importance of newspapers will have taken a severe beating. That, however, is not the case, for a large number of people still believe that it is the printed words that carry conviction. There is no denying that electronic media has invaded our reading space, but it has certainly not replaced newspapers. There is no substitute to reading. If viewership has increased, it has not done so at the cost of readership. **Fleeting** moments may excite, but they do not usually have a lasting impact chiefly because there is no scope for referring back to them. A newspaper has the staying power because it can always be referred back to and retrievals from the archives can be made with comparative ease. Viewing may be a thrill, but reading is always a pleasure. Newspapers, therefore, have created permanent space in the minds of reading public. Newspapers play a very important part in our day-to-day life. Electronic media can never play that role with the same degree of efficacy as newspapers.

Vocabulary

Genre – (n) a kind of literary of artistic work. **Compilation** – (n) something that is compiled (as into a single book or file). **Formulation** – (n) inventing or contriving an idea or explanation formulating it mentally. **Indigenous** – (adj) originating where it is found, aboriginal. **Wriggle** – (v) to move in a twisted or contorted motion (especially when struggling). **Mitigate** – (v) to make less severe or harsh. **Disseminate** – (v) to cause to become widely known, to broadcast. **Adjudicate** – (v) put on trial or hear a case and sit as the judge at the trial of, bring to an end, come to a final conclusion. **Ethics** – (n) motivation based on ideas of right and wrong. **Mushroom** – (v) pick or gather mushrooms, grows and spread fast. **Fleeting** – (adj) lasting for a markedly brief time.

□

33
Population Explosion

Population of a nation should be its asset, not its liability. The moment we talk of population, we talk about its negative aspects. India's growing population is a drain on its limited resources. To that extent this is a liability, a national liability. India's population, according to the latest census report, has gone past 121 crore. It ranks second only to China and at the rate at which we are growing, we will leave China behind in another decade. That means while China's rate of growth has slowed down, ours has not or has increased. Else, it is difficult to explain how a country that had barely 35 crore at the time of independence in 1947 has grown four-fold in little over six decades! Incidentally, our land mass is smaller than that of China. This means we have less space for our growing population than China. This despite the fact that governments have made all out efforts to contain population which means these efforts have not yielded desired results. The reason is nor far to seek. People do not realise the impact of it, or even if they realise, they do not care.

Lack of education is one of the prime reasons for people not understanding the **catastrophe** this population explosion could bring about. Also, government policies are not thrustful enough. There is no uniform policy that could be implemented without any fuss. Governments easily give in to popular demands and submit to unscientific thinking of general people. In our country, there is an unfortunate tendency to leave everything to God's will. This is self-defeating. We allow ourselves this **delusion** that it is God who brings people on this earth and it is God who will ensure his/her survival. Nothing could be farther from truth. But we do not have peers or leaders who could educate illiterate and **ignoramus** masses about the **baneful** effects of population explosion. There is no one to clearly tell them that God plays no role at all in giving birth and death to anyone. God simply has no time or inclination for such things. Fault is our own, not that of God or our stars. It is our problem and it is we who must tackle it. And we need to tackle it with a sense of urgency and on a war-footing. Steps taken so far by the governments have not yielded any positive result.

India's liberal laws on abortion are also to blame for yet another **malady** that is linked to population. Sex determination is a crime as per law, but it is hardly ever implemented with any serious intent. The result is female foeticide. In their quest to have male child, they keep killing girl child when in foetus. Now, a, days, scanning machines are easily available and they help people know beforehand whether the child is male or female. Its alarming impact is being felt in several parts of the country especially in the states of Punjab and Haryana. Getting bride is a serious problem these days. This is one of the side effects of the **skewed** population on the rise.

The explosive population is **nullifying** the progress that the country has made in all spheres. Growing population is leading to growing urbanisation and growing urbanisation is creating civic problems that are becoming unmanageable. This is leading to chaotic situation in most of the cities. Cities are progressively becoming unlivable as more and more people are deserting villages and moving to cities. There is overcrowding everywhere. Trains are overcrowded, buses are overcrowded, and roads are overcrowded. There is crowd everywhere. There is mad rush for seeking admission in schools and patients find it difficult to get medical attention from hospitals. There is no space for walking freely; there is no space for parking vehicles. The situation is simply alarming.

The combined result of all this is that majority of Indians are **languishing** in poverty. Growing population requires more foodgrains, more dwellings, more clothing, more hospitals, more schools and more facilities. But these requirements are not easy to meet as creation of these facilities cannot keep pace with the growing population. Number of mouths to feed is growing at an alarming pace and if this pace is not checked, the day may not be far when there will be hardly any food or any job left for the **teeming** population. In no time, we shall have an army of the unemployed and unfed.

That leaves us with little choice but to come down heavily on this population explosion and the government of the day must formulate a policy that is uniformly applicable to all citizens of the country without any exception. More importantly, the policies thus formulated must be ruthlessly implemented without let or hindrance. Those with more than two children must be made to pay more tax and such families should be denied certain facilities that are routinely available to the citizens of a nation. It's time to take some hard decision on this problem that has acquired **gigantic** proportion.

Vocabualry

Catastrophe—(n) an event resulting in great loss and misfortune. **Delusion**—(n) an erroneous belief held in the face of evidence to the contrary, a mistaken or unfounded idea or opinion. **Ignoramus**—(n) a person who does not have enough knowledge, an ignorant person, uneducated person, knowing nothing. **Baneful**—(adj) exceedingly harmful, deadly or sinister. **Malady**—(n) any unwholesome or desperate condition, illness, sickness, unwellness. **Skewed**—(adj) having an oblique or slanting direction or position. **Nullify**—(v) declare invalid, show to be invalid. **Languish**—(v) to be forced to stay somewhere or suffer something unpleasant for a long time, become feeble. **Teeming**—(adj) present in large numbers. full of people, animals, etc. that are moving around. **Gigantic**—(adj) extremely large.

□

34
Terrorism

If there is one problem that has gripped all nations of the world, it is terrorism. This is a problem that has **engulfed** the entire world and much of the energy that could have been used for the betterment of mankind is diverted towards tackling this problem. But the problem has not **abated**. In today's diction, the word 'terrorism' is the most dreaded and **despicable** word. There is hardly a day when one does not hear about the acts of terrorism in some parts of the world. There is hardly a day when one does not hear about deaths caused by terrorist attacks in some parts of the world. This is the most hated word today. It has created panic all over the world.

Earlier, the acts of terrorism were limited to certain places in certain countries. But now they have spread out to the whole world. There is no part of the world that can claim to be free from this menace of terrorism. There are socio-economic and political factors responsible for the growth of terrorism. While unemployment, regionalism and communalism have provided a platform, politics has fuelled it.

In India, the menace of terrorism originated from Pakistan. This country which was once part of India has not reconciled itself to the loss of Kashmir. India too made some tactical error by taking the matter to the UNO when the accession of Kashmir to India was settled immediately after independence due to alacrity of Sardar Patel. Pakistan has ever since created problems in Kashmir by sending in terrorists to attack civilians and military personnel in the valley. Pakistan is also hell bent on disturbing India because it holds India responsible for **truncation** of Pakistan in 1971. It has not been able to reconcile itself to this loss of East Pakistan and has been **fomenting** trouble for India by sending in terrorists.

India has been highlighting this for a long time. Initially, the world seemed overly inclined to believe the falsehood propagated by Pakistan which sought intervention of the world's only superpower to resolve the Kashmir issue. Failing to force **plebiscite** in Kashmir, Pakistan resorted to terrorist acts. Somehow the misguided elements in Pakistan have succeeded in projecting Muslims as victims and brainwashed many unlettered and unemployed youth to undertake acts of terrorism in the name of *jehad*.

Not content to attack India in Kashmir valley alone, Pakistani terrorists often aided by Pakistani government and military trained misguided youths of Punjab. These youths were **clamouring** for Khalistan. There was a phase when India in the eighties faced serious problems of terrorism in Punjab. Though it was contained, India had to pay a heavy price. Pakistani hand in all terrorist acts was clearly seen and shown to the world.

But since terrorism did not affect the rest of the world in the manner it affected India, no country took India's complaints seriously. India kept on highlighting the matter but the influential parts of the world led by the US did not pay any heed. But once America was hit on 11th September, 2001, they had to take note as the message was loud and clear. The sheer **ferocity** of attack **unnerved** even the mighty Americans who had to sit up and take note. Osama Bin Laden as the head of Al Qaeda was perceived to be the man behind this attack. Twin Towers of America which symbolised America's strength was razed down to the ground in no time. This was a tremendous blow to the American pride. The hunt for Osama began in right earnest as the Americans recognised the need to blot out this **scourge** of terrorism from the face of the earth. George W. Bush declared that they would 'smoke him out', no matter in which hole Osama had hid himself. It was a long search for Osama that ended in Pakistan. Osama was hiding in Pakistan all the time and yet America had waged a war against terrorism in collaboration with Pakistan. The greatest irony is that America had to smoke Osama out from Pakistan without taking Pakistan into confidence. That Pakistan is the picenter of terrorism is known to all, yet for political **expediency**, no country states it in as many words. This gives Pakistan an opportunity to claim that it is a victim of terrorism. Indeed there have been terrorist attacks in Pakistan also. Innocent lives have been lost in Pakistan too. But Pakistan cannot complain because it has created and supported terrorist outfits. Now it is paying for its own sins. But the country has the **gumption** to allege that India is promoting terrorism in Pakistan.

As a matter of fact, terrorists have been creating havoc in Kashmir and other places. While Kashmir has been the regular theatre, terrorists have attacked India at several places including Mumbai. What is required is a concerted effort on the part of all governments, both provincial and central, to tackle this menace of terrorism within the country. And for dealing with this menace internationally, it is imperative for the countries of the world to formulate a policy that should address this problem **holistically**. United States has a special responsibility and it should recognise it as a problem that has to be tackled on war footing if the world has to live in peace. So far, the Americans have taken care of their own interest. It's time it recognised that if the menace of terrorism raises its head in any part of the world, it will impact Americans too. We can no longer live in isolation in this globalised world.

Vocabulary

Engulf—(v) devote oneself fully to, flow over or cover completely. **Abate**—(v) make less active or intense, become less in amount or intensity, die away, slack off. **Despicable**—(adj) very unpleasant or evil. **Truncation**—(n) the act of making something shorter, especially by cutting off the top or end. **Foment**—(v) to create trouble or violence or make it worse; **Plebiscite**—(n) a vote by the people of a country or a region on an issue that is very important. **Clamour**—(v) to demand something loudly. **Ferocity** – (n) violence, aggressive behaviour. **Unnerve** – (v) to make somebody nervous or frightened or lose confidence. **Scourge** – (n) a person or a thing that causes trouble or suffering. **Expediency** – (n) the state of being useful or necessary for a particular purpose, but not always fair or right. **Gumption** – (n) the intelligence needed to know what to do in a given situation, courage and determination. **Holistically** – (adv) considering a whole thing or being to be made than a collection of parts.

□

35
Poverty

Poverty is one such problem that has never deserted India despite several poverty **alleviation** programmes and schemes launched by the governments and despite Indira Gandhi's much **vaunted** slogan *Garibi Hatao*. India has made tremendous progress during these six decades of independence, but poverty has not deserted India. In fact, poverty too appears to have made progress to the **detriment** of nation's health. A large section of our society continues to live below the poverty line. Incidentally, the wealth of India has grown manifold. The distribution of this wealth has been **skewed** and the gap between those 'who have' and those 'who do not have' is **enormous**. This gap between the *haves* and *have-nots* is a disturbing feature of our country.

The **disparity** between those who have and those who do not have is so **glaring** that one is left dazed and lost. While one section has everything it could ask for or desire to have, the other section has little or nothing at all. For this section, day-to-day survival is a matter of concern, for the **affluent** section, the world is at its feet. India is a developing country and this kind of gap in a developing economy is not a good sign. It does not **augur** well for the country. With the rise in prices of all essential commodities, the very survival of this section is seriously **impaired**.

India is integrated with the concept of liberalisation and globalisation. It is no longer f**easible** to think local and prepare for local. There is nothing local in the globalised economy. The preparation, therefore, has to be global. Jobs will be available who can globally compete. Since education is denied to a large section of our society, **lucrative** jobs are taken by those having adequate qualification. Those not adequately qualified cannot get quality and paying job. So, lack of education or illiteracy to a very extent is responsible for poverty of a large section of people. For such people, jobs are few and far between. And because such people are generally disorganised, they cannot influence governments to provide them proper education and environment for improving their lot. This is at the back of it all. Such people are forced to lead a **marginal** life while those belonging to other side of the **spectrum** take away the cake.

One of the reasons why many people **stagnate** in poverty is that they are superstitious in their approach to various progressive aspects of life. They usually discourage their children from learning new things, new arts and new services. This usually applies to those belonging to the lower **stratum** of society. They allow ignorance and illiteracy to determine the course of their life. Instead of encouraging their wards in taking up courses according to their latent talent, they follow **stereotyped** patterns that do not lead them very far. They live in **cocoon** and do not venture out of it to explore new avenues to better their life.

Another important feature of such people is that they are **lethargic** and do not wish to push themselves for doing things. They are more inclined to while away their time without doing any work. If it is possible to survive without exerting themselves, they are happy to do that. Environment being what it is most of such people are discouraged from taking any risk or plunge into some activities that may be new and challenging. They refuse to take challenges; they refuse to take risk. Consequently, they do not grow up.

There is an imperative need to give a **jolt** to this stagnating population. It is absolutely necessary to take them out of this **soporific** zone and push them into an arena of activities. Economically backward should be given incentives to start new entrepreneurship. They should be imparted professional training. Door-to-door surveys in the economically backward areas should be conducted and certain activities should be reserved for such identified persons who could be provided subsidised bank loans for starting their own business or industry. Governments and institutions should willingly come forward to assist such people so that they begin to take interest in career-building exercises. Once benefits begin to **accrue**, they will realise the importance of being entrepreneurial. This will have impact on others as well. What is required is to shake them out of their lethargy and push them into the **cauldron** of action. That will be an ideal way of tackling the problem of poverty.

The important thing is that development should occur and every citizen should be part of the process of that development. Unless development occurs, the country would not be able either to compete on the global scale, or accumulate the wealth necessary to tackle endemic and seemingly **intractable** problems of poverty, illiteracy, hunger and **squalor**.

Vocabulary

Alleviation—(n) assuagement, relief, easement; **Vaunt**—(v) show off, touted. **Detriment**—(n) a damage or loss, hurt. **Enormous**—(adj) extraordinarily large in size, extent, amount, power or degree. **Disparity**—(n) inequality or difference in some respect. **Glaring**—(adj) shining intensely, gross, egregious. **Affluent**—(adj) having an abundant supply of money or possessions of value. **Augur**—(v) be a sign of something to come, especially something important or bad. **Impaired**—(v) make worse or less effective. (adj) diminished in strength, quality or utility. **Feasible**—(adj) capable of being done with means at hand and circumstances as they are, executable, viable, practicable, workable. **Lucrative**—(adj) producing a sizeable profit, money-making, remunerative. **Marginal**—(adj) at or constituting a border or edge, of questionable or minimal quality, bare, fringy, borderline. **Spectrum**—(n) ambit, array, compass, range, reach, scope. **Stagnate**—(v) stand still, be in idle state, exist in a changeless situation, laze, slug. **Stratum**—(n) people having the same social, education or social status (strata is its plural form). **Stereotyped** – (adj) lacking spontaneity, originality or individuality, pigeon-holed, unimaginative; **Cocoon** – (n) silky envelope spun by larva of many insects for protection. a place for retreat. **Lethargic** – (adj) deficient in alertness or activity, unenergetic. **Jolt** – (n) a sudden jarring impact, jerking, saccade, shock. **Soporific** – (adj) sleep inducing, inducing mental lethargy, narcotic, hypnotic. **Accrue** – (v) grow by addition, come into the possession of, fall. **Cauldron** – (n) a very large pot used for boiling. **Intractable** – (adj) not tractable, difficult to manage or mould. **Squalor** – (n) sordid dirtiness, sordidness.

□

36
Corruption

"Corruption is an **insidious** plague that has a wide range of **corrosive** effects on societies. It undermines democracy and the rule of law, leads to violations of human rights, distorts markets, **erodes** the quality of life and allows organised crime, terrorism and other threats to human security to flourish," said Kofi Annan, the former Secretary General of UNO in his foreword to the UN Convention against Corruption. India was one of the countries that did not ratify it. It, thus, gave an impression that India is not keen to **countenance** corruption leave alone tackling it. India endorsed two out of 71 articles of this convention.

Any wonder that corruption in India has acquired **gigantic** proportion and has become institutionalised! According to what is stated in the Convention, it is clear that corruption is at the root of all evils that **afflict** our society today. This evil phenomenon is found in all countries irrespective of their size and shape. It makes no distinction between the rich and the poor and impacts all, everywhere. However, its impact is most destructive and catastrophic in the developing countries. India is a developing country and as Indians we feel the pinch of this menace in every walk of life. Seen from the perspective of India, it can well be said that corruption is the bane of Indian modern society. It would be difficult to trace an individual who is either himself or herself not corrupt or not affected by this scourge of corruption in one way or the other.

Strangely enough, instead of being **frowned** upon, the

menace appears to have gained in respectability. The more corrupt you are the, more acceptable you are. It is a clear pointer to the erosion in the value system of our society. We no longer **despise** the corrupt. We accord them respect and the honest are shown **contempt** or are laughed at. The corrupt are flush with money. Money buys them comfort and peace. This is closely linked to money and status that money provides. No one bothers about how the money or wealth is acquired. All one is concerned with is the acquisition of it. It can buy peace because if someone **pries** into the ill-gotten wealth, money can silence him. The kind of respectability money commands in today's society is nerve-shattering to those who have led their life with the highest degree of honesty. Some people jocularly say that if you are honest, you should be put in a museum. People no longer seem to believe the maxim once so popular: honesty is the best policy.

Corruption hurts the poor disproportionately. It diverts funds meant for development; it undermines government's ability to provide basic services. Corruption is a key element in economic underperformance and a major obstacle to poverty alleviation and development. For instance, we do not have to look far away. MNREGA is a classic example of how a noble scheme has been turned into a vehicle of corruption at mass level. Indian public distribution system (PDS) is the fountainhead of corruption. Foodgrains meant for the poor are siphoned off to markets at a premium leaving the needy high and dry. It is because of the corrupt system that while foodgrains rot, the poor are left unfed. Corruption is the bane of any civilised society. India ranks very high on the meter of corruption. The country is identified as one of the most corrupt nations in the world.

In recent times, India has been discussed in international forum more for corruption than for any achievements. If we are asked to make a list of all scams that have surfaced in India in recent times, we may end up compiling a book. Even if we would like to forget them, 2G, Commonwealth Games, Coalgate, Bofors, security scam, fodder scam and housing scam would keep teasing us for long. Corruption is one of the most important issues. Anna Hazare had to launch his movement to highlight corruption at the high places.

The situation is so grave in India today that one cannot get any work done from a government outfit unless one pays **gratification** money by way of bribe. For those who amass wealth through corrupt means, it is not a problem at all. The problem is for the honest people who do not have enough money even for mere **subsistence**. Finding money for getting a job done is next to impossible and it is his life, the life of an honest person, which is at stake. In a society where corrupt rule the roost, the merit has no takers. For any nation where merit has no takers, it is a dangerous situation.

Every citizen should be deeply concerned about the impact of corruption on the political, social and economic stability and development of our society. It should be recognised by one and all that prevention and combating of corruption is a common and shared responsibility of all and at all levels. It would seem that while the government has surrendered before the corrupt, the judiciary has taken initiative to stem the rot. If it were not for judicial activism, the culprits would never have been brought to book. If it were not for the alert judiciary, the likes of Laloo and Masood would have continued to preside over our destiny instead of being pushed into jail.

Vocabulary

Insidious – (adj) pernicious, subtle, beguiling but harmful, intended to entrap. **Corrosive** – (adj) tending to destroy something by chemical action, spitefully sarcastic. **Erode** – (v) become ground down or deteriorate, remove soil or rock, eat away, wear away, gnaw at. **Countenance** – (v) to support something or agree to something happening, (n) a person's face or its expression. **Gigantic** – (adj) extremely large, enormous, huge. **Afflict** – (v) cause great unhappiness for, distress, cause physical pain or suffering in, smite. **Frown** – (v) to make serious, angry or worried expression by bringing eyebrows closer together so that lines appear on the forehead, to disapprove of something/somebody. **Despise**–(v) to dislike and have no respect for somebody/something. **Contempt**–(n) the feeling that somebody/something has no value and deserves no respect at all. **Pries**–(v) past tense of pry, it means to move or force in an attempt to get something open, be nosey, search or enquire in a meddlesome way. **Gratification**–(n) state of being gratified or satisfied, satisfaction. **Subsistence**–(n) the state of having just enough money or food to stay alive.

□

37
Pollution

One of the gravest challenges facing the mankind is that of pollution. Every part of the world is faced with this problem of pollution. Of all the pollutions, air pollution, land pollution, noise pollution and water pollution are the most striking ones that call for immediate remedial steps. But from the way we are all going about, the solution does not appear to be forthcoming soon. Our preoccupation with development to keep pace with rapidly globalising economy has caused immense damage to the **ecology** giving rise to all kinds of pollution. Indiscriminate deforestation has exposed us to the worst kind of pollution.

Today, the air we breathe is poisonous with so little oxygen. The water we drink is contaminated and full of germs. Noise pollution seems to have turned the entire generation deaf. The air we breathe is no longer natural as we have soaked the oxygen elements from this air we breathe. Air is the cause of many diseases that have emerged as the leading reasons for death in India. The International Agency for Research on Cancer (IARC) has declared that air pollution causes lung cancer. Major components of the poisoned air, according to IARC, are smoke, dust and other dirty by-products of road traffic, factories and construction. They are called **particulate** matter and need to be classified as carcinogen. Carcinogen is a cancer-causing substance just as tobacco, asbestos and ultraviolet radiations are. Studies have shown how poisoned air leads to lower productivity and widespread ill-health, enough to lower a nation's output. Air pollution, studies reveal, costs India about 30 billion dollar or 3% of GDP.

The **depleting** ozone layer has ensured we do not have access to pure and uncontaminated air or water. Air and water are the **quintessence** of life. They are basic needs and they were always available free in the nature. It is no longer. Our greed and **rapaciousness** have destroyed them. Air pollution is one of the major ecological problems mankind is faced with. Since we cannot control the air we breathe, this is the most dangerous pollution of all. All big cities pose serious air pollution problem as they emit smoke from chimneys which mingles with the air we breathe. Smoke emitted from vehicles is another source of air pollution.

Noise pollution is another dangerous menace. It impairs our hearing organ. Most of the city dwellers are deficient in hearing. Constant blaring of horns, loud playing of music at public places contribute to massive discomfiture to human organs besides shooting up blood pressure, sleep loss, mental retardation and other physical disabilities.

Water pollution causes serious health problems. The chief contributor to water pollution is the city sewerage and industrial waste discharged into river beds. Kanpur and Delhi are classic examples in this category. In fact, all cities suffer from this basic problem. We have simply not developed any system to scientifically dispose of our industrial waste and we have no answer to sewerage problems. Consequently, these pollutants enter the groundwater, rivers and other water bodies and we are forced to consume the same contaminated water. The same contaminated water also enters our vegetables and other agricultural produce. And through them it enters our body making our bodies **susceptible** to diseases of various kinds.

Our disposable wastes instead of being disposed of scientifically are thrown or dumped just anywhere. The excessive use of chemicals in the soil and indiscriminate felling of trees, destruction of natural habitats of our wild animals also cause land pollution. If we do not take steps to **replenish** our forest cover with trees and natural **habitats**, the earth may lose its life-sustaining **ingredients**.

Pollution has made the environment unfit for living. It is **hazardous** for health. It causes diseases that take heavy toll. Crackers burst during festivals, especially during Diwali festivals, hugely contribute to air and noise pollution. Its **baneful** effect is being gradually realised and children are taking lead in **dissuading** people from exploding crackers. This is a good sign.

To put a check on pollution, we need to stop deforestation and start a campaign of afforestation in big way. Our immediate concern should be to plant as many trees as possible. Our approach towards containment of industrial waste has to be more scientific. Chambers should be made to trap smoke particles. Gases should be discharged only through exhaust pipes and should be released high up in the sky. Chemical industries should be strictly prohibited in the **vicinity** of rivers and waste materials should be subjected to anti-pollution treatment. Likewise, noise pollution too must be tackled with firmness. The violators should be heavily taxed or penalised. At the same time, attempts should also be made to contain population as the rising population eats into the **diminishing** resources. This also contributes to pollution.

Over the last decade, the **vulnerability** of Indians to overall pollution has increased greatly. In a World Bank report released in July 2013, India ranked 126 out of 132 countries graded for environmental performance, behind China, Pakistan and Bangladesh. For the effects of air pollution on its citizens, India ranked last. This is a wake-up call for India that must be taken in all seriousness.

There is denying that government needs to take credible action to reduce pollution, particularly the air pollution as there is poison in every breath we take. Critics have lashed out at the poor governance and pro-capitalist industries that have left our cities highly polluted. The fact that Delhi, the national capital of India, features among the top five critically polluted cities runs counter to government's claim of improving air quality through various initiatives. Credible actions are required from the government and public which will yield results in the long run.

Vocabulary

Ecology—(n) environmental science. **Particulate** (n) matter in the form of particles; (adj) relating to, or in the form of. **Deplete**—(v) to reduce something by a large amount so that not enough is left. **Quintessence**—(n) the perfect example of something, the most important features of something, essential parts of something. **Rapaciousness**—(n) extreme gluttony, voraciousness. **Susceptible**—(adj) yielding readily to or capable of, easily impressed emotionally. **Replenish**—(v) to fill something that had previously been emptied. **Habitats**—(n) the type of environment in which an organism or group normally lives or occurs, home ground. **Ingredients**—(n) a component of a mixture or compound, an abstract part of something, constituents. **Hazardous**—(adj) involving risk or danger. **Baneful**—(adj) extremely harmful, deadly or sinister, pernicious, baleful. **Dissuade**—(v) turn away from by persuasion, to deter. **Diminishing**—(adj) becoming smaller or appearing to do so. **Vulnerability**—(n) the state of being weak and of being easily hurt physically or emotionally.

□

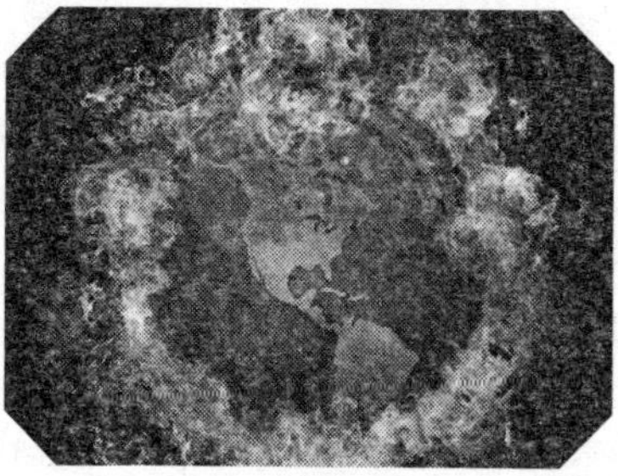

38
Global Warming

If there is one thing that is a serious threat to the ecology, it is global warming. The earth has a natural system of balancing the absorption and release of heat it receives from the sunlight. But, during the last several years, this balance seems to have been seriously impaired and is under constant threat of being irreparably impaired. This could well **jeopardise** the sustainability of life on the earth planet. In the recent past, there has been enormous increase in gases like carbon dioxide, methane and nitrous oxide, etc.

Global warming is caused by rising levels of carbon dioxide in the atmosphere that acts as blanket to contain radiated heat and raises overall global temperatures to dangerous levels, leading to melting glaciers, rise in sea levels, unpredictable weather and changing climate patterns. The rising temperature melts the **glaciers** and ice shields of Greenland and Antarctica and that in turn raises the level of sea. In normal conditions, rising of sea level would have been perceived as a common phenomenon that occurred off and on for a brief period. Those acquainted with the behaviour of seas have learnt to live with these occasional **vagaries**. But with the melting of glaciers in the manner they are now melting raises serious questions about safety of mankind. The predictions about the recurrence of this phenomenon in some of the North Pacific and the West of Greenland raise the question about ecological balance of the concerned regions.

Global warming today is one of the most complicated issues facing the world. Scientific community has been constantly warning about the rising dangers from the ongoing build-up of human, related greenhouse gases. These gases are produced by the burning of fossil fuels and forests. But before this is even addressed, there are issues of technological, economic and political dimension that have to be resolved. Only after these issues are resolved can there be any **concerted** worldwide effort to reduce emissions that are causing global warming. Resolving these issues is not simple in the face of economic slowdown.

Recognising the threat to ecology, more than 190 countries decided to give themselves a timeframe to contain emission level. In what is known as Kyoto Protocol, 40 industrialised countries had pledged to cut emissions by at least 5.2 per cent below 1990 level by 2008-12. Progress was **sluggish** and rich countries were keen to merge Kyoto into a single new accord obliging all nations to fight global warming. Industrialised nations wanted a single track largely because the United States, the second largest emitter in the world, had not ratified the Kyoto Protocol. These rich nations feared to sign up for a binding new Kyoto while Washington slipped away with a less strict regime. It was **doomed** to failure. In principle, it is agreed that the wealthy nations would **trim** their emission level while providing assistance to developing countries to pursue a cleaner energy regime. But the bone of contention is between the rich and the poor countries as to who takes the first step and who coughs up maximum for the changed energy menu.

Global talks on climate change held in Mexico in 2010 led to modest agreements. Without being very optimistic about the likely impact on the warming of the earth planet, the international outreach for tackling the problem received a significant vote of confidence. This was followed by talks in 2011 in Durban, South Africa. Environmental Protection Agency in 2011 in the US began to impose regulations related to greenhouse gas emissions. But the immediate impact on utilities, refineries and major manufacturers was minimal as these rules were applied only on new facilities or on those that were making major modifications to the existing plants. It is envisaged that over the next decade, the agency would virtually regulate all sources of greenhouse gases and would impose efficiency and emission controls on all industries irrespective of region. Tussle between the rich and the poor nations would then perhaps **recede**. Some of the visible adverse effects of global warming can be listed below:

- The annual melt season has lengthened up to three weeks in the last two decades in Antarctica.
- Ice on the Mount Kili Manjaro has been depleting fast since 1912. 75% of it has already gone and it is feared that it will entirely vanish in the next 10 years.
- In May 1998, India lost over 2,500 lives because of excessive heat.
- Polar Bears in Hudson Bay are losing fertility possibly as a result of spring ice break-up.
- A process called bleaching caused by Warmer Ocean is leading to coral reefs losing algae which colours and nourishes them.
- Much of farmlands in Florida in the US is inundated with salt water making the farmland too toxic for crops.

The problem is grave and unless all countries shed their inhibitions and reservations and come forward to work together, mere agreements would not achieve much. We have seen what happened to Kyoto Protocol. According to World Meteorological Organisation (WMO), deaths due to heat waves are to rise drastically all over the world in the next two decades if no immediate remedial actions are taken to contain the global warming. Already, in big cities of the US 1,500 deaths are taking place every year on an average. This could go up to 4,000 by 2020.

Indian Ocean Experiment (INDOEX) has warned that the effects of aerosols (a cloud of solid or liquid particles in a gas) will amplify the warming over several developing countries including India. The findings indicate that **aerosol** may change the precipitation over tropical regions because aerosols have both warming and cooling effects on the climate. Cooling effects of aerosol indirectly help the formation of cloud **droplets** which make clouds brighter and more reflective. Global warming does not merely refer to rising temperatures alone. It could modify rainfall patterns, may cause coastal erosion, may lengthen or cut short growing season in some regions, may melt ice caps and glaciers, and may alter the ranges of some infectious diseases. We have already been noticing some of these changes.

What is still more alarming is that there is a clear division on the question of tackling the problem between the developed and developing countries. No targets have been specified for emission cuts by the developed countries and there is no strong commitment to reduce temperature. Also, there is no clarity on funding for mitigation and adaptation efforts of countries by the developed countries. In short, global warming poses a serious threat to the ecological balance of the earth directly impacting our life. We may be slowly but surely inching towards our doom leading to our extinction too. All nations, particularly the most industrialised ones, owe it to the mankind to minimise and contain the damage if the human race is to survive on this earth.

Vocabulary

Jeopardise—(v) pose a threat to, present a danger to, put at risk. **Glacier**—(n) a slowly moving mass of ice, ice mass. **Vagaries**—(n) alterations, changes, modifications. **Concerted**—(adj) involving the joint activity of two or more, cooperative. **Sluggish**—(adj) moving slowly, not active or brisk, slow and apathetic. **Doomed**—(adj) marked for certain death. **Trim**—(v) reduce, cut down, clipping. **Recede**—(v) pull back, move away or backward, retreat. **Aerosol**—(n) a cloud of solid or liquid particles in a gas. **Droplets**—(n) tiny drops, driblets, dribs.

□

39
Internal Security

Things change so fast that perceptions find it difficult to keep pace with them. Only a few years ago, India seemed to be at peace with itself. The levels of violence had dipped considerably by the year 2011. But the way things have gone ever since, it would be difficult to say India is at peace with itself.

Internal security is national security and it necessarily begins at home, though it is difficult to draw a line of **demarcation** between internal and external security because they are so closely linked, rather so interchangeably linked. Dividing line between the two is nearly **blurred**. Not surprising for a nation that is undergoing social and economic changes at such a fast pace. Seen in this background where aspirations and expectations are rising **exponentially**, it would seem that our society is relatively at peace with itself. But seeming is different from what it actually is.

There is no denying the fact that people by and large are recognising that peace is necessary for stability in life and stability is what one seeks in one's life. Stability cannot come if one is perennially at logger-heads with the establishment. Besides, there is a time in each country's life when the citizenry feels tired of continual fight. Much of the quietude that we see around may be attributed to this rather than to factors like good delivery system at the ground level or overall satisfaction with the establishment. That would be painting a wrong picture. Issues have remained, though, to some extent, appear to have moved below the surface.

Lately, there have been greater instances of Maoists' attacks in some provinces that are **prone** to violence. There are certain pockets where Maoists are very strong and are able to **inflict** casualties on police and politicians at will. In a recent attack, host of political leaders were ambushed and killed in Chhattisgarh. Many police personnel were also killed in similar attacks in various other provinces. Incidentally, these **marauders** possess sophisticated weapons which often our police cannot match.

The reason is not far to seek. Some of our instruments of internal security are out of date or are in total disrepair. They are in crying need of upgrading. Our policing also suffers because we still make do with laws that were enacted in the nineteenth century when things were quieter and simpler. Police reform is overdue. While the political masters have **squabbled** over the issue on the grounds of freedom and federalism, the matter has continued to be neglected. Local and political expediencies have proved to be the biggest stumbling block. Besides, the threats that we face today are far more potent than they were when the laws were enacted. The structures we have designed are simply not adequate to meet the challenge of our times. It is precisely because of this that incidents like 26/11 could happen. The **perpetrators** of crime are today better equipped than our police that is to provide internal security to its citizenry. State-sponsored terrorists have access to weapons of mass destruction, such as chemical, biological and radiological weapons. We have to have a policing force that not only matches the firepower of these perpetrators, but is also capable of inflicting heavy casualty on such elements.

Though governments appear to have made some progress following 26/11 attacks, there are gaps in our internal security system that need to be capped. Even now we see that the enemies of the state carry out their **nefarious** activities with comparative ease and the degree of success simply **baffles** us. We wake up only after attacks are carried out with a great deal of success. One reason for this is apparently our approach to the whole issue. Instead of being proactive, our approach is reactive. We are not prepared beforehand to check and stall any attack. We are not **girded** up for the task. We act only when something happens and casualties have been inflicted on us. This is being reactive. Our counter-terrorism mechanism though existing is not potent enough to instil any fear in the minds of terrorists or Maoists. Rather, it is they who instil fears in our minds. Much needs to be done on this issue. Mere amending of Acts will not serve the purpose. There should be greater stress on implementation.

India certainly needs a peace territory or a peaceful **periphery**. But this must be supported by an external environment if India has to transform itself into a powerful nation both economically and militarily. India faces a strong challenge on this. It has neighbours that have hostile intents. India has conferred the status of the most favoured nation (MFN) to Pakistan, but Pakistan has not **reciprocated** this gesture of India. India has been extending olive branch to China, but China has continued to show eyes to India. Nepal too has not been exhibiting friendly intents lately and is seen aiding Pakistan in exporting terrorism and fake Indian currency into India through its porous borders. Bangladesh that was created with the aid of India too has not been helpful to the cause of India inasmuch as it keeps pushing its poor into Indian territories creating immense logistic problems for India. Even Myanmar in the recent past has shown its ill intents. In short, India is surrounded by countries that are not very well disposed towards India. This makes it absolutely essential for India to have a security instrument that is capable of keeping these forces at bay while it keeps trying to improve relations with its neighbours. India must have a multi-pronged approach to meet the above challenges.

Vocabulary

Demarcation—(n) a border or a line that separates two things. **Blurred**—(adj) indistinct or hazy in outline. **Exponentially**—(adv) in an exponential (an exponent is he/ she who pleads for a cause or propounds an idea) manner.

Prone—(adj) having a tendency to, lying face downward, prostrate. **Inflict**—(v) make someone do something unpleasant. **Marauders**—(n) people or animals going around a place in search of things to steal or people to attack. **Squabble**—(v) argue over petty things. (n) a quarrel about petty points. **Perpetrator**—(n) a person who commits some crime or does something evil or wrong **Nefarious**—(adj) criminal, immoral. **Baffle**—(v) be confusing or perplexing to, cause to be unable to think clearly. **Gird**—(v) prepare for a military confrontation. **Periphery**—(n) the outside boundary or surface of something, fringe, outer boundary. **Reciprocate**—(v) act, feel or give mutually or in return.

□

40
Uniform Civil Code

Almost all nations of the world except India have one civil code for all citizens. No one in any part of the world has any problem with this code. This uniformity is imposed to avoid any possible **discrimination** in the name of religion or religious beliefs. The worst victims are Muslim women who suffer discrimination under personal laws. Why India is exception to this rule, though baffling to many of us, has to be fully understood.

The framers of our Constitution thought that there was a sense of insecurity within minorities. It was thought that with the passage of time this will **evaporate** and then it will be possible to undertake some reforms. But even after six decades, the position has not altered. Blame for this must squarely rest on the shoulders of Nehru who single-handedly blocked it. Article 44 of the Constitution stipulates that "the state shall endeavour to secure for the citizens a uniform civil code throughout the territory of India". The objective behind this Article was to effect integration of India by bringing all communities on the common platform on matters which are at present governed by diverse personal laws but which do not form the essence of any religion, especially with regard to the question of divorce and maintenance for the divorced wife. Even after six decades, public opinion continues to be sharply divided. Religious personal law in matters of marriage, divorce, maintenance, inheritance and child custody continues to be binding on the followers of different religious communities. The central issue that has bogged down today concerns the question of whether religion-based personal law should be continued or a uniform civil code instituted. India has been dithering on this especially when it comes to dealing with the Shariat law of the Muslims. Nehru dithered on it and the Congress has continued to dither on it.

The Supreme Court regretted that Article 44 has so long remained a 'dead letter' and recommended early legislation to implement it. This view was expressed by the Apex Court in 1985 in that famous Shah Bano case. Twenty-eight years have since elapsed. There has been no progress on this matter. In fact, the matter has been given a decent burial by the government led by Rajiv Gandhi; and India remains a country where there is no uniform civil code for its citizens. The Apex Court once again in 2003 pleaded for implementation of the uniform civil code and paved the way by declaring Section 118 of the Indian Succession Act unconstitutional. The Act, the Court said, was arbitrary, irrational and violated the Article 14 of the Constitution. According to this article, all are equal before law within the territory of India. The Apex Court also clarified that Article 25 of the Constitution guaranteed freedom of conscience, freedom to propagate and practise religion, and Article 44 in no way impinged on this freedom. The Court was of the view that marriage, succession and matters of secular characters did not attract the provisions of Article 25/26 of the Constitution either.

This ruling made it absolutely clear that the right to follow one's personal Law was not a fundamental right meaning thereby Muslims were not free to claim that Shariat Law was a fundamental right. Likewise, Christians could not claim that Canon law was a fundamental right. The right of equality was firmly established by the Court and if any member of a community is discriminated against on account of certain provisions of the personal law as Shariat or Canon laws, he/she was free to approach the Apex Court seeking to strike down the unconstitutional part of the personal law. The Court went on to strike down some provisions of Indian Divorce Act that were applicable to Christians.

But instead of taking advantage of this judgement for implementing the uniform civil code, the atmosphere was allowed to get **vitiated** by starting an **acrimonious** debate on the subject. Political outfits according to what suited their political agenda put forth their argument. How unfortunate that while the constitution makers intended to implement the uniform civil code, the vested interests vitiated the atmosphere to such an extent that the matter had to be given a **quietus**. Even though it is clear that it is not a weapon against any religion or minority community, it is exactly this impression which is sought to be created. The nation is thus deprived of a code that should uniformly apply to all its citizens.

A well-known jurist observed that "the genuine concern is that many personal laws relating to marriage, inheritance, guardianship, divorce and maintenance and property matters in all communities are unjust, especially to women. Women are the worst victims of the personal laws, especially the Muslim women". It was this 'genuine concern' which was sought to be addressed by the Shah Bano case in 1985. The then Chief Justice asserted that a uniform civil code would remove **disparate** loyalties to law which have conflicting ideologies. Attempts have been made by many in the past to impress upon the government the need for implementing the uniform civil code as it sought to simplify interpretation and end discrimination.

One of the things the framers of the Constitution should have avoided was to leave certain provisions applicable on the happening of certain events. Reservation is another such provision. Such **contingencies** do not augur well for a nation as huge as ours. Reservation was meant for 10-20 years only. Instead of being withdrawn, the quota is being enhanced on one plea or the other.

Uniform civil code should have been implemented on 26th January, 1950 itself when India adopted its Constitution. So far as the opposition to this provision by certain political class or by certain vested interests is concerned, this is nothing more than posturing and should have been ignored. By **perpetuating** this and by not implementing the provisions of Article 44, we have created an **insurmountable** problem. In the process, India has remained almost the only country in the world that has no uniform civil code. Lack of civil code that uniformly applies to all its citizens means lack of national identity. India has been suffering this identity crisis for long, and it is all our own doing.

Vocabulary

Discrimination—(n) unfair treatment of a person or a group of persons on the basis of prejudice. **Evaporate**—(v) cause to change into a vapour, disappear, vanish. **Vitiate**—(v) to spoil or reduce the effect of something. **Acrimonious**—(adj) marked by strong resentment or cynicism, bitter. **Quietus**—(n) death, or something that causes death, regarded as welcome end to life, something that makes a person or situation calm. **Disparate**—(adj) fundamentally different and distinct in kind or quality, heterogenous, heterogeneous. **Contingencies**—(n) events that may or may not happen. **Perpetuate**—(v) cause to continue or prevail. **Insurmountable**—(adj) that which cannot be overcome, insuperable.

□

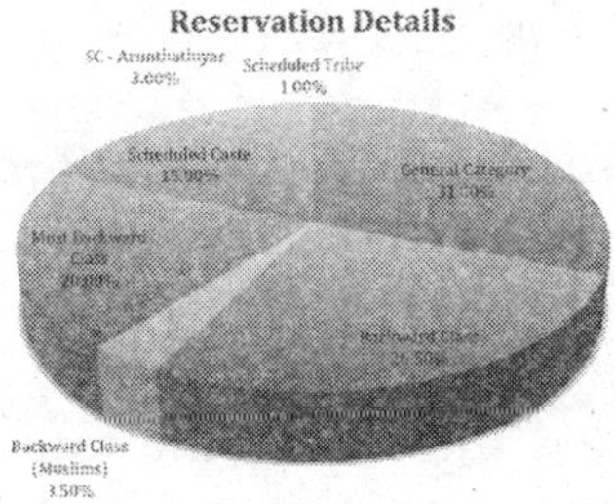

41 Reservation

Reservation in jobs or in the legislative assemblies for the members of scheduled caste and scheduled tribe was meant to be a temporary measure not extending beyond twenty years. That it has continued for over six decades with no signs of its being withdrawn at all shows how serious our governments have been in implementing some of the ideas of the constitution makers. When inserting this provision, the constitution framers assumed that "while making adequate reservation under Article 16(4) care would be taken not to provide for unreasonable, excessive or extravagant reservation". "Reservation provided beyond the permissible and legitimate limits would be liable to be challenged as a fraud on the Constitution". But the 'permissible and legitimate limits' were not defined. So, the reservation has continued and there is a continual **clamour** for more and more of it. That it will ever be withdrawn looks **distinctly** impossible.

But it needs to be appreciated that the constitution framers had little choice but to accept the proposition that reservation must be given to the deprived sections of society who will otherwise not be able to reap the benefits of independence. They have to be brought to the same level so that they have a level playing ground. They had long been denied the basic needs of life and those **bestowed** with riches had kept them under their thumb for a very long time. Equal opportunity, one of the basic **tenets** of our Constitution, can be given only when they were at par with the privileged ones. It was this underlying spirit that the constitution framers provided in the form of reservation for SC/ST which was later extended to OBC and is now sought to be extended to the members of the Muslim community.

But often good intents fail to produce good results, chiefly because some vested interests come into play and spoil the game. It was a temporary measure and should have remained so. No temporary measure should remain long enough to become a sore point. This reservation has become an important tool in the hands of those who do not want India to progress. Some critics of this policy have termed it as 'goitre'. The facility is also extended to internal promotions often bypassing merit. This had created more problems than resolved any. Besides, the benefits of reservation have not percolated down to those sections of the society which needed it the most. Benefits have been pocketed by some influential people and politicians. So, the problem it was expected to address and resolve has not quite been addressed and resolved. But we have the policy in place for the past 66 years. And this was supposed to be a temporary measure!

In the first twenty years of this provision being in place, all that our politicians did was to use this tool for vote bank politics. Instead of honouring the wishes of the constitution framers, Indira Gandhi, the then prime minister gave it a fresh lease of life for another twenty years. Ever since, this extension has become a regular feature and no political outfit thinks it necessary to do away with it because it serves their political purpose. National interest for most of the political parties has taken a back seat.

If it were not for the alert judiciary, the quota of reservation may well have gone past 50%. In 1991, the then Prime Minister V.P. Singh tried to implement Mandal Commission report. Again in 2006, the then HRD Minister Arjun Singh wanted to outdo Mandal Commission by going well beyond the stipulation. In short, most of these politicians were engaging themselves in vote-bank politics. There was a mass outrage against these moves. But these **outrages** could not prevent the policy from being implemented in such premier institutions as

AIIMS, IITs, and IIMs. The result is there for all to see. Studies have revealed that these premier institutions no longer produce quality doctors, engineers or scientists. This is a national loss, but no one seems overly concerned about this loss.

The net result of this policy of reservation is that while in the past Indian schools and universities commanded respectability for their sheer quality, they no longer find place in the list of the best in the world. A country that once attracted students and scholars from all over the world in their famous Nalanda, Vikramshila and Taxila universities have now to send its wards to foreign countries for higher education and quality jobs. This is a sad part of it and calls for some serious thinking by our politicians who lord over us. This is a serious issue and needs to be tackled with a degree of seriousness because it involves the question of nation-building, and nation-building depends on how we treat our new generation. Reservation is certainly not the way to go about it. It's time the policy of reservation was given a re-look.

Vocabulary

Clamour – (v) to make loud demand. **Distinctly** – (adv) clear to the mind. **Bestow** – (v) to give something to somebody, especially to show respect and affection. **Tenets** – (n) a religious doctrine that is proclaimed to be true without proof, dogmas. **Outrages** – (n) anger aroused by some perceived offence or injustice, a wantonly cruel act.

□

42

How the Constitution has Worked

Constitution of India, as we all know, is the product not of a political revolution but of the research and deliberations of a body of eminent representatives of the people who sought to improve upon the existing system of administration. It is this element that makes a retrospect of the constitutional development necessary for the understanding of our Constitution and to examine how it has worked.

Indian Constitution is by far the lengthiest document of this nature in the world. A question that has bothered many a thinker is whether it had to be this lengthy at all. Our Constitution has been altered or amended and trampled over (for some) more than hundred times. This cannot be a matter of comfort at all. Changes have been momentous, to say the least. Should a document that needs to be altered so many times not be re-written? Nearly every provision of the Constitution has been revisited either through interpretation given by the Apex Court or through acts of amendment. Either way, one feels the document has been **mauled** ruthlessly.

These many amendments in the space of six decades cannot be **glossed** over. It raises the question. Has it worked or how the constitution has worked? Our Constitution has vested the power of amending it to the Parliament with or without ratifications by the state legislatures. The American Constitution has vested this power to the judiciary. Even so, the judiciary in America exercises this power only to interpret. There have been fewer amendments to the American Constitution. Our Parliament is not inhibited on this count. It can amend as and when it pleases. Our judiciary examines such amendments to see whether the amendment affects the basic feature of our Constitution. If it does, it is struck down. There have been a number of cases where the government had to backtrack.

The question that vexes the mind is whether it is the judiciary or a constituent body which should be entrusted with the task of introducing changes to accommodate the exigencies of national and social progress. The framers of the Constitution thought it **prudent** to entrust this responsibility bringing about changes to the legislative machinery. Many of the changes that have become part of our Constitution could not have been carried out by the courts with the application of the **canons** of statutory interpretation which are firmly **entrenched** in our courts. At the same time, one cannot help feeling that so frequent and **multifarious** amendments of the Constitution have 'undermined the sanctity of the Constitution as an organic instrument'. In view of the **mutilation** of the Constitution by endless piecemeal amendments resulting in confusion, a commission for the revision of the Constitution should be set up. The commission should objectively examine each of the existing provisions in the light of suggestions **elicited** from the government as well from the citizens and recommend a revision of the Constitution itself instead of just amending it.

The constitution of a nation should be its most sacred and **venerated** document which should be dusted only if absolutely necessary. Americans regard their Constitution nothing short of the Bible of the Nation. One wonders why the same importance should not be given to our own Constitution! Experts have opined that our Constitution should be amplified, by inserting in it provisions relating to matters on which the document is silent. Or, it should be left to conventions or to the goodwill and judgement of those having the responsibility of administering them. These provisions will be codified because in the absence of such codified provisions, much confusion has arisen not only amongst the masses but also amongst administrators themselves.

"The Constitution of India was not intended to serve merely as a charter of government but as a means to achieve the social and economical transformation of the country peacefully and this goal has been achieved to the extent that the government has succeeded in implementing the Directive Principles," observed Durga Das Basu in his Introduction to the Constitution of India. However, the greatest failure of the government is seen in the matter of uniform civil code for the country as envisaged in Article 44 of the Constitution.

On the question of federalism, it can well be said that the changes in the Constitution, formal or informal, have mainly contributed to strengthening the Centre over the States. The most striking part of it is the emergence of the Planning Commission as the super-government which according to a legal luminary has 'disturbed the concept of the autonomy of the states' having impinged on the authority of the states in matters vital to its administration, such as education, health and other welfare services. India though federal in structure has progressively adopted Unitary System. In the process, regional forces have strengthened their bases, thus giving birth to a divide of unforeseen nature. Many of the internal disturbances we faced in the past or are facing today can be traced to this sentiment of being usurped by the Centre. At the same time, if we did not have a strong Centre, it would be difficult to contain the unfortunate happenings in the North-East, Punjab and Kashmir. It was realised by the founders of our Constitution that a federal system was the only system that suited a country like ours, consisting of so many heterogeneous elements. But in view of the external dangers, existing and potential, they sought to impart into the system the elements of adjustments by resorting to which the system might acquire the strength of a unitary system in cases of external aggression or other extraordinary circumstances.

There have been quite a few issues that had to be handled with force. If we did not a strong Centre, some of these issues like terrorism in Punjab and Assam would have continued to nag us. The exodus of refugees from the then East Pakistan would have had a destabilising effect on the country if it was not handled in the manner it was. It's another matter that Pakistan was cut to size in the process. But a strong centre helped.

But then there have been issues of governance that somehow give an impression that governments have chosen to go slow on them. This slowdown has been more visible in the post-liberalisation and globalisation era; and its visibility has become more pronounced in the economic slowdown zone. Government seems to have shut down its eyes on numerous issues that are being progressively dealt with by the judiciary. Those who complain about judicial activism would do well to examine this phenomenon of non-governance, mis-governance or mal-governance. Some consider this as the most remarkable achievement in post-Constitution India. They say "so long as this power is wielded by the courts effectively and fearlessly, democracy will remain ensured in India and, with all its shortcomings, the Constitution will survive". Three crucial elements emerge from this observation. In order that our democracy survives, the courts must wield power (i) effectively, (ii) fearlessly and that (iii) the Constitution has shortcomings.

The surest test of how the Constitution has worked is by seeking to know if this instrument has united the motherland and if it has commanded allegiance of all its citizens without a **demur**. The answer to these questions may not be very encouraging. It may be interesting to note that the constitutions of the Russian Federation and the Chinese Republic command uncompromising allegiance by their citizens. The Russians declared that "betrayal of the motherland is the gravest of crimes against the people". The Chinese declared "it is the sacred duty of every citizen to defend the motherland and resist aggression". In our country, certain citizens would not sing the national song of *Vande Mataram*. We saw this in our Parliament recently when a Muslim parliamentarian walked out of the house when this song was in progress. In our country, a responsible Muslim dignitary can say—"we are Muslims first and Indians afterwards..." Can a country that does not have uniform civil code for its citizens claim that the Constitution has achieved what its framers had intended to achieve? In fact, it can well be said that two of the main problems that afflict India are (i) the mammoth Constitution that promises so much and (ii) the politician/bureaucrat combine that deliver so little.

All said and done, it can be stated that the Constitution of India is neither purely federal nor purely unitary but is a combination of both. It is a Union or compromise State of a novel type. It **enshrines** the principle that "in spite of federalism, the national interest ought to be paramount". An expert described Indian Constitution as "a new kind of federalism to meet India's peculiar needs". The moot point is—has it met that peculiar need or has the national interest been regarded and treated as paramount? In the answer to this question is hidden the answer to the question—how the Constitution has worked.

Vocabulary

Maul—(v) split with a maul and wedges, injure badly by beating. **Gloss**—(v) give a shine to, usually by rubbing, provide interlinear explanations for words or phrases. **Prudent**—(adj) careful and sensible, marked by sound judgement. **Canons**—(n) a rule, especially body of rules or principles generally established as valid and fundamental in a field of art or philosophy. **Entrench**—(v) fix firmly or securely, impinge or impinge upon, occupy a trench or secured area. **Multifarious**—(adj) of many different kinds, having great variety. **Mutilation**—(n) an injury that causes disfigurement or that which deprives one of a limb or some important bodily parts. **Elicit**—(v) call forth, arouse. **Venerate**—(v) regard with feelings of respect or awe. **Demur**—(v) take exception to. **Enshrine**—(v) enclose in a shrine, hold sacred.

□

43

Health Services in India

Right to health is a fundamental right guaranteed by the Constitution and patients are entitled to be treated with dignity irrespective of their social, cultural and economic background or status. This was the observation made by the Supreme Court of India while directing Kolkata's Advance Medicare Research Institute (AMRI) to pay by way of compensation a massive sum of amount to a US-based doctor of Indian origin for the death of his wife. AMRI is a very renowned name in Medicare services and this **momentous** order was passed against this premier health organisation for NEGLIGENCE. There cannot be a more serious charge against a health service provider.

Strictly speaking, there are no hospitals in our country today. They are all shops. The word 'hospital' originated from hospitality which is traced to the word 'host'. A host takes care of the person accommodated in his/her house. Care is the key. But hospitals, having been replaced by service providers often disguised as Medicare outlets, no longer attach much importance to care. We do not imagine of a host who would not take care of guests. Such incidents of negligence which were **sporadic** earlier are becoming more and more pronounced, and regular. Some of them are highlighted and soon forgotten or in some rare cases as cited-above compensation is paid to patients through interventions of courts.

This is rather unfortunate in a country that is in crying need of healthcare. India is a huge country with huge population that can contribute to the making of the country. But unless a person is healthy and free from disease, no tangible contributions can be expected from that person. It is the duty of the state to keep its citizens healthy and free from diseases. Towards that end, it is **imperative** to have sound medical facilities providers. Hospitals are the best outlets where such facilities can be and should be provided. The question is – do we have such outlets?

Outlets are plenty. But, unfortunately, they do not match the requirement. Some outlets are **swanky** and stylish, but hugely expensive. Even where they cater only to the needs of the affluent, they often end up with wrong **diagnosis** and wrong treatment resulting in **fatalities**. What happened at AMRI is just an instance that came to alight. Our medical practitioners are simply not up to it. Often, they look like **mercenaries** who are there only for money. The **solemn** oath to serve the mankind that they take at the time of entering into this noble profession is soon forgotten. Patients have become consumers. Medical practitioners have become service providers, and the outlets to which belong are shops and nothing more.

It would seem India as a nation is not sure whether it is a welfare state or a state that is concerned with the economy part of it where welfare has taken a back seat. Sometimes, we seem to **espouse** the theory of a welfare state and sometimes we become **votaries** of 'there is no free lunch' maxim. It is this kind of **ambivalence** that has put our health service in a state of coma. We have hospitals – government-owned ones – where some of the operations are carried out by untrained people resulting in deaths or permanent disabilities. Innumerable cases keep coming to public domain. But governments do not appear to have learnt any lesson. Public health, it would seem, is not a matter of concern. It is not uncommon to hear about deaths of infants in hospitals. Sheer negligence and incompetence of those entrusted with the **onerous** task of providing health services to the teeming millions runs through all this. The result is catastrophic.

It is not that there are no quality hospitals or service providers in the country. In fact, there are quite a few. India is least expensive destination for **curative** functions. Patients, rather consumers, flock to India from foreign countries as well. At minimum cost, they are provided quality treatment. This clearly shows India has the necessary expertise to provide quality medical treatment. The problem is—all these health-providing institutions are afflicted with the fever of making more profit, more money. Liberalisation of economy has wrought this disease. Therefore, what most of such institutions do is they keep minimum hands to do maximum job so that they earn maximum profit. The result is often disastrous as AMRI, Kolkata will have discovered.

A healthy nation needs healthy citizens who can take the nation forward. Hospitals that look after the health of people are required at every nook and corner and at affordable cost. Swanky hospitals or health services providers may be okay for the rich, but the poor need government—owned hospitals that care for the patients. India has to go a long way in achieving this. Even though government hospitals are there almost everywhere, they are more on paper. We need them to come out of paper and take concrete shape on ground where they can serve the sick and afflicted with care and dignity. The existing scenario is not encouraging at all.

Vocabulary

Momentous—(adj) of very great significance, important. **Sporadic**—(adj) recurring in scattered and irregular or unpredictable intervals. **Imperative**—(adj) requiring attention or action. **Swanky**—(adj) imposingly fashionable and elegant. **Diagnosis**—(n) identifying the nature or cause of some phenomenon or an illness. **Fatalities**—(n) death resulting from accident or disaster, human deaths. **Mercenaries**—(n)persons hired to fight for countries other than their own. **Solemn**—(adj) dignified and sombre in manner or character and committed to keeping promises. **Espouse**—(v) choose and follow, as of policies, ideas, theories, strategies or plans. **Votaries**—(n) bound by vows to a religion or life of worship or service, adherents. **Ambivalence**—(n) mixed feelings or emotions. **Onerous**—(adj) burdensome, not easily borne, wearing, taxing. **Curative**—(adj) tending to cure or restore to health.

□

44

Status of Higher Education in India

The status of higher education in India is nothing to write home about. The fall in its quality is there for all to see. It needs no evidence as Indian universities are not in the first ten or twenty of the top two hundred universities of the world. Quacquarelli Symonds (QS) of UK, one of the major global education ranking organisations, released a list of 200 universities in the world for 2013 wherein no Indian institution found a place. It was the same story with the latest ranking done by Times Higher Education (THE) World University Rankings with no Indian institution finding a place.

The parameters largely responsible for this drop in rankings of our premier institutions like IITs include academic reputation, faculty-student ratio and research capacity. It appears there is a huge gap between what India offers to its students and what the international universities offer. How to bridge this gap? Indian universities can excel only by innovation and research and development. This is the all-important criterion to rank on global standards. One of the surest ways of ascertaining whether Indian universities are innovating is by filing **patents**. We are way behind in this as our ratio is just 10:100000 patents worldwide.

There is no denying the fact that several Indians have made names for themselves. Some of them have landed Nobel prizes as well. But for those achievements, Indian universities can hardly take any credit. The Nobel **laureates** such as Hargobind Khurana, Chandrashekhar and Amartya Sen were, no doubt, Indians, but they were not the products of Indian universities. We cannot remain satisfied with one C.V. Raman, a product of our own university, who got this coveted prize long ago.

Without innovation, and without research and development, it is not possible to claim quality in the higher education. Extensive research is a must if our universities and our students are to make any discernible dent. We may derive some satisfaction when the US president Obama **rues** the fact that Americans are being out-educated by the Indians and Chinese. It simply means American students are doing worse than our students. Maybe, it is their **complacency**. It does not mean the American universities lack quality. It simply means American students lack interest and drive. Their universities are well equipped, only students need to be enthused. But here in India our institutions are failing, not necessarily the students. They are going abroad and excelling there. What then ails our universities?

We have to improve our universities, our faculties and our facilities for research and development. The world is undergoing a change, and at a rapid pace. Educational institutions must keep pace with these changes and prepare students who can cope with changes and also position themselves to meet the challenges of these changes. **Innovation** is the key. Most of the developing economies of the world have made tremendous progress by innovating through technological **prowess**. Resources at our disposal must be deployed wisely. R&D (research and development) should be aimed at creating new resources, maybe by value-addition to the existing resources.

According to experts, the key issue is the research output. While teaching, research, knowledge transfer and international outlook are important, it is the quality of research that takes the cake. This is an area where our institutions are lacking. Other reasons for the **paucity** of Indian higher education are the lack of resources and a profession of higher education. Building world-class universities requires abundance of resources, including capital time, effort and talent. Indian students studying at some of the world's top-ranked universities also believe that it is the quality and quantity of research projects undertaken that sets the best universities apart from the rest. Institutes around the world had recognised the importance of focusing on R&D a long time ago, and now their investments are yielding result. Unfortunately, Indian universities focus only on teaching faculty while failing to lay stress on research. This has led to low ranking. Factors like shortage of funds, sub-par faculty and infrastructure are the primary reasons why Indian institutes cannot **churn** out any noteworthy research.

The first and foremost thing to do to improve the quality of education in our country is to immediately fill in all the vacancies that exist in the premier institutions. The selection of faculty must be carried out in a way that only the quality people get in. Merit should be the only **criterion** of selection. To begin with, we may introduce e-classrooms, Internet and e-medicine to fill the gap of shortage in the universities. This will be an investment. The benefits will accrue, though not immediately.

Higher education has become highly expensive which keeps many a talented student out of the ambit of higher education. Efforts should be made to subsidise higher education so that more and more people from the lower stratum of society get into them. Greater the participation, greater the quality. India is a huge nation and if opportunities are available to all irrespective of where they are placed, it can make a tangible contribution to nation-building which cannot come without quality education. So the question arises—how do we go up the ladder? Governments must allocate more fund for research in pure sciences, provide **incentives** for quality faculty to stay in the universities so that they could give full-time attention. More and more students should be encouraged to take up research projects, and industrial houses should be encouraged to participate. While rankings may not be 'the be-all and end-all' factor, it is important that our institutions deliver what they are supposed to. We may not want to over-fixate ourselves with the ranking phenomenon, but we must create an excellent R&D

environment.

There was a time when India ranked first in the realm of higher education. In ancient India, scholars and students flocked to Nalanda, Vikramshila and Taxila universities for quality education. Ironically enough, it is the Indian students now who move to foreign lands for higher studies. No less a person than the President rued the fact that none of the higher educational institutions in India were ranked among the top as per the international rating of universities. The question is—can we reverse the process? The President of India believes we can.

Vocabulary

Patent—(n) an official document of law granting a right or privilege, especially relating to an invention. **Laureate**—(n) worthy of the greatest honour or distinction, an honouree. **Rue**—(v) feel remorse for, feel sorry for, be contrite about. **Complacency**—(n) the feeling of self-satisfaction. **Innovation**—(n) creation of a new device or process resulting from study or experimentations. **Prowess**—(n) distinguished bravery or courage, especially in battlefields. **Paucity**—(n) an insufficient quantity or number, dearth, shortage. **Churn**—(v) churn vigorously in order to make butter, be agitated. **Criterion**—(n) a basis for comparison, a reference point against which other things can be evaluated. **Incentive**—(n) a positive motivational influence, inducement, bonus.

□

45
Pseudo Secularism

The people of India solemnly resolved to constitute India into a SOVEREIGN DEMOCRATIC REPUBLIC when the Constitution was formally adopted on 26th January, 1950. Was India not a secular state then? It was through 42nd amendment that the words SOCIALIST SECULAR were added in the Preamble of the Constitution in 1976. After 26 years of India's Independence, it was thought necessary to add the words to make it Sovereign Socialist Secular Democratic Republic. The question arises—why? Question also arises as to whether it has helped resolve the vexing problem of secularism and its applicability. According to Dr. Durga Das Basu, the Constitution expert held in high esteem, this insertion of the word 'secularism' in the preamble "has been productive of more mischief than benefit".

The word 'secularism' means "the belief that that religion should not be involved in the organisation of society, education, etc". or "indifference to or rejection or exclusion of religion and religious considerations". As a natural **corollary** to that 'pseudo secularism'—the word 'pseudo' means 'false'—should mean absence of that 'belief' or absence of all those attributes of indifference, rejection or exclusion of religion and religious considerations. A pseudo-secularist is a false secularist or is not secular at all.

We may now examine the matter in the light of above clarification. Now we may turn to the question as to why it was incorporated in the preamble in the first place and then proceed to examine whether it has helped resolve the vexing problem of secularism? The government introduced this amendment to make *explicit* what was *already provided* in the Constitution. But the government thought in the absence of clear emphasis, it was going to be denigrated by the 'vested interests' to promote their 'selfish ends'. As a matter of fact, provisions regarding secularism already exist in the Constitution (Arts. 25-30). The **rationale** provided was that the majority community of the Hindus was oppressing the religious minority, especially the Muslims, **trampling** over the guarantee of equality of all religions. The fact, however, was otherwise.

For a long time in the past, Muslims had been violently resisting Hindu religious processions, and even wedding and other social processions, when accompanied with music. The plea that 'music before the mosque' was against their religious tenet was rejected repeatedly as **hoax** by a **plethora** of authoritative decisions some of which were pronounced by Muslim judges of eminence. Instead of **quelling** such aggression on the part of the minority community, the insertion of this undefined word has been utilised by several political leaders and their outfits to support their own **convoluted** theory that 'secularism' involves appeasing of Muslim sentiments in order to win them on their side, to win their votes necessary to **ascend** to the seat of power. As the Hindu community is divided into numerous political outfits, and the Muslims constitute a single block—united on the foundation of religion—it is the Muslim vote that proves decisive for attaining power. This prompts all political outfits to vie for the Muslim votes by promising to give favours and concession that are against the tenets of the Constitution. Recently, demands have been made for reservation for the Muslim community with even the ruling party espousing this cause. Similarly, a ruling party **succumbing** to the pressure and yielding to a **weird** demand of allowing a Muslim religious procession to carry open swords while disallowing the Hindu processionists to carry **tridents**.

Meeting such demands with an eye on the next election is **tantamount** to discrimination against the majority community in violation of the guarantee provided under Article 14. Besides, it would also breed communalism which the makers of the Constitution sought to ban by abolishing 'communal representation'. It is absolutely essential to understand that what is contrary to the provisions specified in the Constitution cannot be justified with reference to the preamble. The Constitution abolished all distinctions on the ground of religion and did not safeguard anything like 'Muslim sentiments'. There are enough safeguards in the Constitution for the individuals as well as for the collective rights of minorities in a host of provisions. They are justiciable and if ever they are violated, courts can be reached for effective remedies. As a matter of fact, these safeguards have been enforced by the courts on several occasions.

Interestingly, even when the word 'secularism' was not incorporated in the Preamble, the Supreme Court had already defined it in 1973 while explaining the basic feature of the Constitution. It said, "the state shall have no religion of its own and all persons shall be equally entitled to the freedom of conscience and the right to freely profess, practise and propagate religion". This meant the State cannot be a 'theocratic state', i.e. it cannot be governed by religious leaders. It was further elaborated by the Apex Court that secularism not only meant the state shall have no religion of its own, but that any political outfit that sought to capture power must not espouse the cause of any particular religious group, for, if that party came to power, the religion espoused by it would become the official religion and all other religions would come to acquire a secondary or less favourable position.

So, such of those who try to espouse the cause of any particular religious group are not secular in the context of the provisions contained in the Constitution and in the context of various judicial pronouncements made from time to time. Such persons or the political outfits they lead or are part of can be said to be practising pseudo-secularism. Questions are being frequently asked whether Jawaharlal Nehru who introduced 'Haj Subsidy for Haj Pilgrimage' is secular or pseudo secular. Why should India go out of the way to subsidize Haj pilgrimage for the Muslims when no such facility is accorded to the Hindus? Not even the Islamic countries give this facility to their citizens. Obviously, there is an element of appeasement of the minority community. The ruling Congress has generally espoused the cause of this community and has exposed itself to the charge of being 'pseudo-secular'. There is, therefore, a serious need for re-visiting this issue and for taking corrective measure.

Vocabulary

Corollary—(n) a practical consequence that follows naturally, aftermath, inference. **Rationale**—(n) the fundamental reasons or logic behind something, justification for something, principle. **Trample**—(v) walk heavily or roughly over something in order to crush it. **Hoax**—(n) something intended to deceive, raising of false alarm, an act to make someone believe something that is not true. **Plethora**—(n) an amount that is greater than is needed or can be used. **Quell**—(v) suppress or crush completely. **Convoluted**—(adj) highly complex and intricate and occasionally devious. **Ascend**—(v) climb up, rise, go up. **Succumb**—(v) consent reluctantly, be fatally overwhelmed; **Weird**—(adj) strikingly odd or unusual, suggesting the operation of supernatural influences. **Trident**—(n) a spear with three prongs. **Tantamount**—(adj) being essentially equal to something, equivalent.

□

46

The Supreme Court of India

Supreme Court of India came into existence on the day India adopted its Constitution on 26th January, 1950. Initially, it functioned from the Parliament House till it moved to the present building located on Tilak Marg in New Delhi. It has a dome that is 27.6 metres high and has a spacious **colonnaded** verandah. If one wishes to take a look into its interiors, one has to obtain a visitor's pass from the front office.

On 28th January, 1950, full two days after India became a Sovereign Democratic Republic, the Supreme Court came into being. It became operational from this day. Its inauguration took place in the Chamber of Princes in the Parliament building, which also housed India's Parliament, consisting of the Council of States and the House of the People. It was in this Chamber of Princes that the then Federal Court of India had sat for twelve years from 1937 to 1950. This was to be the home of the Supreme Court of India for years before it shifted to its own acquired premises.

The inaugural proceedings were simple but impressive. They began at 9.45 a.m. when the Judges of the Federal Court took their seats. The legal luminaries seated were Chief Justice J. Kania and Justices Saiyid Fazi Ali, M. Patanjali Sastri, Mehar Chand Mahajan, Bijon Kumar Mukherjee and S.R. Das. In attendance were also the Chief Justices of the High Courts of Allahabad, Bombay, Madras, Orissa, Assam, Nagpur, Punjab, Saurashtra, Patiala and the East Punjab States Union, Mysore, Hyderabad, Madhya Bharat and Travancore-Cochin. Along with the Attorney General for India, M.C. Setalvad were present the Advocate Generals of Bombay, Madras, Uttar Pradesh, Bihar, East Punjab, Orissa, Mysore, Hyderabad and Madhya Bharat. Present also were the Prime Minister, other ministers, ambassadors and diplomatic representatives of foreign states, a large number of senior and other advocates of the Court and other distinguished visitors.

The inaugural proceedings, which became part of the record of the Supreme Court, came to an end after it was ensured that the Rules of the Supreme Court were published and the names of all the advocates and agents of the Federal Court were brought on the rolls of the Supreme Court. After its inauguration on 28th January, 1950, the Court began its sittings in a part of the Parliament House. The Court moved into its present building in 1958. The building is shaped to represent the image of scales of justice. The central wing of the building is the Centre Beam of the scales. In 1979, two new wings—the East Wing and the West Wing—were added to it. In all, there are 15 court-rooms in the various wings of the complex. The Chief Justice's court is the largest of the courts located in the centre of the Central Wing.

The original Constitution of 1950 envisaged a Supreme Court with a Chief Justice and seven **puisne** judges. It was left to the Parliament to make laws regulating the constitution, organization, jurisdiction and powers of the Supreme Court. Subject to such legislation, the Supreme Court consists of the Chief Justice of India and not more than twenty-five other judges. In the initial years, all the judges of the Supreme Court sat together to hear cases presented before them. As the work of the Court increased and arrears of cases began to **cumulate**, Parliament increased the number of judges from 8 in 1950 to 11 in 1956, 14 in 1960, 18 in 1978 and 26 in 1986. With the increase in number of judges, separate seating arrangements have been made and they now sit in smaller Benches of two and three, coming together in larger Benches of five and more when required to do so or in to settle a difference of opinion or controversy. At the moment, the Supreme Court has twenty-eight other judges in addition to the Chief Justice. They are appointed by the President of India. The Supreme Court judges superannuate at the age of 65. In order to be appointed as a judge of this apex court, a person must be a citizen of India and must have been, for at least five years, a judge of a High Court, or two or more such courts in succession, or an advocate of a High Court, or of two or more such courts in succession for at least 10 years or he/she must be, in the opinion of the President, a distinguished jurist. Provisions also exist for the appointment of a judge of a High Court as an *Ad-hoc* judge of the Supreme Court and for retired judges of the Supreme Court or High Courts to sit and act as judges of this Court. This temporary measure is resorted to if there is a lack of **quorum** of the permanent judges.

No minimum age is prescribed for the appointment as judge of the Supreme Court, nor any fixed tenure of office. It has been said that the jurisdiction and powers of our Supreme Court are in their nature and extent wider than those exercised by the highest courts of any other country. It is at once a federal court, a court of appeal and a guardian of the Constitution, and the law declared by it, in the exercise of any of its jurisdictions under the Constitution, is binding on all other courts within the territory of India.

The Constitution seeks to ensure the independence of Supreme Court Judges in various ways. A judge of the Supreme Court cannot be removed from the office except through the process of impeachment. The President of India will pass an appropriate order notifying removal of the judge if he/she is impeached by both Houses of the Parliament. The resolution of impeachment has to be carried by a majority not less than two-thirds of members present and voting, and presented to the President in the same session for such removal on the ground of proved misbehaviour or incapacity. The process being so cumbersome, it's no wonder that there has not been any instance of successfully carried out impeachment. A person who has been a judge of the Supreme Court is barred from practising in any court of law or before any authority in India.

The proceedings of the Supreme Court are conducted in English only. Supreme Court Rules, 1966 are framed under Article 145 of the Constitution to regulate the practice and procedure of the Supreme Court.

Vocabulary

Colonnaded – (adj) a row of stone columns with equal spaces between them, usually supporting a roof. **Puisne** – (n) a judge of inferior rank. **Cumulate** – (v) accumulate, amass, gather, pile up, conglomerate. **Quorum** – (n) gathering of a minimal number of members of an organisation to conduct business.

□

47
The High Court

India's unitary judiciary system is made up of the Supreme Court at the national level for the entire country and twenty-four High Courts at the state and union territory levels. These courts have jurisdiction over a state or union territory or a group of states or union territories. Below a High Court, there are a **hierarchy** of subordinate courts such as civil courts, family courts, criminal courts and several other district level courts. High Courts are instituted as constitutional courts under Article 214 of the Constitution of India.

High Courts are the principal civil courts of original jurisdiction in the state along with the district courts which are subordinate to the High Court. High Courts exercise their original jurisdictional powers only when the subordinate courts are not competent (not authorised by law) to try such matters for lack of **pecuniary** and territorial jurisdiction. High Courts may also enjoy original jurisdiction in certain matters if so specifically designated in a state. For instance, matters relating to company laws can be taken up only in a High Court.

However, the work of High Courts primarily relates to appeals filed by the lower courts and writ petitions in terms of Article 226 of the Constitution of India. Writ jurisdiction is also the original jurisdiction of High Court and the precise territorial jurisdiction varies from High Court to High Court. Each state is divided into judicial districts presided over by a district and sessions judge. He/she is known as the district judge when presiding over a civil suit and sessions judge when presiding over a criminal case. He/she is the highest judicial authority below a High Court.

All courts in India including the High Courts are bound by the judgements and orders of the Supreme Court of India by precedence under Article 141 of the Constitution of India.

The Constitution stipulates that there shall be a High Court in every state, but Parliament has the power to establish a common High Court for two or more states. Under this provision, the High Court of Assam (Guwahati) is the common High Court for Assam, Nagaland, Mizoram, Arunachal Pradesh and Tripura. Likewise, Bombay High Court serves both the states of Maharashtra and Goa. The High Court stands at the head of the judiciary in the state. The Chief Justice of the High Court and other judges are appointed by the President of India from time to time in consultation with the Chief Justice of India and Governor of the concerned state. The President may also appoint additional judges not exceeding two years for the clearance of arrear of work in a High Court and an acting judge when a permanent judge is temporarily unavailable for performing his/her duties or is appointed to act temporarily as Chief Justice. Every judge whether permanent, additional or acting may vacate his/her office earlier in any of the following ways:

- By resignation in writing addressed to the President.
- By being appointed as a judge of the Supreme Court or being transferred to any other High Court by the President.
- By removal by the President on an address of both Houses of Parliament (supported by a majority of the total membership of that House and by the vote of not less than two-thirds of the members presented), on the ground of misbehaviour or incapacity. The mode of the removal of a High Court is the same as that of a judge of the Supreme Court, and both shall hold office during 'good behaviour'. This procedure is known as impeachment.

- There are twenty-four full-fledged High Courts in India in addition to ten benches. Latest entrants are Manipur and Meghalaya with High Courts established at Imphal and Shillong, respectively on 25th March, 2013. Madras High Court in Chennai, Bombay High Court in Mumbai, Calcutta High Court in Kolkata and Allahabad High Court in Allahabad are the first four High Courts in India.

The Calcutta High Court is the oldest High Court in the country. It was established on 2nd July, 1862. High Courts which handle a large number of cases in a particular region have permanent benches or a branch of the court established there to cater to the needs of the people of the area. Benches are also present in states which come under the jurisdiction of a court outside its territorial limits. Smaller states with fewer cases may have circuit benches established. Circuit benches also called circuit courts in some parts of the world are temporary courts which hold proceedings for a few selected months of a year.

Besides the power of issuing the writs, every High Court has a general power of superintendence over all the tribunals functioning within its territorial jurisdiction. If the tribunal makes an order which **infringes** a fundamental right of a person, he/she can obtain relief by applying to the Supreme Court or a High Court seeking **quashing** of that decision. This kind of writ is called writ of *certiorari*. If it is filed in the Supreme Court, the writ will lie under Article 32 and under Article 226 if filed in a High Court. As the head of the judiciary in the state, the High Court has got an administrative control over the subordinate judiciary in the state in respect of certain matters, besides its appellate and supervisory jurisdiction over them.

The control over the judges of these subordinate courts is exercised by the High Courts in the following matters:

- The High Court is to be consulted by the Governor in the matter of appointing, posting and promoting district judges.
- The High Court is consulted along with the State Public Service commission, by the Governor, in appointing

persons (other than district judges) to the judicial service of the state.

- The control over the district courts and courts subordinate thereto, including the posting and promotion of, and the grant of leave of, persons including belonging to the judicial service and holding any post inferior to the post of a district judge is vested in the High Court.

The existing jurisdictions of the High Courts are governed by the Letters Patent and Central and State Acts; in particular, their civil and criminal jurisdictions are primarily governed by the two codes of Civil and Criminal Procedure. The High Courts at the three Presidency towns of Calcutta, Bombay and Madras had an original jurisdiction, both civil and criminal, over cases arising within the respective Presidency towns. The original criminal jurisdiction of the High Courts has, however, been completely overtaken by the Criminal Procedure Code, 1973. The original civil jurisdiction of these High Courts has not altogether been abolished but retained in respect of actions of higher value. The appellate jurisdiction of the High Court is both civil and criminal.

Vocabulary

Hierarchy – (n) pecking order, power structure.
Pecuniary – (adj) relating to or involving money, monetary.
Infringe – (v) to break a law or rule, contravene, impinge.
Quash – (v) to officially say that a decision made by a court is no longer valid or correct, to annul, to nullify.

□

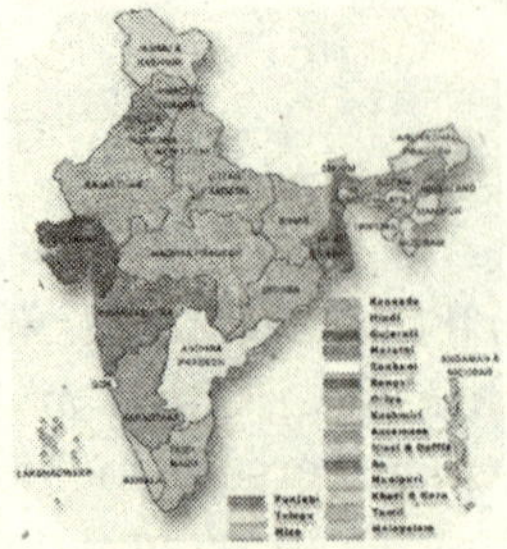

48

Indian Languages

Languages, it is said, posed a special problem for the Constitution makers of India. The plurality of languages spoken by the vast Indian population presented a huge obstacle before them. Where over 1,652 spoken languages, including 63 non-Indian languages, are to pick from, the task was indeed a formidable one.

The framers of the Constitution had, therefore, to select some of these languages as the recognised medium of official communication in order to save the country from a hopeless confusion. Fortunately, for the Constitution makers, the number of people speaking these 1,652 languages was not proportionate. It was consequently possible to pick about 18 languages placed in the 8th Schedule of the Constitution from amongst the major languages of the country. These languages were spoken by about 91 per cent of the total population of the country. Out of all these languages now placed in the 8th Schedule, Hindi along with its **kindred** variants Urdu and Hindustani was spoken by about 46 per cent of the population. Hindi was accordingly accorded the status of the official language of the Union subject to continuation of English as the official language for a limited period of 15 years. For the development of Hindi as a medium of expression, it was recommended to assimilate expressions used in other languages specified in the 8th Schedule into Hindi for its enrichment.

Even though one language was prescribed for the official purposes, the Constitution makers thought it expedient to allow the respective state legislatures to recognise some language or languages other than Hindi as the language for intra-state official transactions. These provisions, therefore, recognise the rights of the majority of the state legislature or a substantial section of the population of a state to have the language spoken by them to be recognised for official purposes within the state. The provisions of the Constitution relating to Official Language have come to be somewhat **complicated** and have created more problems than resolved.

Article 343 of the Constitution laid down that Hindi in Devanagri script will be the official language of the Union. But, for a period of 15 years from the date of commencement of the Constitution, English will continue to be used for all official purposes of the Union for which it was being used immediately before such commencement. Even after the expiry of the stipulated period of 15 years, Parliament by law may provide for the use of:

- The use of English language, or
- The Devnagri form of numerals, for such purposes as may be specified.

The use of English has not only continued beyond 1965, it has become so well **entrenched** that it is **well-nigh** impossible to do away with it. Wherever the Constitution makers have resorted to temporary measures, they have backfired whether it is on the question of language or the question of reservation, and special status to J&K. One of the gravest errors, if it be called so, is the fact that the Constitution of India is written in English. You do not write the constitution of your country in a foreign language. The kind status English enjoys in India, no other language can claim to enjoy. All the suggested measures for appointing of the Official Language Commission at the end of five years and then at the end of ten years and make recommendations to the President have come to a naught and these measures are never going to achieve what the

Constitution makers had assured to achieve. The Commission was to advise to the President on:

- The progressive use of Hindi for the official purposes of the Union;
- Restrictions on the use of English language for any of the official purposes of the Union;
- The language to be used in proceedings of the Supreme Court and High Courts;
- The form of numerals to be used for any official purposes of the Union;
- Any other matter referred to the Commission by the President as regards:
- The official language of the Union, and
- The language for communication between the Union and the states or between one state and another.

Meanwhile, Devanagri form of numerals has been replaced with English numerals. It is, therefore, clear that the measures suggested are not working. They never do. The catch also lies in the brief given to the Commission. The Official Language Commission shall have to have due regard to the industrial, cultural and scientific advancement of India and the just claims and interests of persons belonging to the non-Hindi speaking states/areas in regard to public services. These are **pitfalls** and no commission is ever going to get past these pitfalls. The language, therefore, remains a sore point. Despite so much having been done for Hindi, it has not been able to match English and far from being ousted, English has firmly established itself in India. It would be interesting to note some of the recommendations made by the Official Language Commission. While emphasising on the need for switching over to the use of Hindi, it recommended that there need not be any *rigid date-line for the changeover*. English, it said, should be the principal official language and Hindi the subsidiary official language till 1965. When Hindi is able to replace English after 1965, English should continue as the subsidiary official language. Accordingly, no restriction was to be imposed on the use of English. Hindi, in the meantime, was to be developed in such a way that it could serve as a medium of expression for all elements of the composite culture of India. Hindi must be encouraged to use easy and simple diction.

So, the matter of language stands where it stood at the time of the adoption of the Constitution and will continue to be a sore point just as the reservation and uniform civil code have continued to be the sore points. However, the spirit of liberalisation and impact of globalised economy have made the issue of language a little irrelevant today. The language that commands more acceptability will survive without anyone having to make any special efforts to promote any particular language. Globalised market has provided opportunity for all languages to survive and thrive. What Constitution makers could not achieve market forces are expected to achieve.

Vocabulary

Kindred – (n) family and relatives, the fact of being related to another person. **Complicated** – (adj) difficult to analyse or understand. **Entrenched** – (adj) dug in, established firmly and securely. **Well-nigh** – (adv) slightly short of or not quite accomplished, all but, almost. **Pitfall** – (n) an unforeseen, unexpected or surprising difficulty, a trap in the form of a concealed hole, a booby trap.

□

49
Women Empowerment

Women who account for more than fifty per cent of population in India were held in high esteem in ancient India. The position of a woman in the religious scriptures was that of a deity. According to what is described in the *Manusmriti,* a woman was regarded as a precious being who had to be protected first by her father, then by her husband and finally by her son.

With the passage of time, things have changed radically. Today, women are proving to be one of the main drivers of economy. History has it that it was women who pioneered the Indian economy. Zero economics was their contribution to the concept of economy. It is said that women collected wood and dry leaves in a heap in the jungle, lit fire to it and roasted the borrowed grains on the fire. The resultant merchandise was divided between the donor and the doer. They sold their share and earned profit which helped them **subsist**. This was zero economics. The investment was in the form of labour. This shows women are enterprising by nature. Unfortunately, this entrepreneurship was not encouraged. Instead, they were **subdued** by men. Muscle and money power dominated the society and since men **wielded** these powers, women were left **subjugated**. Men regarded themselves superior to women.

Things have, though, changed in modern times. Government too recognised, though **belatedly,** the role of women and ushered in the new millennium by declaring the year 2001 as 'women's empowerment year'. The Constitution guarantees equality to women. It also empowers the state to adopt measures of positive discrimination in favour of women. Lately, there has been a shift in the approach to women's issues from welfare to development. The empowerment of women has been recognised as one of the yardsticks for measuring and determining the status of women. Attempts are now being made to implement special programmes to ensure flow of benefits, including credit flows through Self-Help Groups (SHGs) channels, to women from other developmental sectors. These are aimed at enabling women to function as equal partners and participants in the development process. Banks, particularly the public sector banks, are playing key role in promoting women entrepreneurs through various schemes and programmes. Today, there are seven Indian banks—private and public—that are headed by women.

For long women were tied down to areas where they could nurture, mould and **cajole**. In a sense, it was an extension of their mothering capabilities. Soldiering, manufacturing, stock broking, banking and finance were kept out from their purview as 'male-only' areas. It was thought these required clinical and analytical skill and ruthless decision making which they with high emotional **quotients** and **empathy** would not be able to execute. The attitude is changing now. In a culture where the woman's role is reversed and the wife is always a homemaker even if an executive, it has taken a shift in mindset.

Empowerment of women became one of the nine primary objectives of the 9th Plan. It attempted 'convergence of existing services' available in both women-specific and women-related sectors. The Tenth Plan is specifically focussed on 'empowering women' as agents of social and economic empowerment, and gender justice. In the recent times, women have scaled heights in several fields. From premium liquor brands and coffee chains to oil drilling majors, companies have begun to hire women employees and executives, allowing them flexible working arrangements including long **sabbaticals** and special counselling. These steps though belatedly taken have helped in substantially improving the position of women. These have brought about an economic **emancipation** of women which, in turn, are having a **salutary** effect on their overall status in society. In this male-dominated society, women are slowly but surely making their presence felt. Women currently occupy 14 per cent of senior managerial positions in corporate India. This demonstrates that the companies employing them have become sensitive to the needs of the women employees. Recently passed Companies Act mandates that listed companies have at least one woman as director on its Board.

It is old fashioned to think women cannot do what men can do. There is hardly any field where women are not competing with men. They are in the armed forces; they are in automobile industries; they are flying commercial aircraft; they have taken to running locomotives; they are running taxis, auto-rickshaws, carrying passengers to their destinations. They are successful bus conductors and drivers. They are everywhere. Who can forget Kalpana Chawla, the women astronaut from India? In various competitive examinations, they are not only excelling, they are beating their male counterparts hands down. Their visibility has improved manifold. They have successfully moved outdoors and made impact. It can no longer be said that they are good only for indoor activities. In ancient times too, there were women philosophers like Maitreyi and Gargi who were much respected for their wisdom and knowledge and participated in discussions and discourses on equal footing with men. They played a significant and important role in Indian freedom struggle as well. History seems to be repeating itself.

Yes, the fact of the matter is—much needs to be done to improve their lot at all levels of society. It would appear as though some of us have not been able to digest their success and have continued to deny them their rightful place in society. Often, their success is looked down upon as concessions allowed to them. The fact of the matter is, they have been subjugated for so long that it has become a habit with many of us to want them to play second fiddle to men. That they are emerging out of men's shadow is not going down very well with a section of society.

On the one hand, they are progressing by leaps and bounds; on the other hand, atrocities are being committed on them day in and day out. It would be difficult to believe that the instances of gangrape of women that are on ascendancy are attributable to men's criminal mentality alone. Somewhere it is the **dormant** but violent tendency of men being superior to women that is expressive of these mass scale rapes taking place with **impunity**. **Foeticide** is also indicative of the same mentality. Even though it is long established that it is the girl child who is more helpful to parents, there is a growing tendency to commit **infanticide**. This is already having an impact on the population pattern of the country; and that is dangerous.

Empowerment of women should not just be a slogan. It must be a well thought out, well-worked policy of the government. A woman on any given day is a better cementing force than man insofar as integration of society is concerned. If the value system, which has taken a beating in the recent times, has to regain its lost sheen, women must be given the place of pride in society. Crimes against them must be firmly dealt with. Far from being weaker sex, they are the most powerful element in our society. A nation or a society can realise its full potential only when women are allowed to realise their potential without let or hindrance. It is not for nothing that women are called 'better half'. So, this better half, which is also the other half of the population, should be treated with care and respect. If we neglect this half, our progress will remain limited to the half of it only. As per the Gender Gap Survey 2013, India ranks as one of the lowest in women's education, health, economic participation and opportunity. The survey cautioned that these are detrimental to India's growth. The heartening news is that 23 per cent of senior positions in the field of human resources, 16 per cent in financial sectors and 10 percent in the sale segment are held by women in India.

The government too should show its firm commitment to empowerment of women. Mere tokenism would not serve the purpose of nation building. Women's Bill awaiting passage from the Parliament would go a long way in empowering women as it will put them in a **vantage** position from where they can help initiate steps for improving nutrition and health issues of women as also steps to contain and eliminate cases of foeticide and infanticide.

Vocabulary

Subsist—(v) support oneself, exist, live, survive. **Subdued**—(adj) in a softened tone, restrained in style or quality, quieted and brought under control, chastened, kept down. **Wield**—(v) have and exercise, handle effectively. **Subjugated**—(adj) reduced to submission. **Belatedly**—(adv) later than usual or expected, tardily, late. **Cajole**—(v) influence or urge by gentle urging, caressing or flattering. **Quotients**—(n) numbers, ratios. **Empathy**—(n) fellow feeling, sympathy. **Sabbaticals**—(n) a leave usually taken every seventh year. **Emancipation**—(n) freeing, liberation, release; **Salutary**—(adj) tending to promote physical well-being, **Dormant**—(adj) in a state of biological rest or in suspended animation, inactive. **Impunity**—(n) exemption from punishment or loss. **Foeticide**—(n) the act of destroying a foetus, aborticide. **Infanticide**—(n) a person who murders an infant, murder of an infant. **Vantage**—(n) place or situation affording some advantage.

□

50
Inter-State Relations

The Indian Constitution provides that "full faith and credit shall be given throughout the territory of India to public acts, records and judicial proceedings of the Union and every State". This is because though a federal Constitution involves the sovereignty of the units within their respective territorial limits, it is not possible for them to remain in complete isolation and the very exercise of internal sovereignty by a unit would need recognition by and cooperation of the other units of the federation. All federal constitutions therefore lay down certain rules of **comity** which need to be followed in their treatment of each other. These rules relate to:

Recognition of the public act, records and judicial proceedings of each other, extra-judicial settlement of disputes, coordination between states, freedom of inter-state trade, commerce and intercourse.

Accordingly full faith and credit means that statutory instruments, judicial orders of one state will be recognised in another state in the same manner as in the state of origin. As to the mode of proof of such acts or orders and records thereof, the Parliament has the power to legislate on them.

As states usually act as an independent unit in the exercise of its internal sovereignty, conflicts of interests between units keep arising from time to time. One of the most glaring examples is the issue of sharing of water between Karnataka and Tamil Nadu. Dispute between Maharashtra and Karnataka over their claim on Belgaun is yet another example. In order to maintainthestrengthoftheUnion,itisessentialthatthereshouldbe adequateprovisionforjudicialdeterminationofdisputesbetween the units and for settlement of disputes by extra-judicial bodies as well as their prevention by Constitution and joint action. The Supreme Court is vested with the power of exclusive jurisdiction in the matter.

Inter-state councils set up by the President not only advise on disputes, they also investigate and discuss subjects in which some or all of the states or the Union and one or more of the states have common interest. In exercise of this power, some of the constituted councils are Central Council of Health, Central Council of Local-Self Government, Central Council of Indian Medicine, and Central Council of Homeopathy and several more. This is for institutionalising inter-state coordination. Towards this end, the Parliament has created zonal councils which are statutory bodies to advise inter-state matters. There are five zonal councils within the territory of India and they are Northern, Southern, Eastern, Western and Central Zonal Councils. The point to note here is that while inter-state councils are the product of the Constitution, zonal councils are the product of Parliament.

Each zonal council consists of the Chief Minister and two other ministers of each state in the zone and the administrator in the case of union territory. There is provision for holding joint meetings of two or more zonal councils. Union Home Minister acts as the common chairman of all zonal councils. In addition to the above five zonal councils, there is also a North-Eastern Council to deal with the problems of the seven member states of Assam, Manipur, Meghalaya, Tripura, Arunachal Pradesh, Naglanad and Mizoram. This council came into existence in 1971 under the North-Eastern Council Act, 1971. Also, there is The River Boards Act, 1956 that provides for the establishment of a River Board for the purpose of advising the governments interested in relation to the regulation of or development of an inter-state river or river valley. The Inter-State Water Disputes Act, 1956, provides for the reference of an inter-state river dispute for arbitration by a Water Disputes

Tribunal, whose award is binding on the disputing states as per the provisions of the Constitution (Article 262[2]).

The biggest challenge for any federal structure lies in removing the inter-state barriers so that people feel that they are members of one nation. One of the ways of guaranteeing this freedom is by ensuring freedom of movement and residence throughout the country. This is guaranteed by Article 19(1)(d)-(e) of the Constitution. More importantly, it is the movement or passage of commodities from one point to another and freedom for commercial transaction that shows efficacy or otherwise of inter-state relations. The progress of a country as a whole requires free flow of commerce and intercourse as between different parts without any barrier. This is one of the surest tests of successful federal system.

But such a freedom is never **absolute**. Non-discriminatory restrictions are imposed by Parliament from time to time in the public interest. Parliament has accordingly enacted the Essential Commodities which empowers the Central Government to control the production, supply and distribution of certain essential commodities such as coal, petroleum, iron and steel and cotton. If there is **scarcity** of goods in any particular part of the country, Parliament can enact even discriminatory or preferential provisions for a limited period of time to **tide** over the scarcity. In short, reasonable restrictions may be imposed by a state in the public interest. These restrictions instead of causing any disruption in the smooth inter-state relation tend to lay down some ground rules that need to be followed in order to maintain a hassle-free inter-state relation.

It is important to note that any federal scheme involves the setting up of dual governments and division of powers. The success and strength of the federal **polity** depends on cooperation and coordination between the governments. Even though the Union giving directions to the states is foreign and **repugnant** to a truly federal system, the Constitution prescribed a **coercive** sanction for the enforcement of directions. This position is taken by the framers of the Constitution in view of the peculiar conditions of this country and, particularly, the circumstances out of which the federation emerged.

Vocabulary

Comity – (n) a state or atmosphere of harmony or mutual civility or respect, concord, symphony. **Absolute** – (adj) perfect, complete or pure. **Scarcity** – (n) a small and inadequate amount, scarceness. **Tide** – (n) the periodic rise and fall of the sea level under the gravitational pull of the moon, surge. **Polity** – (n) the form of a government of a social organisation, a politically organized unit, civil order. **Repugnant** – (adj) offensive to the mind, abhorrent, detestable, repulsive, obscene. **Coercive** – (adj) serving or intended to coerce, powerful.

□

51

The Public Services

"The system of responsible government, to be successful in practical working, requires the existence of a competent and independent Civil Services staffed by persons capable of giving to successive ministries advice based on long administrative experience, secure in their positions, during good behaviour, but required to carry out the policy upon which the government and legislature eventually decide." That was the observation of the Joint Select Committee on Indian Constitutional Reforms, 1933-34.

If we contrast the above observation of JPC with the latest ruling of the Supreme Court on the same subject, the rot that has set in this steelframe of India will become clearly visible to one and all. The Court observed that in and "the present political scenario the role of civil servants has become complex and onerous. Often, they have to take decisions with far-reaching consequences in the economic and technical fields. Their decisions must be transparent and in public interest. They must be fully accountable to the community they serve".

This matter was taken to the Court by a group of former bureaucrats including a former cabinet secretary and a former election commissioner. They contended that public servants were not private servants. Mal-governance affected people and quality of administration. It was also contended that good governance is critical to good democracy. They alleged that most of the transfers, promotions, postings and foreign assignments were decided on whims, not on merit, by the political executives. The Apex Court **minced** no words in stating that repeated shuffling and transfer of officers was **deleterious** to good governance. Minimum assured service tenure was necessary for ensuring efficient service delivery and increased efficiency. The apex court almost echoed the sentiment expressed by JPC. Its 'secure in their positions' is the same thing as the 'minimum assured service tenure' of the Apex Court. The JPC had made that observation in the thirties and the Apex Court has made this observation after almost eight decades. This clearly means that if the JPC was **wary** of politicians, then Apex Court is wary of them now which means not much has changed on the surface.

Are we then to believe that this latest order from the Apex Court is going to alter the situation? Will the politicians fall in line and bring about the desired change that the Supreme Court has ordered? Looking at the way, several similar orders in the past were dealt with by the political executives, it may not be an occasion to celebrate. The Court had issued similar directions in 2006 on police reforms, but most of its directives are yet to be implemented.

It is important to understand that in the parliamentary system of government that India has the policy of the administration is determined and laid down by the ministers responsible to the legislature. But the policy is implemented and the administration of the country is run by a large body of officials not concerned with politics. In the language of the political science, the officials form the 'permanent' executive as distinguished from the ministers who form the 'political' executive. The political executive is chosen from the party in majority, the permanent executive is appointed differently and it does not belong to the party in power. This executive maintains the continuity of the administration as also the neutrality in politics that is characteristic of civil servants. They constitute the permanent executive and account for their efficiency. While ministers cannot claim any **expertise** on the technique of administration and the details of the administrative departments, the civil servants, as a body, are supposed to be experts in the detailed working of their departments. The **inherent drawback** in this system of carrying on the administration with the help of these civil servants is that they tend to be more and more tied down to rules and regulations and lack flexibility or responsiveness to fresh ideas which the political executive is bound to maintain as it is responsible to the legislature. But for all of these shortcomings, the civil servants are **indispensable** to the parliamentary form of government. It is, therefore, necessary to shield it from being abused or misused by the political executive.

Governance is not just an art, but also a science and, to that extent it is a business for experts, Governance has accordingly fallen into the hands of this large army of officials who have taken up the business of running the government as their profession career while being in the service of the government itself. As they cannot be **dispensed** with despite a recent clamour by some ministers from a provincial government, it is necessary to prevent them from converting the democratic system into a bureaucracy or officialdom. At the same time, the technical and **enormous** task of governance cannot be left in the hands of the political executives alone.

Solution lies in firstly having a team of officials who will not only be efficient but also honest and can be trusted with the confidence that they would not abuse their position and would be strictly impartial, having no political or personal bias and that they would faithfully carry out the policy once that policy is formulated by the government in power. They must also maintain a proper discipline so that they have proper relationship with the employer, i.e., the state; and ensure that for breaches of the rules of discipline they can be brought under proper departmental action. In the case of breach of law, they can be made answerable before the courts of law.

Once the security of the state is thus ensured, it is equally important that the security of tenure of public servants should also be ensured. That precisely was the **angst** of the JPC in the thirties and that is the angst of the Apex Court in its recent ruling. All of these can be achieved if there are definite rules and proper safeguards in respect of what is broadly known as the 'conditions of service' of public servants and the Constitution has sought to lay down some basic principles in this behalf.

The two issues that are substantially dealt with by the Constitution makers are (a) tenure of office of the public servants and disciplinary action against them and (b) the constitution and functions of the Public Service Commissions, which are independent bodies to advise the government on some of the vital matters relating to Services.

Now, the Apex Court in its latest ruling has directed the government to set up a board to advise the governments on transfer, postings, promotions and disciplinary action. These matters, the Court directed, should be handled by a civil services board (CSB). It is hailed by many as a landmark **verdict** aimed at **insulating** bureaucrats from political interference. The Supreme Court gave the Centre, the states and union territories three months to implement its direction. The boards that are to be constituted are to function till the Parliament brings in a proper legislation to set the CSB. It will be interesting to see how the government reacts to this order.

Vocabulary

Mince—(v) make less severe or harsh, walk daintily, cut into small pieces. **Deleterious**—(adj) harmful to living things, injurious, hurtful. **Wary**—(adj) marked by keen caution and watchful prudence, leery, mistrustful, suspicious. **Expertise**—(n) skillfulness by virtue of possessing special knowledge, expertness. **Inherent**—(adj) existing as an essential constituent or characteristic, in the nature of something though not readily apparent, built-in, integral, inbuilt, underlying. **Drawback**—(n) the quality of being a hindrance. **Indispensable**—(adj) essential, not to be dispensed with, absolutely necessary, vitally necessary. **Dispensed**—(v) given or provided in small portions, administered. **Enormous**—(adj) extraordinarily large in size, amount, extent, power or degree, enormous, tremendous. **Angst**—(n) an acute but unspecific feeling of anxiety, usually reserved for philosophical anxiety about the world or about personal freedom. **Verdict**—(n) judgement, finding of fact; **Insulate**—(v) protect from heat, cold or noise by surrounding with insulating material, to isolate.

□

52

The State of Jammu and Kashmir

The Constitution of India has accorded a special status to Jammu and Kashmir. To understand why J&K enjoys special status, we have to go into the history of this state. Under the British regime, it was an Indian state ruled by a **hereditary** Maharaja. On 26th October, 1947 when the state was attacked by the Azad Kashmir Forces with the support of Pakistan, the Maharaja Sir Hari Singh sought the help of India after executing an Instrument of Accession. This was similar to the ones signed by other Indian States similarly placed.

By the **accession**, the dominion of India acquired jurisdiction over the state with respect to the subjects of Defence, External Affairs and Communication, and like other Indian States which survived as political units at the time of the making of the Constitution of India. The State of J&K was included as Part B State in the First Schedule of the Constitution of India as promulgated in 1950. This category of Part B was abolished in 1956 and Jammu and Kashmir was included in the list of the States of the Union of India, all of which now stood included in one category. Nevertheless, the special Constitution position which the state enjoyed under the original Constitution (Article 370) was retained. This means that the provisions of the Constitution relating to the states in the First Schedule are not applicable to the State of Jammu and Kashmir, even though it is one of the states specified in that schedule. Here lies the catch: it both belongs to it and does not belong to it. This Article 370 of the Constitution of India has remained a bone of contention.

This peculiar position, legal experts and political thinkers concede, was due to the fact that having regard to the circumstances in which the state acceded to India, the Government of India had declared that it was the people of J&K acting through their Constituent Assembly, who were to finally determine the constitution of the state and the jurisdiction of the Union of India. The substance of the provision embodied in Article 370 of the Constitution of India was this: the applicability of the provisions of the constitution regarding this state was to be in the nature of an **interim** arrangement. The interim arrangement has become a **perennial** interim arrangement.

In *White Paper on Indian States,* the government has **averred** that the Instrument of Accession signed by Maharaja Hari Singh on 26th October, 1947 was in the *same form* as was executed by the rulers of numerous other states which had acceded to India. So, the legal consequences are the same for J&K and other states. It was, however, due to lapse of **paramountcy** under Independence Act of 1947 that Indian states regained the position of absolute sovereignty which they enjoyed prior to the assumption of suzerainty by the British Crown. These states then became competent to accede to either of the newly created dominions of India and Pakistan. The states that had signed the instrument of Accession to Pakistan had signed the same document. Both countries enjoyed the same legal rights. Without an **iota** of doubt, the accession of J&K to India is legally and irrevocably unassailable. India was well within its rights to exercise complete jurisdiction over the state in terms of the Instrument of Accession. Yet, India had given an assurance that accession or the constitutional relationship between India and the state will be subject to confirmation by the people of the state. There was no role for a third party intervention at all. One might say in **hindsight** that this assurance by India was uncalled for.

The act of accession was given an unequivocal legal effect by declaring Jammu and Kashmir as integral part of India. However, the other provisions of the Constitution were made subject to eventual approval of the constituent assembly of the state. Irony is that only Articles 1 and 370 of the Constitution would apply on J&K on its own while application of the remaining provisions would be determined by the President in consultation with the Government of the State as provided in Article 370. Accordingly, the legislative authority of the parliament over the state would thus remain confined to the items specified in the Instrument of Accession. This interim arrangement will continue so long as the constituent assembly does not make its decision. Only after this decision is made by the state constituent assembly and recommendation is sent to the President, Article 370 will be **abrogated**. It is in **pursuance** of these provisions of the Constitution that Union Parliament is made competent to enact laws relating to defence, external affairs and communication for Jammu and Kashmir.

Constituent Assembly of J&K ratified in 1954 the Instrument of Accession to India and future relation of the state with India. Thereafter, the President made the Constitution Order. According to this order, the jurisdiction of the Union extended to all Union subjects under the Constitution (with some alterations) instead of only three subjects of defence, external affairs and communications. This order as amended from time to time deals with the entire constitutional position of the state within the framework of the Constitution of India leaving aside only internal constitution of the State Government.

The first official act of the constituent assembly was thus aimed at putting an end to the hereditary rule of the Maharaja and to transfer power to the popular government headed by an elected *Sadar-i-Riyasat*. J&K thus became the only state having a separate constitution for its administration. This constitution declared that Jammu and Kashmir was 'an integral part of Union of India'; and its territory will comprise all the territories which were under the sovereignty or suzerainty of the ruler of the state as on 15th August, 1947. This included the areas that were under Pakistani occupation. The provision is **immune** from amendments. Under the original constitution of the state there was a difference between this state and other states of India as regards the head of the government. It was

Sadar-i-Riyasat in J&K against 'governor' in other states. This distinction was done away with in 1965 by an amendment in the Constitution of J&K.

Despite several liberal measures, the pro-Pakistani elements in the state have continued their demand for a plebiscite to determine whether the state should accede to India or to Pakistan. They formed a Plebiscite Front and organised violent demonstrations with the **avowed** objective of seceding from India. Sheikh Abdulla too lent his open support to such a demand. He was put under preventive detention in 1955. He was released in 1964 on showing change of heart, but had to be placed under preventive detention again in 1965 as he kept blowing hot and cold which led to his being **externed** in 1971. An agreement was finally reached in 1975 whereby the demand for plebiscite was abandoned. It was also decreed that the special status under Article 370 would continue. The process of integration that had started in 1954 was thus halted and Indian Parliament was clipped of its jurisdictional powers over the state and autonomy of the state was re-emphasised in certain matters. The state is bestowed with privileges that no other state enjoys.

In short, J&K is a sovereign state within a sovereign state with very little restrictions imposed on it. Bharatiya Janata Party has demanded that the President declare cessation of Article 370 to remove the tag of special status to bring the state on a par with other states. The party reasons (a) the makers of the Constitution of India had granted special status to J&K only as a temporary measure and (b) the people of the state have misused and abused the special status and entered into a conspiracy with Pakistan to cause disturbance in India. The government has not met the demand on political grounds and it remains to be seen if and when this party will come to power and take steps in this direction to make Jammu and Kashmir a normal state of India.

Vocabulary

Hereditary–(adj) occurring among members of a family usually by heredity, ancestral. **Accession**–(n) a process of increasing by addition. **Interim**—(adj) serving during an intermediate period of time, meanwhile, meantime. **Perennial**—(adj) lasting an indefinitely long time, suggesting self-renewal. **Aver**—(v) to declare or affirm solemnly and formally as true. **Paramountcy**—(n) the state of being paramount, the highest rank or authority. **Iota**—(n) a tiny or hardly detectable amount, little, whit. **Hindsight**—(n) understanding the nature of an event after it has happened. **Abrogate**—(v) revoke formally, get rid of, abolish. **Pursuance**—(n) the continuance of something begun with a view to its completion, pursuit, quest. **Immune**—(n) secure against, resistant. **Avowed**—(adj) openly declared as such (an avowed enemy). **Extern**—(v) though this word is a noun which refers to a person who works in an institution, yet does not live there. In the essay, the word is used as verb to mean that a person has been ousted from the place where he ordinarily resided as in the case of Sheikh Abdullah.

□

53
The Malaise of Non-Governance

We had gained our independence after sacrificing a great deal and had come to believe that independence was going to be the panacea for all our ills. Nehru talked about the 'commanding heights of economy', and set about the task of governing the nation. Some of the lofty and avowed aims and objectives of the government were mixed economy, land reforms, improving the lot of the economically weak and of those belonging to schedule castes and schedule tribes, establishment of an **egalitarian** society, abolition of *zamindari* system and providing dignity and respectability to women.

Nehru began his long innings with a special thrust on industrial and technological advancement. But his problem was he wanted to achieve Indian goals with British administrative set-up. The only discernible change was that Indian Civil Service (ICS) became Indian Administrative Service (IAS) eliciting a comment that "steel frame of ICS has been replaced by the wooden frame of IAS". *Zamindari* has just about changed its garb. The benefits hardly went to those who needed them most. Governance essentially meant attending to the basic problems and delivering of facilitating inputs. The basic problems not only remained, they also grew rapidly because of the **galloping** increase in population. People were, nevertheless, willing to wait.

Nehru was a dreamer, a visionary. He was a bird that wanted to scale the sky and to fly out into distant lands. He wanted to grow out of India's borders, and succeeded in no small measure. But this did not help the cause of governance. When Nehru declared that he would tie the corrupt to the nearest lamp post and flog him publicly, it raised the hopes.

Lal Bahadur Shastri's brief stint was only a bridge between Nehru and Indira Gandhi. It neither marked a beginning nor an end of any era. History will judge him by his own standards. His resignation as Railway Minister following a train accident is cited even today as a sterling example of morality in public life. Cited, not **emulated**. Morality in public life is a scarce commodity in the **burgeoning** market of politics today. Shastri wanted to chart out a different course, especially on economic matters, on the matters of governance. Some notable steps in that direction were already taken – decontrol of cement, for instance – and some were in the pipeline. In fact, just before his premature death at Tashkent, he had directed his secretariat to prepare a scheme to reduce public expenditure and taxation to remove most of the shackles on the economy. Well, did we not smell liberalization here – liberalisation with a humane touch?

When Indira Gandhi took the mantle, people were disillusioned and **restive**. People's disenchantment was matched by the growing dissension in the ruling Congress Party. Political manoeuvring was the order of the day. Having lost much of its **sheen**, the Congress was also investing much of its time and energy on manoeuvre and counter-manoeuvre and by the end of 1968, the spirit of sacrifice which was the **hallmark** of the party was replaced by a naked greed for power and pelf. To her was available a fertile ground for political ascendancy and she made the best possible use of the same for self-projection and self-promotion.

Malaise of non-governance became all the more pronounced under Indira Gandhi despite nationalization of banks and abolition of privy purses and the vote catching slogan of *Garibi Hatao*. Even though governance was a casualty under her, '71 Indo-Pak War that culminated in the creation of Bangladesh enhanced her political stature. She could unabashedly take credit for '71 War victories, but would **apportion** the blame for emergency excesses on her **overzealous** officials. She suffered no **compunctions** for thrusting an extra-constitutional power on the hapless people of the country in the form of Sanjay Gandhi and after his death on Rajiv Gandhi. In the later years, the sense of insecurity gripped her so much that she would not trust anyone. Bhindranwale in Punjab was the result of her political distrust. This creation of hers ultimately led to her political and personal doom. While her politicking went on, governance remained a casualty. People felt cheated by her slogan of *Garibi Hatao.* There was total distrust which found expression in JP Movement.

India did not have real governance during the entire period of over six decades. Not even under Nehru. Whatever little was happening or had happened was largely due to the process of evolution. Mark Tully was reported to have said, India did not inherit from the British the Westminster model, rather it inherited the British colonial spirit which was more concerned with commerce than with governance. So, non-governance was inherent under Nehru's rule as well. But few would have questioned the *bona fides* of Nehru or Shastri.

If governance occupied backseat during normal times, people tasted the real governance for a while during the internal emergency which Indira had brought in to save her own political career. The much **maligned** trains began to move on time. Offices opened in time and employees were found in their seats. It looked as though there was a government, perhaps for the first time, that seemed willing to govern for a change. Suddenly, things appeared to have fallen in grooves. Everything was moving like well-oiled machine. There was no dearth of people who wanted continuation of the **draconian** emergency only because it gave some **semblance** of governance. So much starved of governance was India that it found virtue in emergency.

Morarji Desai with the blessings of JP took oath of the office after Indira was ousted from power in 1977. People expected governance from them. But they chose to quarrel amongst themselves. The government survived for some time, but governance continued to suffer. Disenchantment with the fledgling government was so strong that people voted Indira Gandhi back to power.

Though she returned to power, she was not her original self. She appeared to have lost her political acumen and was gripped with a sense of insecurity. Punjab was charting out a different course largely because of her own political instability or the sense of it. She had propped up Jarnail Singh Bhindranwale to keep her political opponents at bay. But soon he grew into a Frankenstein ready to **gobble** her up. The nation, it seemed, was heading for disaster. Disaster did strike the nation: first in the form of Operation Bluestar; and then in the form of Indira's assassination.

The nation passed into the hands of Rajiv Gandhi, a co-pilot with the Indian Airlines. Even though Rajiv Gandhi won the elections, he failed to govern. He made long winding speeches that took him nowhere. There were some pacts signed here and there. Rajiv-Longowal accord was perhaps the most notable one, although one does not quite see how it benefited anyone. He promised to rid the Congress of power brokers, but ended up being surrounded by a **coterie** that brokered power. His biggest political blunder however was also a foreign policy blunder. By sending troops to Sri Lanka, he helped no one's cause. He was soon assassinated.

Charan Singh, V.P. Singh and Chandrashekhar took their turn to become India's prime ministers. They had no time for governance **enmeshed** as they were in intense politics. V.P. Singh did two things for which his name will always remain in the pages of history. First, it was the waiver of bank loans up to rupees 10,000 and second, it was the expansion of the ambit of job reservation that sort of derailed Indian polity. If the banking industry has not yet recovered from this most unbank-like act, the nation will perhaps never recover from the shock of further division of already divided society on the basis of caste which the *Mandalisation* brought about. It must, however, also be said that it also brought in its wake a kind of social awareness that perhaps has no immediate parallel in the contemporary Indian history.

During all these turbulent years, governance did not even have a semblance of it. India continued to suffer under the impact of non-governance. Narasimha Rao had to be *recalled to life* from his near political hibernation to lead a minority government. He had to use all his erudition, **ingenuity**, political skill and the money power of the worst kind to stay afloat and in power. With the disintegration of the Soviet Union and the unification of Germany, a new political order was emerging all over the world. Most of the communist countries were encountering **simmering** discontent largely because of economic hollowness. These events had an impact that was of far-reaching consequences, not only for the concerned countries, but also for the developing countries like India. The spirit of globalisation and liberalisation was sweeping across the world. This provided Rao the opportunity to take India away from Nehruvism.

But with the liberalisation of economy also came the **spectre** of scams. Initially, they were only spectres. But soon real faces of scams became visible and Rao came under tremendous pressure brought about not only by the opposition, but also by the members of his own party.

India was once again in turmoil, because while scams were silently **fructifying**, Babri Masjid was demolished throwing India into a cauldron of communal riots. If Indira Gandhi was held directly responsible for extensive damage to the Golden Temple in 1984 that led to her death, Naraimha Rao too was largely blamed for the demolition of Babri Masjid which was ultimately to lead to his political death. Congress was ousted from power.

Atal Bihari Vajpayee formed the next government, but it did not last beyond thirteen days. Strangely enough, the parties that were cutting at the throats of one another before and during the elections **huddled** together to form a government with the Congress extending support from outside. A government of thirteen parties led by H.D. Deve Gowda who was quietly functioning as the Chief Minister of Karnataka came into being. *India thus entered an era of politicians ruling without mandate.*

Deve Gowda did not last for long. He was replaced by Inder Kumar Gujral. Congress supported him from outside. Gujral would **antagonise** no one, particularly the one who had the ability of rocking his boat. Even though Gujral had the **rudder** in his hand, the nation was **drifting** like a rudderless boat, for the man holding the rudder in his hand did not know how to navigate. Gujral's agony too did not last for long. Fresh election threw up a new government led by Atal Bihari Vajpayee who ran the show for about six years. He tried to bring about some semblance of governance, nothing more than that. Dr. Manmohan Singh, a non, political entity, took up from where Atal Bihari Vajpayee had left off and seemed to be doing well with India recording remarkable growth on all fronts of economy. Everything seemed to be going well until the Left parties supporting from outside decided to pull the **rug** from under its feet on the question of nuclear deal with the U.S. Government. The government survived, but governance suffered from then on. On its second coming, the government was **beset** with problems of governance from the very beginning and scams of the worst dimension began to surface one after another and in quick succession too. This killed the spirit of governance. The kind of corruption that India witnessed under Dr. M.M. Singh is unprecedented and the paradox is he is himself regarded as honest. Governance continues to get bogged down.

We have been celebrating our independence and republic days with fanfare, patting ourselves on being the largest democracy of the world. One fondly hopes we are also rid of the malaise of non-governance.

Vocabulary

Egalitarian—(adj) favouring social equality, classless, equalitarian. **Gallop**—(v) to move fast like horse, extend. **Emulate**—(v) strive to equal or match, especially by imitating, copy, imitate. **Burgeon**—grow and flourish. **Restive**—(adj) being in a tense state, edgy. **Sheen**—(n) the visual property of something that shines with reflected light. **Hallmark**—

(n) a distinctive characteristic or attribute. assay-mark, authentication, trademark, stylemark, earmark. **Apportion**—(v) distribute according to a plan or set apart for a special purpose, give out as one's share or portion. **Overzealous**—(adj) excessive enthusiasm or intense devotion to a cause or an idea, fanatic, rabid. **Compunction**—(n) a guilty feeling about doing something, remorse, self-reproach, conscience-prick. **Malign**—(v) speak unfavourably about, traduce, badmouth. **Draconian**—(adj) overly harsh or strict. **Semblance**—(n) an outward or token appearance or form that is deliberately misleading, an erroneous mental representation. **Gobble**—(v) east hastily without proper chewing. **Coterie**—(n) an exclusive circle of people with a common purpose. **Enmesh**—(v) entangle or catch in a mesh, ensnarl. **Ingenuity**—(n) the power of creative imagination, the property of being ingenious. **Simmering**—(adj) to cook something by keeping it at a boiling point, to be filled with a strong feeling, especially anger so difficult to contain or control. **Spectre**—(n) a ghostly appearing figure, an apparition, phantasm, ghost. **Fructify**—(v) to make or become productive or fruitful. **Huddle**-(v) crowd or draw together, crouch or curl up. **Antagonise**—(v) provoke the hostility of, act in opposition to. **Rudder**—(n) steering mechanism consisting of a hinged vertical plate mounted at the stern of a vessel. **Drift**—(v) be in motion due to some air or water current. **Rug**—(n) carpet, carpeting, wig. **Beset**—(v) annoy continually or chronically, assail or attack on all sides, decorate or cover lavishly.

□

54
Importance of English in India

The fact that the Indian Constitution is written in English should clearly show the importance the language of English enjoys in India. The question of ignoring the language does not arise as the first President Dr. Rajendra Prasad had said, "India cannot afford to ignore this language". India inherited English language from the British who ruled over the country for over two centuries and left an indelible mark on every aspect of our life.

After India became independent, many wanted English to go with the English. According to their way of thinking, English language was considered as an **embodiment** of Western culture and they feared that the continued use of this language could corrupt our culture and our values. Mahatma Gandhi was also not very well disposed towards the language. But his main thrust was more on the manner of teaching English than on the language itself. He said, "the manner in which it is given to us has **emasculated** the English educated Indians, **constrained** our intellect and rendered us **effeminate**". There are a large number of people who believe that English has created a wide gap between those few who are English educated and those who are not.

If these were extreme views, there were moderate voices as well that wanted this language to stay as there was no unanimity about the official language India should have. They wanted English to continue as an option during the period of **transition** so that Hindi, the language known and spoken by over 40 per cent of the population, could finally replace English. These moderates thought a sound knowledge of English was necessary for acquiring higher education. They thought and they still think that without adequate knowledge of English it is not possible to make any tangible progress in the matters of technical education in India. It was contended that Indian languages were simply not in a position to offer developed study materials in Hindi or in any other Indian language. English, therefore, for them was and is inevitable. English, they aver, should be compulsorily taught in our schools so that our children do not fall behind others.

There are two theories. One, English should be made medium of instruction for all educational institutions; and two, it should be made compulsory for higher education alone. It is recognised almost by all that knowledge of English is necessary for scientific and technical education, but they contend making it compulsory at school level would tax our students who find it **cumbersome**, irritating and painful to **cram** up their lessons in English. India's is a rural-based society whose mother tongue is Hindi or any other regional language. Asking them to master a *foreign language* is asking for too much.

The catch lies in this that some of us still want to believe that English is a foreign language. A language that has remained with us for nearly three centuries now is anything but a foreign language. You do not write your constitution in a foreign language. If English is difficult for some people who find it hard to clear English papers, it is not because it is really hard. It is because they think they are learning a foreign language. The moment they shed this thought, the language will cease to be a problem. A person whose mother tongue is Hindi will find it hard to clear Tamil or any other regional language paper simply because he/she has it in his/her mind that the language he/she is required to pass is not his/her mother tongue. For him/her Tamil and English will pose the same problem. It is just a question of how we learn.

There is no dearth of Indians who have excelled in their knowledge of English. There have been great writers who have made quality contribution to English literature. Nirad C. Choudhary was one Indian who used to teach **nuances** of English language to the English. Not just that he used to educate the English on English manners. His mother tongue was not English, but he never regarded English as a foreign language just as we do not regard Urdu as a foreign language. We learnt Urdu because of our association with the language and we learnt English because of our association with English language. Indians have never lacked intelligence and they enjoy a reputation of being a quick learner. Today Indians receive **accolade** all over the world for their knowledge of English. I have known of Indians who possess quality knowledge of English and this quality is recognised all over the world.

In today's world, English has become all the more important. In a globalised economy, we cannot remain cut off from the world. English is the link language. This language connects us to other parts of the world as also to the other parts of our own country. Without the knowledge of English, we cannot progress and prosper in the world. China is trying hard to catch up with us in acquiring the knowledge of English because they clearly see the advantage the knowledge of the language gives in expanding its business interests. If you are armed with the knowledge of English, you can face any situation in any part of the world. It helps you connect with the people and without connecting one cannot achieve any success in this globalised economy.

Problems also arise because we often think that English is the competitor of Hindi or that its growth will stunt the growth of other languages. The fact of the matter is there is space for all kinds of languages to grow and occupy a rightful place. Besides, this is the age of competition. Let all languages compete with one another. Competitions bring the best out of you. Hindi or other languages too can grow and play their part. English can always be a supplement. It need not be seen as **supplanting** our mother tongue. The knowledge of English is absolutely essential not just for acquiring higher education but for keeping pace with fast growing world economy. The knowledge of this language enables us to communicate with the corporate world. It opens us to the emissaries, leaders and host of others who make a difference to our life.

If we regard English as our own language, the progress will be smooth and the benefits that will accrue from this knowledge can steer India well ahead of many countries in the days to come. We must not tamper with English and should allow it the rightful place it enjoys amongst the Indians not just in India but all over the world.

Vocabulary

Embodiment – (n) a new personification of a familiar idea, incarnatioin. **Emasculate** – (v) deprive of strength or vigour, remove the testicles of a male animal. **Constrained** – (adj) lacking spontaneity, not natural. **Effeminate** – (adj) having unsuitable feminine qualities. **Transition** – (n) the act of passing from one state or place to the next. **Cumbersome** – (adj) difficult to handle or use especially because of size or weight, not elegant or graceful in expression. **Cram** – (v) crowd or pack to capacity, study intensely as before examination. **Nuances** – (n) a subtle difference in meaning, opinion or attitude. **Accolade** – (n) a tangible symbol signifying approval or distinction, award, honour, laurel. **Supplant** – (v) take the place or move into the position of, replace, supervene upon.

□

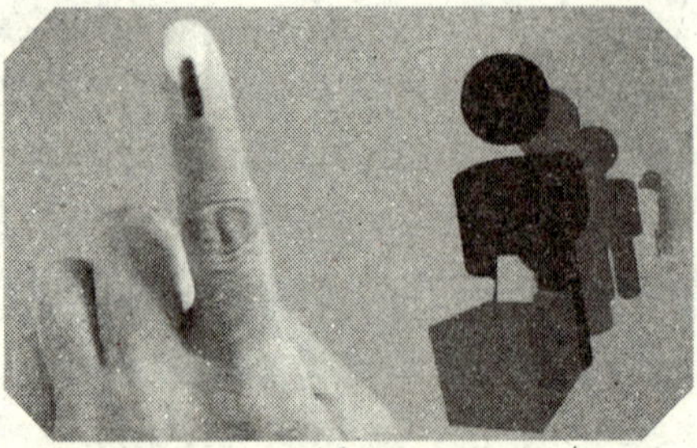

55

Practising Democracy in India

Generally speaking, when one talks about democracy, one talks only about what defines democracy. And when that is done, one ends up with some **lofty** expressions on democracy and democracy-related aspects. In the process, one loses the sight of the real faces of democracy. Before proceeding further into this discussion, let us take a look at what democracy actually means or signifies. Democracy, dictionaries say, is the political orientation of those who favour government by the people or by their elected representatives. It refers to a political system in which the supreme power lies in a body of citizens, who can elect people to represent them. It is a **doctrine** that the numerical majority of an organised group of people can make decisions binding on the whole group. In the same category, we can place the famous statement that a democratically elected government is 'of the people, by the people, for the people'. Without doubt a democracy is all that and much more than that.

But we must draw a line between the democracy we z**profess** and the democracy we practise. The two are different. In the context of our country, they are far too different. India became a sovereign democratic republic on 26th January, 1950 with the adoption of the Constitution. But if we look at the history of the past six decades, we cannot help concluding that we have lost our way. The **cherished** path of democracy that was **bequeathed** to us by our peers has long been forgotten and we have embarked on a path that is full of potholes. The democratic values that were so dear to our founding fathers have been consigned to dustbin and the institutions that were so **sacrosanct** have been violated beyond recognition. The way we have allowed things to drift, those who have shed their blood for the country must be wondering whether it was worth it.

There is no **gainsaying** the fact that this country so full of heterogeneous elements belonging to different races and religions can remain one only if it is inspired by a national sentiment. Unity in diversity should not just remain a slogan with us. It must be so in reality as Americans demonstrate it. One will find it hard to locate an original American. People from all over the world have **converged** on America and serve it as their own country despite inherent differences. The situation in India is just to the contrary. Here we determine everything from the point of view of power politics. All matters whether constitutional or legal are viewed from political angle. No one seems to think from the nation's point of view. It is very difficult to find space for impartial or **disinterested** elements to give a non-political interpretation of the Constitution. All political parties and leaders express their allegiance to the Constitution and yet almost all of them violate both the letter and spirit of the Constitution with **impunity**.

The blame for this mess must be shared by all. We have simply failed to live up to the expectations of our founding fathers. It is the failing of all politicians, bureaucrats, the business people, the professionals and people from all walks of life. We violated institutions and statutes with total disregard. These institutions and statutes that reinforced the foundation of our democracy have been **trampled** upon with ruthless regularity leaving our democracy **bruised** and shattered. That is the kind of democracy we have practised over the years and are still practising.

Some practising politicians would have us believe that communal harmony and the political unity of the country can be achieved only through bestowing more and more extra-constitutional privileges. They forget the **adage** that 'once an infant always an infant'. India chose to be a secular republic and the Muslims who stayed back in India knew they were in secular India where no religion commanded special attention of the establishment. Yet, some of them kept chanting 'Islam in danger' and this gave birth to Hindu fundamentalism. Likewise, the slogan of 'Muslim sentiments' gave rise to 'Hindu sentiments'. This is an unstoppable vicious circle that has been responsible for various communal riots in the country. This is because of the democracy we practise.

Some of the ills can be attributed to mushrooming of civil societies and non-governmental organisations and to the emergence of new and regional political aspirations and practices. Disenchantment of the backward and deprived class with the existing establishment may also have contributed to this fall. These civil societies and various groups, political or otherwise, keep making fresh and new demands on the political system seeking to have their share in political **pie**, economic resources and social standing. Much of success or failure will depend on how the political system responds to these demands, or how it balances the interests of the nation's heterogeneous society with the requirements of national unity. In the face of the questionable legitimacy of the Indian state and continuing progression of civil society, it will be a difficult exercise for the Indian state to reclaim its legitimacy as it will be called upon to redefine the line of demarcation between state and society. No doubt, India has encountered these issues in the past and these should continue to guide Indian democracy in the process of its evolution. India has borrowed heavily from the Western legal traditions to formulate its principles of liberal democracy which reflect the aspirations to end the inequalities and to enhance social welfare of its people. Now, this is India's position by choice.

But what actually the politicians have practised for long runs counter to what is proposed in the Constitution and what is set forth as guiding principle in its Preamble. There has been a steady Concentration of power in the Central Government even as increasing assertiveness is shown by various **ethnic** and caste groups. Instead of addressing their issues, the government has responded with greater ruthlessness in curbing them. Increasing uses of coercive power have eroded government's legitimacy. Besides, the present political set-up is highly criminalised. There is unholy nexus between politicians, bureaucrats and criminals at the hands of which the citizenry suffers untold misery. The ruling party is guided more by the lust of power than by desire to serve people. Opposition parties too have failed to espouse people's cause. People have lost faith in the political parties and have grown increasingly cynical. Increasing role of money and muscle power has further **alienated** people from the polity. If the Supreme Court and Election Commission had not been active, India would have drifted into chaos. Some of the recent rulings of the Apex Court have instilled some hope.

It is hoped that the political class will see the writings on the wall and will start practising the democracy that matched the aspirations of people and also, in the process, lived up to the expectations of the Constitution framers.

Vocabulary

Lofty—(adj) of high intellectual or moral value, elevated in nature and style, of imposing height especially standing out above others. **Doctrine**—(n) a belief as authoritative by some group or school, philosophical system, school of thought. **Profess**—(v) practise as a profession, teach or claim to be knowledgeable about. **Cherish**—(v) be fond of, be attached to, hold dear, treasure, care for. **Bequeath**—(v) leave or give by will after ones death. **Sacrosanct**—(adj) must be kept sacred, inviolable. **Gainsay**—(v) challenge, dispute. **Converge**—(v) be adjacent or come together. **Disinterested**—(adj) not influenced by personal feelings, not prejudiced or biased, quality of being neutral and impartial in judgement. **Impunity**—(n) exemption from punishment or loss. **Trample**—(v) tramp down, tread down, step on somebody and crush under feet. **Bruise**—(v) hurt, injure, spite, wound, offend. **Adage**—(n) byword, proverb. **Pie**—(n) dish baked in pastry-lined pan often with a pastry top. **Ethnic**—(adj) denoting or deriving from or distinctive from the ways of living built up by a group of people. **Alienate**—(v) arouse hostility or indifference where there had been love, affection or friendliness.

□

56

Fundamental Rights

The Constitution of India has **embodied** a number of Fundamental Rights which are to act as limitations not only upon the powers of the executive but also upon the powers of the legislature. These rights are seen as **inalienable** rights of an individual, which every individual is entitled to in order that he/she is able to lead a life of dignity and self-respect. These may also be called basic human rights essential for the actualisation of the highest good of an individual citizen. Courts have the power to declare as **void** laws **contravening** Fundamental Rights.

Our Constitution draws extensively from the *unwritten* Constitution of England and from the Constitution of the United States as also from various other constitutions of the world. In England, individual liberty is secured by judicial decisions determining the rights of individuals in specific cases brought before the court. But while courts in England have the power to protect the individual against executive tyranny, they are powerless against legislative aggression upon individual rights. In other words, there are no fundamental rights in England that can bind the legislature. Parliament in England is **'omnipotent'** and it can change any law. The English courts have no power of judicial review over legislation at all. No law enacted by the British Parliament can be struck down as unconstitutional on the ground of contravention of any supposed fundamental or natural right.

The framers of the American Constitution, on the other hand, were apprehensive of tyranny not just from the executive but also from the legislature. There is what we call 'judicial supremacy' in America as opposed to 'parliamentary supremacy' in England. In India, our Constitution makers adopted Fundamental Rights to safeguard individual liberty and also for ensuring social, economic and political justice for every member of the community. Indian Constitution effects a compromise between the doctrines of parliamentary sovereignty and judicial supremacy. As Indian parliament is created and limited by a written Constitution, whatever this Parliament enacts must broadly conform to the limitations and prohibitions imposed by the Constitution. In case any of these limitations are **transgressed,** the Supreme Court and the High Courts are competent to declare a law unconstitutional and void. As far as the contravention of Fundamental Rights is concerned, this duty is specifically enjoined upon the courts by the Constitution by way of abundant caution [Article 13].

Fundamental Rights can broadly be categorised as under:

Right to Equality

Art. 14 – Equality before law and equal protection of the law

Art. 15 – Prohibition of discrimination

Art. 16 – Equality of opportunity regarding employment

Art. 17 – Abolition of untouchability

Art. 18 – Abolition of Titles Right to Freedom

Art. 19 – Freedom of speech and expression; assembly; association; movement; residence and settlement; profession

Art. 20 – Protectioin in respect of conviction for offences

Art. 21 – Protectioin of life and personal liberty

Art. 22 – Protection against arrest and detention in certain cases

Right against Exploitation

Art. 23 – Prohibition of traffic in human beings and forced labour

Art. 24 – Prohibition of employment of children in hazardous employment

Right to Freedom of Religion

Art. 25 – Freedom of conscience and free profession, practice and propagation of religion

Art. 26 – Freedom to manage religious affairs

Art. 27 – Freedom as to payment of taxes for promotion of any particular religion

Art. 28 – Fredom to attendance at religious instructions in certain educational institutions

Cultural and Educational Rights

Art. 29 – Protection of language, script or culture of minorities

Art. 30 – Right of minorities to establish and administer educational institutions

Right to Constitutional Remedies

Art. 32 – Remedies for enforcement of the Fundamental Rights conferred by part writs of habeas corpus, mandamus, prohibition, certiorari and quo warranto.

One of the fundamental rights – the right to property – has been withdrawn in 1978. This means if a legislature makes a law depriving a person of his/her property, he/she cannot challenge the reasonableness of the restrictions imposed by such law. Some of the rights such as under Articles 15, 16 and 19 are available only to the citizens of India. Some of the other fundamental rights, on the other hand, are available to *any person* on the soil of India – citizen or foreigner – under Articles 14, 18, 20-25-27, 28 and 32.

Absence of right to work and right to education has been criticised by many as they feel these rights are more fundamental than some of the Fundamental Rights. Another criticism that merits attention is that these Rights are **couched** in a language that is not easily understood. They are provisions that are hedged with so many qualifications, exceptions and explanations which make them very difficult for any individual to fully grasp the meaning of it all. These criticisms apart, these rights can be enforced through courts of law. Right to work, right to education and right to information have since been incorporated through legislations as separate law and they serve the same purpose as these Rights. The Fundamental Rights are aimed at limiting the power of the government and prevent the executive and the legislature from becoming **authoritarian** and dictatorial. Besides, they provide opportunities to individuals to develop to their full potential and lead a life of dignity and self-respect. The **pious** aim of any democracy should be to allow its citizens to grow to their full potential. Fundamental Rights help produce a free society where an individual is not unnecessarily **hemmed** in by restrictions. Only a society where an individual lives with dignity and enjoys basic freedom can have all round progress for its members which, in turn, helps build nation and therein lies the importance and significance of Fundamental Rights.

Vocabulary

Embodied—(adj) possessing or existing in bodily form. **Inalienable**—(adj) incapable of being repudiated or transferred to another, not subject to forfeiture. **Void**—(adj) lacking any legal or binding force, containing nothing. **Contravene**—(v) go against, as of rules or laws, deny the truth of. **Omnipotent**—(adj) having unlimited power, all powerful, almight. **Transgress**—(v) act in disregard of laws. **Couch**—(v) formulate in a particular style or language. **Authoritarian**—(adj) autocratic, despotic, dictatorial. **Pious**—(adj) having, showing or expressing reverence for a deity. **Hemmed in**—(v) surrounded in a restrictive manner, encircle as a military tactic.

□

Citizen's Fundamental Duty

Environmental protection is a fundamental duty of every citizen of this country under Article 51-A(g) of our constitution, which reads as follows.

Article 51-A(g): " It Shall be the duty of every citizen of India to protect and improve the natural environment including forests, lakes, rivers and wildlife and to have compassion for living creatures"

57

Fundamental Duties

The constitution makers had not given any thought to fundamental duties. Hence, these duties that came into existence in 1976 did not form part of the original Constitution. The Fundamental Duties – ten in number – were introduced by way of an amendment (42nd Amendment Act, 1976), mainly to achieve the objective of limiting the operation of the Fundamental Rights as they were devised in the 1949-Constitution. It is incorporated in Article 51A inserted in the Constitution by above amendment. Under this Article, it will be the bounden duty of every citizen of India

To abide by the Constitution and respect National Flag and the National Anthem;

To cherish and follow the noble ideal which inspired our national struggle for freedom;

To protect the sovereignty, unity and integrity of India;

To defend the country;

To promote the spirit of common brotherhood amongst all the people of India;

To preserve the rich heritage of our composite culture;

To protect and improve the natural environment;

To develop the scientific temper and spirit of inquiry;

To safeguard public property;

To strive towards excellence in all spheres of individual and collective activity;

To understand the true import and significance of 'composite culture', it may be desirable to acquaint ourselves with

> the observations of the Supreme Court. The Court pointed out that the foundation of this composite culture is the Sanskrit language and literature, which is the great binding force for the different peoples of this great country and it should be preferred in the educational system for the preservation of that heritage—apart from the duty of the government. The reason is not far to seek. The original population of India was Hindu. Thereafter this country was subjected to Muslims and British rule. Because of its wonderful tolerance, the Hindu culture **imbibed** these alien cultures and, thus, grew up a 'composite culture' in India.

There is no provision in the Constitution for directly enforcing these duties on the citizens or for any sanction to prevent their violation. But if in determining the constitutionality of any law, if a court decides to give effect to any of these duties, it may consider such law to be reasonable in the context of Article 14 or 19, and, thus, save such law from unconstitutionality. It would also serve as a warning to the **recalcitrant** elements in the citizenry against anti-social activities such as burning the copies of the Constitution, destroying public property and the like. The Apex Court held that since these duties are **obligatory** for the citizens, the state should also **strive** to achieve the same objective. The court may, therefore, issue suitable directions in these matters in appropriate cases.

It will perhaps be in order to examine as to what led to incorporating this provision of Fundamental Duties in the Constitution when the framers of the Constitution had not envisaged it. But there were some exceptions. One, Parliament invested with the power to modify the application of the fundamental rights to the members of the armed forces or intelligence organisations so as to ensure proper discharge of their duties and maintenance of discipline amongst them. Two, in the event of martial law being in force, Parliament is empowered to indemnify any person in the service of the union or a state for any act done in connection with the maintenance or restoration of order. Three, the fundamental rights would remain suspended under the nation is under emergency. During the period of emergency Article 19 of the Constitution will remain suspended. These exceptions to fundamental rights gave rise to the demand for fundamental duties.

Though these fundamental duties are not enforceable in the courts nor their violations punishable, a court may decline to enforce a fundamental right of an individual if he/she is shown to have violated any of the ten fundamental duties specified above. Besides, in the light of the observations of the Supreme Court that the fundamental rights are not absolute, the significance of the fundamental duties becomes all the more pronounced. This also conforms to the maxim that every right has a corresponding duty.

Vocabulary

Imbibe—(v) take in, receive into the mind and retain. **Recalcitrant**—(adj) marked by stubborn resistance to authority, fractious, refractory. **Obligatory**—(adj) doing of an act because necessitated by law, rules. **Strive**—(v) to exert much effort or energy, endeavour, reach, strain.

□

58

Central Bureau of Investigation

Certain things, certain institutions and certain systems are so well entrenched in our psyche that we take them for granted. We do not look or **pry** into their origin because we do not find them questionable. For instance, the institution of Central Bureau of Investigation or its more familiar shortened version, CBI is so well settled in our psyche that we would never have looked into the question of its legitimacy if it were not for the order passed by the High Court at Guwahati. The honourable High Court has termed it illegal as it is not the creation of law. CBI is the country's premier investigating agency and it is said to have been created by a home ministry resolution on 1st April, 1963. If it were not for this order that came as a bolt from the blue, we would not have known in ordinary course that CBI functioned under Delhi Special Police Establish Act, 1946. This investigating agency is also the Interpol agency in India and according to one view it was created in 1941 as the Special Police Establishment tasked with domestic security. It is said to have been renamed the Central Bureau of Investigation in 1963 with the motto **insignia** of 'industry, impartiality and integrity'.

A **peep** into the history of this premier investigating agency, therefore, becomes **imperative**. As Special Police Establishment (SPE), its function was to investigate bribery and corruption in transactions with the War and Supply Department of India. It was set up during the World War II with its headquarter at Lahore in Pakistan. After the end of the war, there was a continued need for an investigating agency to keep a tab on the central government employees for acts of bribery and corruption. It was transferred to the Home Department by the 1946 Delhi Special Police Establishment Act. Its scope was enlarged to cover all departments of the Government of India. Its jurisdiction was extended to the union territories and could be extended to the states with the consent of the concerned state governments.

Sardar BallabhBhai Patel, who was the Deputy Prime Minister and also the Home Minister then, wanted to **weed out** corruption from the erstwhile princely states such as Rewa, Tonk and Jodhpur. He asked the then legal advisor Karam Chand Jain to monitor criminal proceedings against the dewans and chief ministers of those states. SPE became CBI with the passage of a resolution on 1st April, 1963. This was the bone of contention in the High Court of Guwahati. In fact, the honourable High Court **quashed** that very resolution by which the agency was formed. The contention of the court was that the 1963 resolution was not even a proper executive order as it was neither a cabinet decision nor was it signed by the President. The court said that the **impugned** order could at best be regarded as a departmental instruction. A departmental instruction cannot be termed law, the court ruled. Delivering the order, the bench said, "we do hold that the CBI is neither an organ nor a part of the DSPE and the CBI cannot be treated as a police force constituted under the DSPE Act, 1963".

Majority of the legal **luminaries** have, **prima facie**, concurred with the view of the High Court. Few however doubt that the Supreme Court will grant a stay simply because the **ramifications** of this ruling are huge. It will be overturned not so much because the order is 'erroneous and strange' as some officials have chosen to call it, but because the CBI draws legitimacy from the Supreme Court and various High Courts that have entrusted the agency with the task of investigating cases from time to time. Many of the entrusted cases are being monitored by the Supreme Court. So, the question of illegitimacy is ruled out. In all probability, the Apex Court will direct the government to enact a law through legislation to legitimise its creation. The government too will go for a 'legally tenable solution' to a problem regularly encountered by the investigative agency. That, in all probability, will set the matter at rest. But it raises a question. How can we be so casual towards such things and why for decades no step was taken in this direction, especially in view of the recommendations made from time to time? It was also pointed out in 2009 by a ruling party MP, a Supreme Court lawyer, in an Observer Research Foundation. He had termed the legal architecture of the central investigating agency as '**dubious**'. Accordingly, the CBI had no independent standing in law. Simply put, it is a piece of legislation whose underpinnings in law are **tenuous**. CBI draws its powers from the *antiquated* 1946 DSPE Act. In fact, it is now revealed that the present government had snubbed the CBI for demanding a new law; it had also refused to heed the warning of the parliamentary panels for terming the 1946 law as 'outdated and grossly inadequate'. The question is – why did the government ignore CBI note that sought the replacement of the old law with a new law? The government is reported to have explained that while the proposal to give statutory backing to the CBI has been under consideration, there is no need of any new law in view of the legal opinion given by the Attorney General. This clearly shows the government failed to read finer law points and allowed the matter to **escalate**.

While these issues are legal and they will be tackled at the appropriate level, we need to take a look at the kind of work CBI has done over the years to earn the esteem it enjoys today. No doubt, there are issues of CBI being partisan and is often accused of toeing the government line. But these issues do not take away the good work this agency has done over the years. Besides resolving many individual and tricky cases to take them to their logical conclusions, if it were not for CBI we would not have seen the resolution of the fodder scam. Today the chief **protagonists** of the scam are in prison. Even now it is preoccupied with various important cases involving people at the very top. It is hoped that this premier investigating agency will be freed from the control of the government so that it no longer remains 'caged parrot'. Now that it is sure to have a law legislated to give it the legal legitimacy, it is possible that the demand of making it autonomous will be met.

Vocabulary

Pry—(v) to move or force, be nosey, search or inquire in a meddlesome way, make an invited or presumptuous inquiry. **Peep**—(v) to look furtively, appear as though from hiding, to make short high sound, cheep, chirrup, chirp. **Imperative**—(adj) requiring attention or action. **Quash**—(v) declare invalid, to annul, cancel, to put down by force or intimidation. **Impugned**—(adj) attack as false or wrong, challenged. **Luminary**—(n) a person who is an expert or a great influence in a special area or activity. **Prima facie**—(adj) based on what at first seems to be true, although it may be proved false later; (adv) at first sight.**Ramification**—(n) [Usually plural] one of the large number of complicated and unexpected results that follow an action or a decision. **Dubious**—(adj) fraught with uncertainty or doubt, open to doubt or suspicious. **Tenuous**—(adj) so weak or uncertain that it hardly exists. **Escalate**—(v) to become or make something greater, worse, more serious etc. **Protagonists**—(n) main characters in a play, movie or book.

□

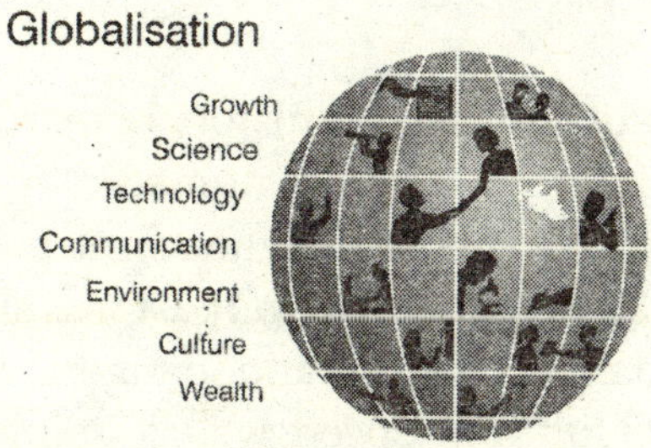

59
Globalisation

The way the word 'globalisation' is referred to these days, it makes one wonder if it is something new and unheard of. That however is not the case. The word might evoke concerns of various kinds in various minds but as a concept it is not new. Only the thrust is new. The fear that it could lead to economic and, therefore, political **hegemony** of some is also misplaced. It can lead to no such hegemony whether in physical or in ideological form if we understand the underlying spirit of globalisation.

Economic globalisation was practised by our ancestors too. Simply understood, it is the concept of one globe one market. Earlier too, when the civilisation was in its cradle, people did business with people from all over the world. The only **constraint** then was the establishment of contact. There was no business **taboo** of any kind. The only issue was of how to reach all parts of the world. Man by nature is nomadic. It is this nature of mankind that has made civilisation or globalisation a possibility. If man were not a nomad, the world would not have made the kind of progress it has. The greatest example of this is the United States of America. There are fewer original Americans than those who settled there from different parts of the globe and made America their home. This is the effect of globalisation with a difference. This globalisation that we are discussing now is different from the one just cited above because this globalisation deals mainly with trading relations and activities with all barriers dismantled.

This globalisation is as old as history of mankind, beginning with the great migrations (man is **nomadic** by nature; he will settle anywhere in pursuit of livelihood) of people across the great land mass. But the process in the past was slow and fraught with risks and dangers. Risks and dangers never inhibited man from the pursuit, but speed was certainly an important factor. But today we live in a different world. The technology has made it possible to reach out to any part of the globe in a **jiffy**. Communication has become so fast that we and our products can reach any part of the globe without any difficulty at all. This has lent a new meaning to globalisation. The globe has truly become squeezed into a ball. Globalisation derives special meaning and content from this fast and subtle means of communication. This need not be seen as a disadvantage even if for the time being we are not able to match the ability of some nations in providing cheap and easy merchandise. For instance, China has flooded our local markets with their goods. It may be a momentary setback, but in the long run it may and it should prove beneficial. It is a challenge to our **ingenuity** to produce better merchandise at a lesser cost.

Globalisation is expected to generate the spirit of competition which is so important in today's liberalised economy. If it were not for globalisation, our information technology would not have made an inroad into the world market. Today we are the best and the most sought-after IT providers in the world. It has given a fillip to our economy and it has provided better job opportunities to our own wards that have excelled. They have excelled thanks to globalisation.

Today's world is so well connected that it is no longer possible to remain isolated from one another. We can no longer stay shielded from the impact of what happens in other parts of the world. If 9/11 happened in the US, it impacted the entire world. If Tsunami happened in the Andaman and Nicobar Islands, it impacted the other parts of the world as well. 26/11 happened in India, but several other countries were impacted by it and are still feeling the heat of the same. The economic slowdown that began in the US and Europe has left every country of the world affected.

Globalisation is both a process and a phenomenon. The two will have to be understood in their **entirety**. Breaking down of distances measured by time is an important factor and it is a phenomenon that marks globalisation. This phenomenon far from getting slowed down will further intensify as we make more technological advances. We have to live with this phenomenon. In fact, we should adjust ourselves expeditiously with this phenomenon so that we can reap the benefits that would **accrue** therefrom. Adjusting to these technological advances is what we call process. This process has to be continual if we are to constantly reap the benefits of globalisation. It is a never-ending process; it is a dynamic process. Each country of the world is a part of this process and it must be the **endeavour** of each one of them to ready itself to meet the challenges – and opportunities provided by these challenges – so that it is not bypassed by the massive institutional and technological changes that are taking place so rapidly. Globalisation as a process is expected to absorb these changes.

To expect that globalisation as a process will have the same and equal impact on all parts of the world will be expecting too much. Nothing can ensure uniformity. There are various reasons for that. Much of it depends on the absorption capacity of each nation and that usually depends on the economic structure and political frame and work of individual countries besides the entrepreneurial traits of the citizens of the countries. No two countries are identical in their economic structures, political patterns, and in entrepreneurial skills. Market mix also varies from state to state and from country to country making uniformity a distant dream.

However, it is no longer possible to remain insulated from the rest of the world. Today, it is possible to have a common thread running through all economic systems. While this will enable us to enjoy the fruits of a multi-civilised world, it will also expose us to the attendant risks. That is the **quintessence** of globalisation which we must be ready to **countenance**.

Vocabulary

Hegemony – (n) the dominance or leadership of one social group or nation over other. **Constraint** – (n) the state of being physically constrained or restrained, a device that retards the progress or movement of something. **Taboo** – (adj) excluded from use or mention. (n) a prejudice that bans or restricts the use or mention of something because of its sacred nature. **Nomadic** – (adj) having no fixed home, changing location frequently as required for work or food, peregrine, roving, wandering. **Jiffy** – (n) a very short time, blink of an eye, instant. **Ingenuity** – (n) the power of creative imagination, inventiveness. **Entirety** – (n) the state of being total and complete. **Accrue** – (v) grow by addition, come into the possession of. **Endeavour** – (v) a purposeful or industrious undertaking, earnest and conscientious activity intended to do or accomplish something. **Quintessence** – (n) the purest and most concentrated essence of something, the perfect example of something. **Countenance** – (v) consent to, give permission, allow. (n) the human face, the appearance conveyed by a person's face.

□

60

The Crumbling Institution of Marriage

The institution or marriage once regarded as **sacrosanct** in India is fast losing its social **sanctity** in addition to legal. All over the world the traditional views on matrimony are undergoing change and new domestic arrangements are evolving. It would, therefore, be interesting to see where and how India stands with regard to these changes, especially as courts too have begun to take a fresh look at this institution.

The idea of an Indian marriage has undergone a drastic change in the recent years. Increasing urbanisation and migration from rural to urban centres may be one of the primary causes for this change. Rural economy is breaking out into urban culture, thus exposing people from rural but lower social strata to modern trends and spaces. A peep into the matrimonial ads will show how they are getting **acclimatised** to urban lifestyles. 'Caste no bar' figures prominently in the matrimonial ads. This shows people are rising above deep-rooted **disparities** like castes and religion. With the **patriarchal** control over women slackening and joint family structures almost having collapsed, more changes and more drastic ones cannot be ruled out.

It would be wrong to suggest that the institution of marriage has collapsed in reality. Far from it, however, the fact remains that it is no longer sacrosanct. But despite **monogamy**, live-in relationships, single-parent households, deliberate single statuses, late marriages and homosexual partnerships getting and gaining acceptance, there is still space for the institution of marriage in the society. Marriages are no longer a given, at least in the urban centres of India. Society is no longer unanimous about the **efficacy** of the institution. Differential treatment comes from different sections. The youth today is exposed to new lifestyles necessitating exploring of their sexual identities. One of the reasons for this may well be the excessive breakdown of marriages in the West.

Changing marriage **prototype** is also the result of progress in women' education and income and the rights granted to them over property. Besides, young Indians do not necessarily feel as bound by duty and are more conscious of working towards fulfilment in the relationship than merely playing the role of husband or wife. The changing norms are making the institution of marriage less an institution and more of a personal human relationship determined by emotionality and companionship than by rigid legal, familiar or social **diktats**. Economic disparity plays a significant role in determining the quality of relationships. Formal or informal relationships depend on economic factors as it is easier to make decisions and live through them if one is economically independent. It helps in handling the social barriers. It would not be an exaggeration to say that marriages are no longer planned. They are all situation based. But the biggest thing is that people now have a choice before them to suit their situation.

What also helps relationships outside the institution of marriage is the realisation that living-in is simpler to get out. Courts are also recognising the rights of women in living-in relationships. The Madras High Court ruled in 2006 that couples having premarital sex will be considered equivalent to married couples. Orissa High Court too ruled and introduced new law for those living-in relationships. The changed outlook has made it easier to accept life outside marriage. What are the **impelling** factors that are driving our youth to go for such **radicalised** living style? It is the evolving work culture, say many and still many say for them vocation or career is more important than marriage. Still, some others say there is no space for children in their life. Life, many say, is a water-tight compartment where there is no space for anyone and anything except their personal happiness. What, however, is most important for them all is that they are saved the trouble of having to waste years for getting a divorce in case they want to part ways. This kind of relationships they are now having makes it so easy to part ways. Clearly, marriages are also affected by the fast food culture.

A survey has revealed that the marriage rate in the US is at its lowest point in more than a century and the number of marriages across the country fell by over 5% during the recent recession. A research estimated that the number of single-person households globally will rise to 331 million or 15.7% of total households by 2020. India, it revealed, will be the fourth largest number of households in the world after the US, China and Japan. According to a matrimonial website, the number of divorcees under the age of 25 in India has gone up to 8% in 2011 from a mere 2% in 2008. Though alarming, only one out of every 100 Indian marriages end up in divorce unlike in US where 50% marriages end in divorces or break-ups.

No doubt, there is concern in parts of the world about the decline of the institution of marriage; and UK has initiated steps to give **incentives** to those who still **cling** to this institution that many see as crumbling fast. The British Prime Minister David Cameroon unveiled a marriage tax breaks plan, which would help married couples to get tax breaks up to 200 Pounds a year. It is also reported that the Australian Government has decided to cut welfare payments to single parents. According to another report, grandparents in Edinburgh are being given legal rights to maintain contact with their grandchildren after a family breakdown or divorce. All these are a pointer to the recognition that the institution of marriage is crumbling, falling apart and there is a need to prevent what looks **inevitable**.

Same sex marriages too have played a part in lessening the importance of the conventional institution of marriage. There are at present 14 jurisdictions (including 13 states) in the US that recognize the same sex marriages and eight states recognise some form of same sex union. Russia passed an anti-gay legislation in June 2013 against what it termed the 'propaganda of non-traditional sexual relations'. This stringent law of Russia is seen as a measure to stigmatise gay people and it seeks to ban giving children any information about homosexuality. This law empowers the police to arrest and detain tourists and foreign nationals suspected of being **gay**. It has outlawed 'homosexual propaganda' as **pornography**. Brazil is one of the five Latin American countries to have recognized same-sex unions and is one of the three, along with Argentina and Uruguay, to have legalised same-sex marriage. There are 15 countries across the world where same-sex marriage is permitted. Eight of these including England and France are in Europe. India too recently decriminalized homosexuality, though India does not as yet recognise gay marriage.

So, the institution of marriage has taken a knock of the worst kind. Whether or not it will survive is difficult to say with any degree of certainty. However, if the constraints that this institution suffers from are removed, the crumbling institution may still survive despite radicalism all around.

Vocabulary

Sacrosanct—(adj) inviolable, sacred. **Sanctity**—(n) the quality of being holy. **Acclimatised**—(v) getting used to a certain climatic conditions. **Disparities**—(n) inequalities and differences in certain respects. **Patriarchal**—(adj) characterisc of a social organisation in which male is the head of the family and title is traced through the male line. **Monogamy**—(n) having only one spouse at a time, monogamousness. **Efficacy**—(n) capacity or power to produced a desired effect, efficaciousness. **Prototype**—(n) a standard or typical example. **Diktat**—(n) an order issued by someone with authority, often unpopular or harsh. **Impelling**—(adj) markedly effective as if by emotional pressure, forcing, propelling. **Radicalise**—(v) to make people more willing to consider new and different policies, ideas, etc. to make them more radical in their political orientation. **Incentive**—(n) a positive motivational influence, bonus, inducement. **Cling**—(v) to remain emotionally or intellectually attached, to adhere, to cohere. **Inevitable**—(adj) incapable of being avoided or prevented, imminent, invariably happening or occurring. **Gay**—(adj) bright and pleasant, homosexual or arousing homosexual desires. **Pornography**—(n) creative activity (writings or pictures or films) to arouse sexual desire.

□

61

How Should We Treat Our Elders?

When we refer to a person as elder or elderly, we usually have in mind a person who is past his/her prime. Calling them old might sound a little harsh. So, we call them elderly or senior citizens. Refer to them by whatever word we may, the fact of the matter is we place them on the other side of the **spectrum** called life. We no longer think of them in terms of being a contributory factor to life. We often sideline them and try to put them in an unproductive mould. It is unfortunate that those who, prior to their retirement—if they were in some kind of a service where retirement came as a matter of rule—were so relevant for us should suddenly become as irrelevant as to be **stacked away**. Things may or may not happen exactly that way, but the tendency is to write them off and treat them differently. No one likes to be called old.

The problem is while there are many who celebrate youth and childhood there is hardly anyone celebrating the old. If Wordsworth says, "bliss was it that dawn, to be young it was heaven", T.S. Eliot has this to say, "I grow old, I grow old; I shall wear the bottoms of my trousers rolled". Eliot will roll his trousers so that he does not look old. This in spite of the fact that there is no dearth of people who have continued to contribute their might even after having grown old! Is it really that very bad to be old or does it mean being old is being **decrepit** and being of no use to the society and to the economy?

The facts do not quite testify to that. If there were the case we would not have Khushwant Singh in our midst; we would not have Amartya Sen, A.P.J. Abdul Kalam to just name a few. Their contribution to literature, to social economy and to science will remain unquestionable. But yes, not all old people are like them. For that matter, not all young people are like Sachin Tendulkar or Sania Mirza. Excellence cannot be tied down to age. So, does the world really care for the aged? The first World Assembly for the Ageing was held in 1983 and the second after two decades. This is clearly indicative of the importance given to the issue. And what was the outcome of these deliberations? Attempts were made to define the parameters for building a society for all ages. The matter has not gone beyond that.

In the Western countries, the elders are usually kept out of the family, but certain basic facilities are provided to them. They are spared all **hustle and bustle** of the daily life. Social security, shelter and healthcare are taken care of so that they are spared the strains of life. This is a far cry in India. One reason for this is—India is new to this concept. Till sometime back, joint family was the order of the day here. But the joint family system has disintegrated fast enough to warrant fulfilment of bare necessities to the aged who are left to fend for themselves; so that they may spend the evenings of their life in relative calm and peace. This is the responsibility of the young India which it must take.

Darwin's theory of the survival of the fittest would perhaps apply more to the present world than it applied to the previous generations. The concept of the liberalised economy and globalised market has overwhelmed the world with a **vengeance**. Only those who are bodily and mentally strong have lived up to the rigours of this changed environment and those with weak muscles and reflexes have been thrown **asunder**. It is the duty of the society to pick out those thrown asunder to provide **succour** and care. The good thing is the world is awaking to the fact that these elderly people are a storehouse of knowledge which could be profitably transferred to the young generation. Also, the world is gradually but surely veering to the idea that the aged are not a spent force and that their services and knowledge can still be utilised for bettering the quality of the world.

The UN has belatedly recognised that the neglect of the aged was a criminal act of negligence and so it took up the agenda of building a society for all ages. UNO was alarmed at the rate of atrocities and indignities heaped on the elderly. In the developed economies, the situation was comparatively less alarming than in the developing economies. The cases of neglect, abuse, physical torture and indignities were on the rise in all developing economies without exception. In our own country, there are more than eighty million senior citizens which is seven per cent of the population. With the rising rate of life expectancy, this number is going to rise. So, we already have an army of the aged. Instead of pushing them to the brink, we need to find ways and means of utilising their knowledge. It must be kept in mind that a large number of them are retirees from various services. Their immense experiences can be put to profitable use.

It will of course not be possible to return to the old joint family system where the elderly were respected and their guidance in all social and economic matters was considered mandatory. Their authority was unquestionable. That status can no longer be restored in this changed milieu. At the same time, there is no reason to subject them to total neglect which is becoming more and more noticeable in our society, and that is a matter of concern. As stated earlier, the experiences of the retirees can be profitably utilised. As for those who have no experiences to back them, such elderly people can be given some vocational training. Adult education is a step in this direction. In short, these people who are considered a liability can be turned into asset. There are many things that these elderly people can do without much physical exertion. This will not only give them job satisfaction, it will also give them much needed economic freedom.

There is no denying that the senior citizens deserve better treatment, greater care from the society to the making of which they have contributed a lot during their heyday. Just because they are in their **twilight** years, we cannot leave them to fend for themselves. If we cannot personally attend to their needs, we can certainly create institutions that can take care of their needs. One day we too would need the services of such institutions. Meanwhile, there is no dearth of people who strongly believe that life begins after sixty. Not just believe, they live their life in entirety. There is no dull moment in their life as they keep themselves busy doing things they could not do when they were young and kicking.

Vocabulary

Spectrum – (n)ambit, array, scope, range. **Stack away** – (v) keep or lay aside for future use. **Decrepit** – (adj) lacking muscular strength or vitality, feeble, infirm, rickety. **Vengeance** – (n) the act of taking revenge, retribution, payback. **Asunder** – (adv) into parts or pieces, apart. (adj) widely separated especially in space; **Succour** – (n) assistance in times of difficulty. **Twilight** – (n) the time of day immediately after sun set.

□

62

Tenants and Landlords

Tenants are usually the **accursed** lot. They are forced by the circumstances to live in a house they do not own; for which they have to cough up a sizeable chunk of their hard-earned money. But their **travail** does not end with just paying the rent. In fact, it begins from there. Of course, there are quite a few tenants who give torrid time to their landlords. But such cases are more an exception than rule. A tenant is always at the mercy of his landlord or landlady. Landlords, it would seem, like to keep their tenants on **tenterhooks**.

Relation between a tenant and his landlord is rarely, if ever, a very **cordial** one. It may begin on a cordial note. But certainly does not end on the same note. Sometimes the process gets reversed too. But such occasions are rare, few and far between. For, if it did not begin on a cordial note, the deal would never be struck. The word cordial, however, is not appropriate here, because cordiality begins with the tenant and ends with him. It is not for him to expect that the landlord would return cordiality. It is the tenant who needs a roof over his head. The landlord can afford to ignore a number of tenants even for an indefinite period of time.

So, a prospective tenant makes a cautious approach to his prospective landlord who subjects him to a grilling interview before deciding to **condescend** a proper hearing. The prospective tenant answers every question in great **trepidation**, for he does not know which answer of his may disqualify him. The prospective landlord extracts every bit of information about his hapless victim, but reveals very little about himself or herself. If the prospective tenant crosses the first **hurdle** successfully and unscathed, he then faces another crucial area of settling the rent. If this hurdle is also crossed successfully and without being bruised, then he faces the most crucial one. That is the area of dos and don'ts.

These dos and don'ts are like Ten Commandments. The tenant has no choice but to follow them **meticulously**. While listing all those dos and don'ts here may not be desirable, we can afford to take a look at some of the **queer** conditions that bind a tenant to what may be called a **tether post**. One of such conditions must relate to **rational** (it is rationed, actually) use of water. At the time of striking a deal, water would usually not pose any problem at all and would hardly be a matter of discussion then. But once the house is occupied and the advance rent is paid, water becomes a perennial problem which is resolved always at the cost of the poor tenant. The poor tenant has no choice but to acquiesce to whatever arrangement is made, for he cannot afford to change house so quickly yet again. Besides, he can never be sure that he will not be meted out the same or worse treatment elsewhere. So, he stays out. If he has small children, he is specifically asked to keep them restrained. They must not make noise, nor must they pluck flowers, if there are any in the close vicinity. They must not dare to socialise with the landlord or his family. Landlords are a class apart. They would not approve of too many guests, or of parties. Ceremonies of all kinds are best avoided. Tenants must lead as sedate a life as can be possible.

Nowadays, it is a fashion to seek to **enhance** rent every year. If the tenant does not agree to it, he is asked to vacate the house. Landlords are entitled to yearly rent enhancements, but tenants are not entitled to ask for yearly whitewash. Small repair works are not the headache of the landlord. If there is an electricity breakdown, it is expected that the tenant will have it rectified at his own cost. But in case he does not, the landlord sees to it that the amount spent on it is duly recovered from the tenant at the earliest opportunity. Even for settling the electricity bill, the rate payable by the tenant is different from the one that is paid by the landlord to the electricity board.

A tenant cannot claim privacy as a matter of right. So, a tenant need not be surprised to see his landlord and his wife walk in unheralded and unannounced to survey the house they had let out, but thought they continued to command the same occupational rights they enjoyed before letting it out. Pity the tenant because first he thought it was he who enjoyed the right to privacy because he had paid rent and second because he was not aware of new concepts that had **surreptitiously** crept in.

Vocabulary

Accursed—(adj) under a curse, accurst. **Travail**—(n) an unpleasant experience or situation that involves a lot of hard work, difficulties and/or sufferings. **Tenterhook**—(n) to be very excited or anxious while waiting to find out something or see what is to happen. **Cordial**—(adj) diffusing warmth and friendliness, politely warm and friendly. **Condescend**—(v) to behave in a patronising and condescending manner. **Trepidation**—(n) a feeling of alarm or dread. **Hurdle**—(n) obstacle, impediment. **Meticulously**—(adv) in a meticulous manner, things done by taking extreme care of details. **Queer**—(adj) beyond or deviating from the usual or unexpected. **Tether post**—(n) restraint consisting of a rope or light chain used for tying down animals to a post. **Rational**—(adj) consistent with or based on or using reason. **Enhance**—(v) make better or attractive. add something extra to make better or more intense. **Surreptitiously**—(adv) in a clandestine manner, something done sneakily, stealthily.

□

63
Obscenity for Obscenity's Sake

Every time there is an outcry against the growing **obscenity** in our films churned out by our film industry, there is a momentary cooling down. But once the public outcry abates or dies down, it returns to the **fore** again with vengeance. Not that there is actually any toning down during the period (however short) of protest. Lull is only on the surface. It is only played down a little. That is all. Everything else continues as ever before. In fact, they continue with renewed vigour.

The matter is hotly debated in the media and elsewhere. The government on its part makes some ritualistic changes in the censor rules and lets the matter rest. Here too politicians who run the government show more concern about their own negative projection in films rather than about obscenity and vulgarity as such. Consequently, not much actually happens. The films continue to purvey sex in its vilest and ugliest forms. There is a kind of competition amongst the film-makers to 'show' as much as they could. And there is no dearth of filmy **damsels** who are only too willing to 'reveal everything' as long as they got paid.

When they are criticised, they retort that they show because they have things to show. But the question is—if they show only because they have 'things' to show, then it's a pity that they have 'nothing' other than what they actually show. And pray, who does not have 'things' that they so shamefacedly and **flagrantly** show! And the way they are going about it—showing it all—they may soon face a situation when they may not have anything to show at all. Or maybe, by this over exposure they may only succeed in **cloying** the appetite of the viewers who may have initially **lapped it up** all. Novelty wears thin when it ceases to be novel.

Some of the film-makers have justified presentation of sex (the word is used here in the limited sense of vulgarity and obscenity and nothing else) as being essential to their kind of films. How true? *Their* kind of films! Those who oppose them and *their* kind of films are termed **prude** and **snob**. Similarly, the guardians of public morality continue to **lambast** these people who are selling sex and vulgarity in their **variegated** forms. While this goes on, the impressionable minds take in unfiltered, unalloyed though processed sex in adequate measure. None seems greatly concerned or **perturbed** over the matter. No government worth the name tackles the situation with any commitment and firmness the issue demands.

True, an individual's likes and dislikes cannot be allowed to be shaped by government diktats. But it is equally true that constant exposure to this kind of **morbidity** is doing immense harm to the upcoming generation. The freedom of expression does not give us the freedom to spoil others; or it does not give us the right to feed the **gullible** on what is **putrid**. A child who is in the formative stage of his life is not expected to decide for himself what is right and what is wrong for him. His elders, his mentors decide for him and he accepts it. Indeed, he has to be sexually educated, though I am not very sure if our ancestors were any worse off without this education. Anyway, that is beside the point. But the films and magazines and advertisements that are **accosting** him are not the ones to impart any lesson worth emulating. They could only lead them astray. To be fair to the purveyors of sex, they never pretend to be moralists or opinion makers. True, nobody would make the mistake of disbelieving them. They are the entertainers and they have their own ways, however skewed, of entertaining. But what they are doing in the name of entertaining is unpardonable. It is not the end alone that is important; means is equally, if not more, important. So, when they parade obscenity as a means to an end which is entertainment in the present case, it is just **nauseating** and humanly **demeaning**. This is obscenity for the sake of obscenity.

This has a baneful effect on those watching it, particularly if they happen to be children and adolescents. The argument that if you do not relish it do not take it is the absurdest of all absurd arguments. They perhaps mean to say that if their product is found unpalatable, they should be cast away. This is like asking one to taste the poison and upon finding that it is poison, it should be thrown away. To know it is **unpalatable**, you have to take it on your palate first and then decide whether it is palatable or otherwise and suffer the consequences in the process. And if each individual decides about its quality after tasting it, then each is exposed to its baneful effect and the damage is done.

The other argument advanced by these film-makers is—those opposing their brand of films are hypocrites. Why? Because, they argue, these hypocrites themselves indulge in all kinds of obscenity and vulgarity within their four walls, but they would not like to see them enacted on the screen. They are right and I for one am ready to buy this argument. It is better to be a hypocrite than to be animalistic. There is a grain of truth in their argument. Man is a *social* animal, not an animal. He is social because he is hypocrite. And because he is hypocrite, he does not, like an animal, do it all in full public view.

Whenever someone in his **exuberance** and in over enthusiasm tends to do it all in full public view it becomes revolting to our sensibilities. Even those votaries of openness are hypocrites because they themselves would not use public places as their bedrooms. Dogs and bitches mating in the streets are a common sight, yet we do not seem to enjoy it. They are not hypocrites nor do they have any inhibitions. But we have it all and we are better off for that.

We are all naked under our shirts and pants. There cannot be a greater truth than this. Yet how many of us are ready to shun our shirts and pants? Yes, a civilised man is a hypocrite and the day he ceases to be so, this world will cease to be a worth living place. We are inhabitants of a civilised society. We are duty bound to conform to civil behaviour. Whenever someone tries to be uncivil at the cost of others, others have a duty to make him behave.

Sex, like food, is essential. No one denies it. But **gluttony** of any kind is not desirable though permitted within your own confines, not in public domain which these film-makers and others like them are doing. Obscenity and vulgarity cannot and must not be accorded a place of respectability if we wish to live in a livable society.

Vocabulary

Obscenity – (n) the trait of behaving in an obscene (vulgar, indecent, lewd) manner. **Fore** – (n) front part of a vessel or aircraft. (adj) situated at or toward the bow of a vessel. (adv) near or toward the cockpit of a plane or bow of a ship. **Damsel** – (n) a young unmarried woman. **Cloy** – (v) supply or feed to surfeit. **Lap up** – (v) take up with the tongue, lick. **Prude** – (n) a person excessively concerned about propriety and decorum, puritan. **Snob** – (n) a person regarded as arrogant and annoying, prig, snoot. **Lambast** – (v) beat with a cane, censure severely and angrily. **Variegated** – (adj) having a variety of colours, varied, motleyed. **Perturbed** – (adj) rattled, thrown into a state of agitated confusion. **Morbidity** – (n) an abnormally gloomy or unhealthy state of mind, unwholesomeness. **Gullible** – (adj) naïve and easily deceived or tricked. **Putrid** – (adj) in an advanced state of decomposition and having a foul odour. **Accost** – (v) speak to someone, approach with an offer of sexual favours, come up to. **Nauseating** – (adj) causing or able to cause nausea. **Demeaning** – (adj) causing awareness of one's shortcomings, degrading, disgracing, humiliating. **Unpalatable** – (adj) not pleasant or acceptable to the taste or mind, distasteful. **Exuberance** – (n) joyful enthusiasm, ebullience. **Gluttony** – (n) habitual eating to excess, gula, overeating.

□

64
Growing Population and Thinning Families

Travails of a thinning family are many, said a business executive. Economically, well-off, perhaps. Soundly placed in the society, maybe. Yet, roundly unhappy. Upon being pressed further, the executive said—he was just one person around whom the whole of his world revolved. He was the **pivot**. What he meant was—he had no one to fall back on, particularly at the moments of crisis. Crises never give prior notice of their coming. He was the bread winner of the family; he was the master of the family and he was the attendant of the family. He was the guide; he was the provider. In other words, he had to attend to every **sundry** detail of whatever concerned him or his family in person. His wife and his two children constituted his world.

What was his problem actually? Well, he reflected, when his parents were alive, they all lived together as a joint family. There were his uncles and aunts, their children and others. There were quite a few male members and there was no dearth of female members either. There was no pressure on any particular individual for transacting any family business. There was a central authority who was more like a **titular** head than anything else. But his words were final. Everything seemed to have been going on so very well. Clearly, our executive was being **nostalgic** about the life of the yesteryears. He has been suffering from the longing of returning to the past.

Is it not a **paradox**, he asks, that while the population of the world is increasing, man is becoming more and more lonely! It is a paradox indeed. But this paradox is what we had bargained for, or we may say that this is the price we must pay for our progress and economic prosperity. This is the price we must pay for our consumerism. *Datoons* had to be replaced by toothbrushes, for in the kind of **cubicles** we live in or are moving into there cannot be space for collecting and storing the used *datoons*. Besides, toothbrush is the symbol of the present while *datoon* represents the past we have long abandoned and discarded. There is no way we can return to that. If some people are still able to find some **twigs** for brushing their teeth, it is just because they are able to locate some trees here and there. Not many can do that, and how many really have time for *datoons*!

But why should a situation like this bother him when he and many like him had worked overtime to break the system of joint-family? If the system was good enough, why did it break in the first place? Shall we say that our executive is 'overwhelmed by the change' that is affecting us all in several ways? Our happiness or otherwise depends on the ways in which we respond or fail to respond to this change. Is our protagonist scared of 'tomorrow and tomorrow and tomorrow' that 'creeps in this petty pace from day to day to the last syllable of recorded time...'? Is he afraid of the prospects he sees or is he frightened by the shape of tomorrow that he foresees? Or is he scared of the steps we are taking to reach our tomorrow? Thinning of families could just be one of the ways leading to that.

It is time to sit up and **chronicle** the subtle changes that are roaring past us; it is time to take note of the current of change so powerful as to overturn institutions, so demanding that it shifts our values and so **invigorating** that **shrivels** our lives. Our protagonist would certainly have been better equipped to deal with the situation if he had taken into account small and minute details of everyday life. Commonplace and everyday matters—the things we buy and discard; the places we leave behind and host of other things that keep clipping through our lives.

What the business executive is suffering from is 'the disease of change', a sickness from which increasingly large number of people suffer. This disease of change is essentially a psychological condition. In the midst of growing population, man has become more and more lonely. He tries to return to the nostalgic past for finding that familiar psychological cue that helps an individual to function in a society. Unfortunately for him, this psychological cue has long been withdrawn and he is thrown in the cauldron of unfamiliar set of cues which he is unable to adapt to. The paradox of growing population and thinning family can be understood in the light of this revelation.

For our protagonist the future appears to have arrived a little too soon. He has not been able to withstand the superimposition of new culture on the old one which he has himself shunned long ago, but now **craves** to return to. Not because of his sudden love for it, but because of his failure to respond and adapt to the change that has taken place around him. For if had he done that, he too, like many similarly placed individuals, would have **delegated** some of his powers and responsibilities to his wife and children to begin with. Who knows our protagonist must already be doing that, but is perhaps not satisfied with the result?

Vocabulary

Pivot—(n) the person in a rank around whom others wheel and manoeuvre. **Sundry**—(adj) consisting of a haphazard assortment of different kinds, mixed. **Titular**—(adj) of or relating to legal title of something, nominal. **Nostalgic**—(adj) unhappy being away and longing for familiar places or persons. **Paradox**—(n) a statement that contradicts itself. **Cubicles**—(n) small room in which a nun or monk lives. **Twigs**—(n) a small branch or a division of a branch. **Chronicle**—(n) a record or narrative description of past events. **Invigorate**—(v) heighten or intensity. **Shrivel**—(n) wither as with a loss of moisture, shrink. **Crave**—(v) have an appetite or great desire for, plead or ask for earnestly. **Delegate**—(v) transfer power to someone, allocate a task to someone.

□

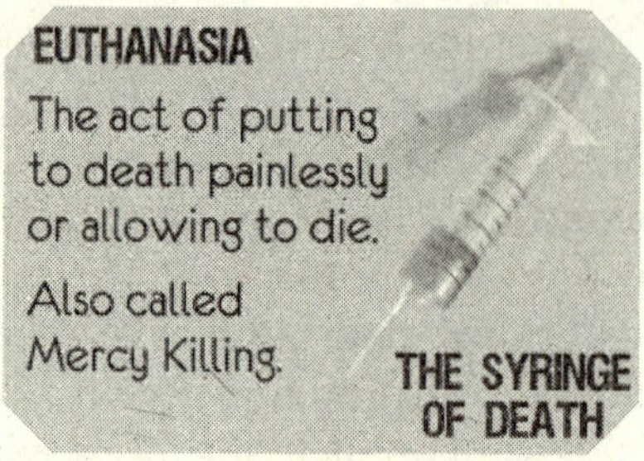

65
Euthanasia—Mercy Killing

Aruna Asaf Ali had just passed away leaving her mourners behind. But it was not an easy and quick death for her. She had to battle it out for quite some time before breathing her last. No one has ever conquered death, though efforts are on at various levels to at least postpone death or to elongate life, if that can be done with a measure of success. But to talk of voluntarily ending life!

The first voluntary Euthanasia Law that came into force on 1st July, 1669 in the Northern Territory of Australia, provides that doctors are empowered to give **lethal** injections of drugs to the terminally ill. No doubt, there is a great furore over the law. This has given rise to fresh debate whether or not a human's life was his inalienable right. While those advocating it argue that the terminally ill people have a right to decide for themselves whether or not they wish to live on, others equally forcefully argue that "once the basic principle is violated, in practice there will be found even more justification to suppress the life of a person who is a burden on family and society". Now, there is no doubt there can never be any **unanimity** on this. In fact, more and more people would rise against this. The Vatican has already banned it and with the majority of the governments it is not an issue at all.

In India, it cannot even be thought of. Not because we recognise and honour the right of the people to life. If that were the case, we would not have had 'state-facilitated' killings we have every other day. We may not have the sanction of Euthanasia

Law, but we can always leave live electric wires hanging loose at some vantage points or leave gaping manholes unattended as death traps which adequately serve the purpose. On paper, our civilised, responsive and responsible governments will always honour *sanctity of life.* In practice, however, they will always be guided by the principle of **expediency** or **exigency** depending on what meaning is assigned to these expressions and who the assignors are. So, in India we may never have Euthanasia Law. We do not need them. Enactment of such laws requires some pondering and lots of political courage and political responsibility which most of our politicians cannot assure us they have.

When the provincial government of Northern Territory in Australia implemented the first voluntary Euthanasia Law in 1996, there was much hue and cry. Rejecting the theory of supreme right to life, Tom Pauling, the Chief Lawyer of the Northern Territory government said that "there is no inalienable right to life". Understandably enough, it raised lot of dust. Euthanasia aims at affording a painless death to those for whom life is a curse because of the terminal illness. Euthanasia means 'easy death' or 'mercy killing'. It is based on Greek theory that incurables should be painlessly removed. Obviously, the idea is to **mitigate** the sufferings of a person who if not put to easy death will continue to suffer.

While on sufferings, I am reminded of Raskalnikov, the protagonist of Dostoyevsky's immortal work *The Crime and Punishment*, bowing down to Sophia, a **weakling**. She hurriedly retreats as Raskalnikov makes the bow. Did she think he was bowing down to her, he asked. He was, he said, bowing down to her sufferings. Human sufferings have moved many in the past and will continue to do so in future as well, no matter how insensitive we grow. It is this sentiment that moved the heart of those who advocated the Euthanasia Law and it is the same sentiment that agitates the minds of those who oppose this law. The **moot** point is—does this mercy killing have any relevance in India? Do we need anything of this kind at all? Here in India our approach is more philosophical, though less humane. We do not like to enter into an argument whether or not life is sacrosanct. To be more precise, we do not debate the question of 'right to life'. For us, life itself means suffering for a vast multitude. If we were to have this law on euthanasia, it will be a **cumbersome** task to find specialists and psychiatrists for each of the sufferer whose death is contemplated to be caused. Sheer number would be mind-boggling and the whole machinery may collapse under its weight. The important thing is the elimination of sufferings. If death is what will secure this elimination, the stress should be on death. And there are several ways of securing death. We do not require any Euthanasia Law. It smacks of *sophistication* and *elitism* which need to be frowned upon. No, we do not need anything that has anything to do with sophistication. If death is what is required to end sufferings, death it shall be and there are quite ingenuous and **pragmatic** ways of achieving it. The methods may be crude or cruder or even the crudest at times. They are result-oriented, time-tested and unfailingly successful. Few countries can match our ingenuity and rate of success. What is more heartening is the fact that we achieve the objective without actually engaging our official machinery. For instance, the official machinery did not have to do anything to cause the death of a journalist and his young and beautiful wife a few weeks ago in our cities. All that was needed to perform the feat was to leave a live electric wire hanging on a busy road. The poor couple! They thought they were armed with an *inalienable right* to life! The sufferings of a young couple thus came to an end without giving a bother to euthanasia. Well, it was a crude method of achieving success. There are cruder methods as well. There is no need for showing any specific instances. There are more safe methods of securing mortality. If buildings are collapsing more frequently these days, if trains are going off the rails more systematically, if buses are falling into valleys and rivers more regularly and if occasional hooch tragedies are claiming more and more lives, they are not without a design. The design is to put an end to their sufferings. We have far too many ways of achieving this. Our ingenuity (those who call it insensibility are being unfair) must be appreciated. We do not believe in stereo-typed methods of providing *relief* from sufferings. We can have scores of pilgrims frozen to death as those proceeding on a pilgrimage to Holy Amarnath did not even livc to discover for themselves, or those working in coal mines did not live on to recall and recount how their sufferings came to an end. Not that we can cause only mass deaths. We can also perform individual feats. And **providence** too seems to come to the aid of the ruling oligarchy everywhere. Rainy season is the best season for this. If the gaping manholes have gobbled up many individuals individually, the **innumerable** ditches that our roads specialise in have broken ribs of several other individuals. And to top it all, we have this free for all traffic system that keeps multiplying to accidental deaths. Death is important, how it comes is not.

The promoters of euthanasia law in the Northern Territory of Australia have to do lot of explaining, and even then they may not be sure that their explanations would be accepted. We have to do no explaining at all. Pauling's problem is—he has become an apologist for death. He has to find, as the opponents of this law say, more justifications to suppress the life of a person who is suffering, or who is a burden on family and society. Besides, the procedure as entailed in this law is very cumbersome. Under this law a general physician and a specialist have to sign a form confirming terminal illness and a psychiatrist to certify that the patient is not suffering from treatable depression. True, getting them to sign those forms here would not be a difficult job. But when death can be achieved without all this fuss, why not settle for something that is least cumbersome!

So, while elsewhere a debate is raging on the desirability or otherwise of Euthanasia Law, we in our own country certainly do not require this kind of **barbarous** law that tends to seek permission of a person whose life is to be 'put out'. Imagine, could we have got the permission of that journalist and his young and beautiful wife to electrocute them to instant death! These sophisticated laws are best left for those so-called civilised people. We have our own methods: the crude, the cruder, and the crudest methods of securing death. And we offer no apologies.

Vocabulary

Lethal—(adj) of certain death, deadly. **Unanimity**—(n) full agreement between a number of people. **Expediency**—(n) the quality of being suited to the end in view, useful for a particular purpose not necessarily fair or right. **Exigency**—(n) an urgent need or demand that must be urgently met. **Mitigate**—(v) to make something less harmful. **Weakling**—(n) a person who is physically not strong. **Moot**—(adj) open to argument or debate, of no legal significance. **Cumbersome**—(adj) large and heavy, difficult to carry. **Pragmatic**—(adj) being practical and sensible rather than having fixed ideas or theories. **Providence**—(n) God or a force that some people believe controls our lives and the things that happen to us, usually in a way that protects us. **Innumerable**—(adj) too many to be counted, very many. **Barbarous**—(adj) extremely cruel and shocking.

□

66

Illiteracy—The Malaise that Afflicts India

Illiteracy is a malaise, an evil that needs to be defeated. The longer it lasts, the worse India will suffer. An illiterate person is the one who can neither read nor write. This inability to read and write is at the root of many problems that India faces today. A country's progress is hugely affected if its population is illiterate. A country's progress is directly proportional to the literacy of that country. To say that illiteracy is a curse in a modern society of this twenty-first century will hardly be an exaggeration. An illiterate person is unable to fully understand the values of life; and the benefits of developmental activities are not reaped by an illiterate person because of ignorance about such activities that can bring about a revolutionary change in his or her life. Inability to read and understand what is going on in the world around is a huge disadvantage in this modern world. Only a knowledgeable person—one who knows how to read and how to write—can appreciate the intricacies of things around that can contribute to his or her well-being. Literacy is therefore a must and it is only the first step towards settling into the **realm** of knowledge for which education is necessary. Literacy helps, but mere literacy does not help.

Though steps have been announced for providing the right to free and compulsory education, these will have to be implemented at the ground level with all **earnestness** and sincerity. It has no doubt been made mandatory for the state to provide children in the age group of 6 to 14 years not just free schooling but also quality education. It is important to see that this is implemented without exception. The picture right now is not very encouraging though. We still have schools in the open, in tents or under trees. In the absence of basic infrastructure, enactment of laws alone will not help.

Elementary education in most of the countries is the responsibility of the state. Most of these countries have implemented this without let or hindrance, for they have realised the importance of this investment. India has made a **belated** entry into this group insofar as the enactment of law is concerned. It has, however, not yet been able to match up to other countries with regard to building of infrastructure. Some of the key Asian countries where this law has been enacted have achieved near total literacy. These countries are Japan, Korea (South), Singapore and Hong Kong and some others like China, Mauritius and Malaysia are not far behind. India's position is not something to write home about. One of every three illiterate persons of the world is an Indian. This should shame us as a nation.

Things are beginning to brighten up on Indian horizon lately because of the initiatives taken by the governments. While in 1951 the literacy rate was a bare 18.33 per cent, it rose to 52.21 per cent in 1991 and stood at 64.84 per cent in 2001; and according to the provisional input the literacy rate has further risen to 74 per cent for male and 65 per cent for female in 2011. Census-related data have revealed that the highest illiteracy rate is among the agricultural labourers. Poverty is certainly one of the prime causes of illiteracy. The poor find it difficult to send their wards to schools. They are usually in dire need of **augmenting** family income by engaging their wards in various works. Sending them to schools means shortage of working hands. They prefer to send their children to workplaces instead. They are employed both in organized and unorganized sectors. Incidence of school drop-outs is the highest in the rural areas chiefly because governments' monitoring mechanism is **inadequate** in rural areas. Mid-day meal for the school children helped improve attendance in schools, but they also became a **dampener** lately because of the quality of food served in schools. Many parents withdrew their wards from schools because a large number of schools are found to have purveyed **spurious** foods that caused death and other ailments. This is criminal and effective steps must be taken to curb this and to improve attendance rate. Several provincial governments have initiated steps to give incentives to students. It is hoped these **sops** will really help. However, quality continues to be a casualty in a large number of government-owned schools. If our aim is to educate our young ones, the emphasis must be given to quality.

Prior to 1976, education was the responsibility of the states. But as their resources were **jejune**, the programme suffered. However, after effecting necessary amendment in the Constitution, the Union Government has assumed larger responsibility. National Policy on Education was formulated together with Programme of Action. These policies brought about the much-needed uniformity in education which helped make Adult Education Programme a mass movement. The policy also laid special thrust of the education of girls. *Navodaya Vidyalayas* in each district was the result of these initiatives. Sarva Shikasha Abhiyaan (SSA)—education for all—was launched in 2001 and it covers the entire country. The idea is to impart quality elementary education to all children in the age group of 6 to 14. The stress is also given on opening of schools in the areas where there are no schools and to improve the existing infrastructure of schools. Emphasis is also laid on providing teachers, to equip all schools with computers to make rural children computer literate. Likewise, the aim of the National Literacy Mission is to impart functional literacy to the unlettered in the age group of 15-35. This is an important tool to wipe out illiteracy from the country. This programme has subsequently been upgraded to *Sakshar Bharat* with focus shifting on female. Female literacy is of utmost importance as she plays the most important role in shaping the life of her children. Empowerment of women is the underlying philosophy of this scheme and the target of the government is to impart functional literacy to 70 million in the age group of 15 and beyond. Budgetary allocations too have been enhanced. Out of a total outlay of ₹ 1,300 crore in the financial year 2011-12 for adult education, a substantial amount of ₹ 1,167 crore has been allocated to *Sakshar Bharat* scheme. Though there is need to pump in more money in this area.

While these schemes may take time to yield desired results, the important thing is the realisation at all levels that literacy is an important tool in the hands of people with which they can tackle the problem of poverty and various other ills plaguing the society today. This realisation has **dawned** not only on the governments but also on the people themselves. Literacy and more importantly education is seen as an investment and people are willing to invest. Governments have a very special role to play as it is they that will have to provide infrastructure and quality teaching facilities. Without quality there is no possibility of gain. If there is a vast multitude of people in the formative years of their life hankering after knowledge, there is also a large population of knowledgeable people in the later years of their life who have both time and inclination to impart quality. Important thing is to give them outlets where they can deliver their knowledge and expertise to those willing to take. Illiteracy will then be a matter of the past.

Vocabulary

Realm—(n) a domain in which something is dominant, kingdom, land, region. **Earnestness**—(n) an earnest and sincere feeling, serious-mindedness. **Belated**—(adj) after the expected or usual time, delayed. **Augment**—(v) enlarge or increase. **Inadequate**—(adj) not sufficient to meet a need. **Dampener**—(n) a device that dampens or moistens something. **Spurious**—(adj) plausible but false, intended to decieve, unauthentic. **Sop**—(n) a concession given to mollify or placate, a piece of solid food for dipping in a liquid. **Jejune**—(adj) lacking in nutritive value, lacking interest, significance or impact, insubstantial. **Dawn**—(n) the first light of day, the earliest period. (v) to become clear, apparent or enter one's consciousness or emotions, to appear or develop, to become light.

□

67

History of the Origin of Indian Literature

When unfurling the pages of history on Indian literature to trace its origin, the first thing that comes to view is the Vedic literature, primarily the four Vedas, the Brahmanas and the Upanishads. In their literary aspects, some of these scriptures are of high merit. The hymns of Rig Veda—1028 of them—are the work of many authors and they show variation in style and merit. The real history of Indian literature would invariably begin with the great epics of the *Mahabharata* and the *Ramayana* which give clear evidence of their origin as martial legends. These are basically martial **ballads** into the hands of the priesthood who, in the process of transmitting them, altered their superficial character, and **interpolated** passages on **theology**, morals and statecraft to suit their own design of propagating religious sentiments and beliefs or to court the favours of their lordships.

Of the two epics, the *Mahabharata* with over 90,000 stanzas is perhaps the longest single poem in the world's literature. The authorship is attributed to Vyasa. The poem tells of a great civil war in the kingdom of the Kurus. The style of the *Mahabharata* is direct and vivid. The characters are delineated in very simple outline with an individuality that makes them real personages.

The second epic the *Ramayana* is rather different in style and content. In size, it's a little over one quarter of the *Mahabharata*. Of the seven books or chapters, the first and the last appear to be later additions. The poems are brief and mostly **didactic**. The style of this epic betrays kinship with the classical Sanskrit poetry. The traditional author of the epic was Valmiki. The style of the *Ramayana* is less rugged than that of the *Mahabharata*. While the first of the two contains occasional grammatical and prosodical errors, the other contains almost none. The *Ramayana* is a work of greater art, but less vigour. It contains many dramatic passages and presents a beautiful descriptive writing. This is lacking in the *Mahabharata*.

The earliest surviving Sanskrit poetry is that of the Buddhist poet Asvaghosa who created a metrical life of the Buddha (*Buddhacarita*) in a simple classical style. The earliest example of courtly Sanskrit prose in Indian literature can be traced to the *Girnar Inscriptions* of Rudradaman dated A.D. 150. But the classical Sanskrit literature has not quite impressed the Western world though Goethe was delighted with Kalidas. Sanskrit literature taken as a whole has been considered artificial, over-ornate, lacking in true feelings, or even an example of wasted and **perverted** ingenuity. It is said Indians themselves were not quite satisfied with it.

The main ingredients of the Indian poet were love, nature, **panegyric**, moralising and storytelling. Religious subjects in the sense of legends of the gods are common enough, but deep religious feeling is generally missing in courtly literature. A few like Bhartrhari wrote occasionally on religious themes, yet classical Sanskrit poetry is predominantly secular, for gods have often been portrayed as enlarged human beings. But love was passionately physical as in *Kumarsambhavam*. The phenomena of the seasons, day and night, birds and beasts and flowers are employed to frame human emotions, or are personified as counterparts of the human subjects of the poet as in *Meghdootam*. Kalidas was particularly fond of including generalisations of a **sententious** or moral nature in his verses and this was regarded as a legitimate *alamkara* (adornment) of Sanskrit poetry. **Gnomic** verses were very popular.

Many other poets after Kalidasa wrote epics, but none so ably as he. Kumarada's *Janaki-harana* continued his tradition while Bharavi's *Kiratarauniya* is somewhat **florid**. Bhatti wrote *Bhattikavya,* a remarkable poem on Rama which contained some passages of real beauty. Magha was even more ingenious in his long poem *Sisupala-vadha.* After Magha narratives became progressively less important and longer poems often became mere displays of verbal ingenuity.

Caurapancasika (Fifty Stanzas of the Thief) by the Kashmiri Bilhana of the 11-12th century described the secret love of a bold housebreaker and a princess. These stanzas are full of 'intense emotion recollected without tranquillity'. It certainly qualifies as an important piece of Indian literature. *Gita Govinda* (Songs of the Cowherd) of Jaidev is a series of dramatic lyrics intended for singing. It describes the love of Krishna and Radha and the milkmaids. His lyrics are rhymed and they look forward to verse forms of vernacular literature.

Sanskrit prose literature mainly comprises a few narrative episodes in the Brahmanas, followed by the Pali Jatakas. In the Gupta period, however, this very prose acquired a style of **ornate** prose narrative called *kavya* which means poetry. One branch of this narrative literature was **fable**. These cheerful little stories whose characters are often talking animals had some influence on the literature of the West as well. The ***Panchtantra*** and Narayan's ***Hitopdesha*** belong to this category. The chief writers in this genre were Subandhu, Dandin and Bana and they all lived in the late sixth and the early seventh centuries.

The Pali literature was generally simpler in style, though it was considered largely prosaic and repetitive. But Pali language was much closer to the speech of the ordinary people than Sanskrit. Much of what Pali poetry is known for can be traced in *Theragatha* and *Therigatha.* Some of the verses are attributed to Amrapali, the beautiful courtesan of Vaishali who became a Buddhist nun. A fine example of Pali descriptive poetry is found in *Mahavamsa* which tells the tale of the capture of the capital of the Tamil invader Elara by Duttagamani. Prakrit literature mainly comprises the Prakrit scriptures of the Jainas. Their poetry is better than prose. Some of the important works are *Setubandha,* describing Rama's invasion of Ceylon,

Gaudavadha, describing the exploits of the king of Kanyakubja, and a drama by the 10th-century dramatist Rajasekhara. The most important literary work in Prakrit is *Saptasataka* of Hala.

The oldest Tamil literature goes back to the early Christian era. Tamil tradition speaks of literary academies. The earliest available literary works include Tamil grammar *Tolkappiyam* and 'Eight Anthologies' (*Ettugotai*). These are the greatest monument of ancient Tamil literature. The poetry of *Ettugotai* is little known outside the place of its origin and its language is so **archaic** that the modern educated Tamil cannot unfurl meaning without aid. One important feature of Tamil literature is that its style is much closer to folk literature than the style of courtly Sanskrit. Tamil poets wrote long poems which they called *kavya. Silappadigaram* is the earliest and greatest in this genre written by the grandson of the great Chola King Karikalan. This together with *Ramayanam* by Kamban is regarded as the national epics of the Tamil people. It needs to be said here that the early literatures of Canarese (Kannad), Telugu and Malayalam, though quite a force, are less important than those of Tamil and do not play big part in tracing the origin of Indian literature.

The literatures discussed above are the products of literary schools with formal conventions and long traditions which the modern writers and poets have extensively drawn upon to build on them.

Vocabulary

Ballad – (n) a narrative poem of popular origin, a narrative song with a recurrent refrain. **Interpolate** – (v) insert words into texts often falsifying it thereby. **Theology** – (n) the rational and systematic study of religion and its influences. **Didactic** – (adj) instructive (especially excessively) **Perverted** – (adj) having an intended meaning altered or misrepresented, showing or appealing to bizarre or deviant tastes (especially used of sexual behaviour). **Panegyric** – (n) formally expressing praise. **Gnomic** – (adj) relating to or containing gnomes: gnome is a legendary creature resembling a tiny old man, or one who lives in the depths of the earth and guards buried treasures. **Florid**—(adj) elaborately or excessively ornamented. rubicund, flamboyant. **Ornate**—(adj) highly or excessively decorated, flowery, marked by elaborate rhetoric. **Fable**—(n) a deliberately false or improbable account, a short moral story (often with animals as characters), a story about mythical or supernatural beings or events. **Archaic**—(adj) antiquated, primitive, or so old as seeming to belong to an earlier period.

□

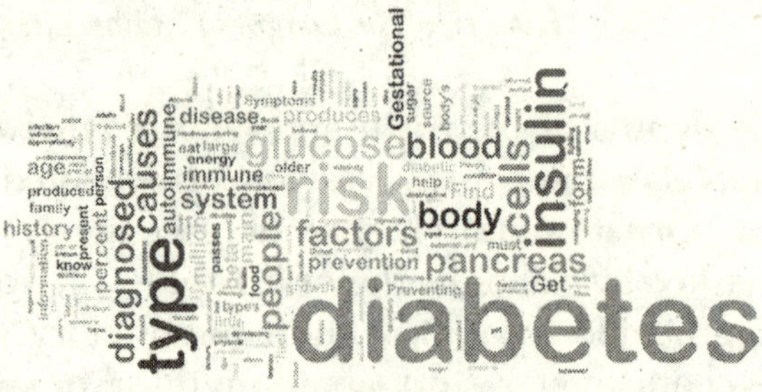

68

Diabetes—A Sure Killer

It is said that there are 382 million in the world who are afflicted with the deadly disease of diabetes of which 175 million are undiagnosed. That means almost one in every two is remains undiagnosed, untracked. Globally, 46% of 382 million people with diabetes are undiagnosed. In India, 50 to 60% of the estimated 63.1 million diabetics is undiagnosed.

What exactly is diabetes and why is there so much hue and cry about it in all parts of the world? Well, the food we eat gets broken down to a simple sugar called glucose. This glucose is transported to cells and organs by the blood. Now as things stand, glucose cannot, on its own, **penetrate** into cell walls. It needs the support of **insulin**. This is a **hormone** produced in the body by the **pancreas**. This carries glucose into the cells. When we eat, the sugar in the blood rises and that in turn triggers the pancreas to release insulin. It is this released insulin that is the essential part of the system. Therefore, we often hear of a diabetic patient getting shots of insulin.

Diabetes occurs when either pancreas fails to produce insulin or does not produce enough insulin or when the body cannot efficiently utilize the insulin so produced. The unutilized portion of insulin remains in the blood, which deprives the body of the energy it needs to function. This is the most critical element. If not detected in time, poorly or ill-controlled diabetes can cause serious complications which include heart disease, stroke, blindness, **amputations**, kidney disease, nerve damage, and even early death.

A patient had a wound in his right leg had been suffering this would for full fifteen years and did not know how to get rid of this nagging problem. Finding himself lying back in a transparent coffin-like **contraption** to breathe in pressured oxygen to heal his wound would have looked **bizarre** to him earlier. No matter what medicine was administered on the wounded part, it would simply not heal. He tried all systems of medicine, nothing worked. It was much later that he discovered he had diabetes and that was what was preventing the wound from healing. On being diagnosed with an infected diabetic ulcer, his wound was cleaned; it was treated by using a technique called vacuum-assisted closure (VAC) dressing and he was prescribed a dozen sittings of hyperbaric oxygen therapy (HOT). That is how a diabetic patient could actually end up in a pressurised chamber to inhale several lungs-full of pure oxygen.

But it is not necessary that all diabetic patients must undergo the same kind of treatment. If things are controlled in time, diabetes need not become the silent killer it has tended to become. Ask a medicine practitioner, he would advise you to:

- keep your haemoglobin A1C to less than 7%
- keep total cholesterol to below 200, artery-blocking LDL (bad cholesterol) to below 100, heart protecting cholesterol (good cholesterol) to over 45, triglycerides reading, which tend to be higher in diabetics, to below 150
- do not smoke
- keep your blood pressure to 120/80. The risk of heart disease and stroke is two to four times higher in diabetics
- exercise regularly
- eat fresh high-fibre, low calorie food.

Diabetes is usually categorized as Type 1 and Type 2. When a person's own immune system attacks and destroys the cells in the pancreas that produce insulin, decrease it and finally stop its production completely it is called Type 1. When the body cannot utilize the produced insulin efficiently, Type 2 diabetes is said to have occurred. It is also called adult onset diabetes.

What actually happens is—in a person with insulin-resistance, the glucose remains in the blood and forces the pancreas to overwork to produce more insulin, finally wearing it out.

One in every twenty people with diabetes has foot problems. Nerve damage is so severe that it causes **numbness,** burning sensation or pain severe enough to keep you awake at night. While ulcers are rare, more than 50% of the diabetic patients have nerve damage with symptoms of numbness, pain or weakness in hands, feet and legs. If not detected and treated in time, the complications begin to multiply. For many the first inkling of the trouble is the **tingling** in the feet or acute weight loss. By then some damage is already done and it leads to complications such as heart disease, stroke, blindness, amputations, kidney disease, nerve damage, and early death. Diabetic foot, the doctors say, is the leading cause of hospitalisation among people with diabetes. "About 15% of India's total diabetic population develops foot ulcers, which leads to approximately 45,000 lower limb amputations each year," said the Director of Narayana Institute of Vascular Sciences. He further said that "amputations and complications are preventable with appropriate diagnosis and management at the right stage".

The important thing is to recognise the **enormity** of the problem and initiate steps to check its spread. There is no reason to give a free run to this silent killer when there are ways and means of tackling them. Diabetes, the experts say, can certainly be managed, with most people leading a productive life decades after diagnosis. Medicines can certainly help; lifestyle modifications too can play an important role in tackling the problem to a great extent. Weight loss, exercising and eating healthy can elongate life span. Awareness is the key.

Vocabulary

Penetrate—(v) pass into or through, often by overcoming resistance. **Insulin**—(n) a chemical substance produced in the body that controls the amount of sugar in the blood. **Hormone**—(n) endocrine, internal secretion. **Pancreas**—(n) a large elongated endocrine gland located behind the stomach, secretes pancreatic juice and insulin. **Amputations**—(n) a surgical removal of all or part of a limb. **Contraption**—(n) a device or control that is very useful for a particular job. **Bizarre**—(adj) conspicuously or grossly unconventional or unusual, freakish, eccentric, outlandish. **Numbness**—(n) partial or total lack of sensation in some part of the body, a symptom of nerve damage or dysfunction. **Tingling**—(n) a somatic sensation as from many tiny prickles. (adj) exciting by touching lightly so as to cause laughter or twitching movements. **Enormity**—(n) great importance, scope or extent.

□

69
The Indian National Flag

National flag of a country is its national symbol. It identifies a nation; it gives the nation its exclusivity and a citizen of that nation takes pride in his or her national symbol, national identity and national entity through the national flag. So the paramountcy of the national flag is unquestionable. According to Mahatma Gandhi, it is the bounden duty of every Indian, irrespective of which religious belief he or she subscribed to, 'to recognise a common flag to live and to die for'.

The Constituent Assembly which met in 1946 for the first time adopted the national flag on 21st July, 1947. When in 1947 India gained freedom from the British, a committee headed by Dr. Rajendra Prasad decided to adopt the Congress flag as the national flag of India with a few modifications. With this in mind the flag of 1931 was adopted as the national flag of India, but the spinning wheel (charkha) in the middle was replaced with Ashok Chakra. Thus, the Indian national flag was born. It is a horizontal tricolor in equal proportion of deep saffron on top, white in the middle and deep green at the rock bottom. The ratio of the width to the length of the flag is 2:3. The saffron colour on the top stands for courage, sacrifice, and the spirit of **renunciation**; the white in the middle stands for truth and purity, and the green at the bottom represents faith, **fertility** and righteousness. At the centre of the white band there is a wheel in navy blue colour that indicates the *dharma chakra* (the wheel of law). The wheel has twenty-four spokes. The Indian national flag was designed by Pingali Venkayya as a symbol of freedom. Nehru called it a "flag not only of freedom for ourselves (sic), but a symbol of freedom to all people".

The Indian national flag represents India's long struggle for freedom and it is a national treasure besides signifying India as an independent republic. It was the national flag of the Dominion of India from 15th August, 1947 to 26th January, 1950. Thereafter, it became the national flag of the Indian Republic.

The history of Indian flag dates back to 1904 when the first Indian flag came into being. It was made by Sister Nivedita, an Irish disciple of Swami Vivekananda. It was coloured red and yellow and in the middle of it 'Vande Mataram' was inscribed in Bengali. The red stood for struggle and yellow for victory. The flag contained a symbol of 'vajra', the weapon of God Indra, and a white lotus in the middle. While 'vajra' stood for strength, lotus stood for purity. Another flag was designed in 1906. It was a tricolour with three equal strips of blue (top), yellow (middle) and red (top). The blue strip had eight stars of slightly different shapes. The yellow strip had 'Vande Mataram' written in Devnagari and the red strip had two symbols: the first one was the sun and the second one had a star and a crescent near the fly. There was yet another flag designed the same year which was often known as 'Calcutta Flag' or 'Lotus Flag', as it had eight open lotuses on it and was believed to have been designed by two Bengali gentlemen by the name of Sukumar Mitra and Sachindra Prasad Bose and was hoisted by Sir Surendra Nath Banerjee on 7th August, 1906 at Parsi Bagan Square in Calcutta to register protest against partition of Bengal. The day was celebrated as 'protest day'. Yet another flag surfaced in 1907 which was slightly different from the one discussed above. The same year India had yet another flag known as Madam Bhikaiji Rustom Cama's flag. The flag was collectively designed by Madam Cama, Veer Savarkar and Shyamji Krishna Verma. It was hoisted by Madam Cama on 22nd August, 1907 at Stuttgart in Germany. This was the first time that an Indian flag was hoisted in a foreign country. It is also referred to as 'Berlin Committee Flag'. The flag consisted of three colours—the topmost being green followed by golden saffron in the middle and the red colour at the bottom. It had 'Vande Mataram' inscribed in the middle.

In 1916, Pingali Venkayya designed a flag and sought the approval of Mahatma Gandhi. Gandhi advised him to incorporate *charkha* in the middle to symbolise economic regeneration of India. Bal Gangadhar Tilak adopted a new flag in 1917. This flag had Union Jack at the top. The rest of the flag contained five red and four blue strips. It had seven stars on it in the shape of 'saptarishi'. 1921 saw a new flag designed at the instance of Mahatma Gandhi, who wanted a flag that included all communities in it. It had three colours with white on the top followed by green in the middle and red at the bottom. The pattern of this flag was based on the Irish flag. The colour interpretation of this flag went like this: the white represented the minority communities of India while green represented Muslims and the red represented the Hindu and Sikh communities. But this colour interpretation was not liked by many. So, in 1931, a new flag was designed by Pingali Venkayya with the spinning wheel in the middle. This flag was approved by the Congress Committee in 1931 and was adopted as the official flag of the committee. This very flag was adopted, with modifications, in 1947 after India gained freedom. *Charkha* was removed and in its place was put Ashok Chakra and, thus, Indian flag came into being. The *Chakra* symbolises the power of the state governed by the principle of Righteousness or *Dharma,* the **primaeval** system of justice in India. This has been the bedrock not just of governance, but that of the socio-politico-economic edifice itself. The wheel also denotes motion which is symbolic of life. There is life in movement and death in **stagnation**. Wheel stands for dynamism of a peaceful change. The Indian national flag symbolises all of these; and, therefore, it becomes the moral duty of all Indians to respect and honour the flag. There is a Flag Code in force. This code has been revised after fifty-two years and it now enables the citizens of India to fly the national flag over their homes, offices and factories on any day. But certain basic rules have to be conformed to while flying the flag. There are some dos and don'ts that need to be kept in mind.

The Dos

The national flag may be hoisted in educational institutions under an oath of allegiance (included in the flag hoisting manual for schools).

A member of public, a private organisation or an educational institution may hoist/display the national flag on all days and occasions, ceremonial or otherwise consistent with the dignity and honour of the flag.

The new revised code accepts the right of all citizens to fly the flag on their premises.

The Don'ts

The flag cannot be used for communal purposes, drapery or clothes. It should be flown only between sunrise and sunset irrespective of weather.

The flag must not be intentionally allowed to touch the ground or the floor or trail in water. It cannot be draped over the hood, top and sides or back of vehicles, trains, boats or aircraft.

No other flag or bunting must ever be placed higher than the national flag. No object, including flowers or garlands or emblems can be placed on or above the flag. The tricolour cannot be used as a **festoon, rosette** or bunting.

There is a provision in the Flag Code for putting flower petals inside the national tricolour before it is unfurled on special occasions like Republic Day or Independence Day. This provision was incorporated on 24th January, 1997. Our national flag is our national pride and it is a citizen's bounden duty to uphold the dignity of our national flag at any cost.

Vocabulary

Renunciation – (n) an act of rejecting or disowning something or somebody. **Fertility** – (n) the state of being fertile. **Stagnation** – (n) the state of being stagnant, of not developing, not growing, of having come to a stand-still position. **Festoon** – (n) a curtain of fabric draped and bound at intervals to form graceful curves. **Rosette** – (n) a round decoration made of ribbon, rose window.

□

70
Poverty Alleviation

One of the key objectives of the Independent India was to build a prosperous, democratic and progressive nation, and to create social, economic and political institutions which will ensure justice and fullness of life to every man and woman. These objectives are the part of the Constitution of India wherein the Directive Principles direct that the state shall **strive** to promote a social order in which justice, social, economic and political, shall inform all the institutions of the national life and in particular shall ensure that the citizens, men and women equally, have the right to an **adequate** means of livelihood. After six decades of our independence, we can ask ourselves as to what has been the extent of achievement on these avowed objectives.

There is no denying that India has made significant progress in various social and economic spheres during the last sixty-six years. We can justifiably claim to have got the largest pool of scientific manpower in the world. We can also claim to have got a **robust** and **resilient** agriculture economy with self-sufficiency in food production. We can also claim to have built a diversified industrial and service structure with a large pool of skilled manpower and ample entrepreneurial capabilities.

But country's record in reducing poverty is not that encouraging. The performance on this front does not correspond with the achievements made in other spheres. We were one of the poorest countries in the world at the time of our independence. The situation has not greatly altered. A disturbingly large **chunk** of population continues to live below the poverty line. Poverty continues to remain a major challenge for India.

The question that is upper-most in everyone's mind is—who are the poor? Officially speaking, a person who does not get the minimum required calories per day to keep the body and soul together is poor. The minimum food requirement is 2,400 calories per capita per day in rural areas and 2,100 calories in the urban centres. The Planning Commission in 1993 declared that families living in rural areas whose annual family incomes were less than ₹ 11,000 at 1991-92 prices were below the poverty line. In order to get the minimum food to meet the calories required, a family of five will need an income of ₹ 1,150 (rural) or ₹ 1,300 (urban) at that price level. Although there is no **unanimity** on this, it is generally agreed that agriculture and forest labourers, small and marginal farmers, village artisans, non-farm manual labourers and workers in then unorganised sectors in urban centres are poor. On an average, agriculture labourers get between ₹ 15 and ₹ 40 per day. This too varies from season to season and area to area. On an average, a male worker finds work for 230 days in a year. On occasions, the workers are forced to sell their **limbs** to survive. On occasions, they borrow money from landlords or moneylenders to meet their day-to-day requirements. In the process, they end up being bonded labourers for years on end. According to an estimate, there are 2.6 million bonded labourers in India. Usually, the small and marginal farmers migrate to other states for greener **pasture**. There are about two million inter-state migrant workers occupied in agriculture and non-agriculture activities such as brick-kilns, construction works, etc. They are usually employed through third parties and, therefore, do not get the **stipulated** wages. Needless to say, they do not get other privileges prescribed by the government as well.

Low calories—when poverty is multi-dimensional—do not wholly explain the nature of poverty. Generally, the poor have larger family. For them larger family is a necessity as more hands mean more income, though it also means more mouths to feed. A child is seen as a social security for old age. In India, there are more than 20 million child labourers. The poor are not only badly off, they are equally **vulnerable** to diseases who perennially suffer from malnutrition. The living conditions are **deplorable**. This is the situation after six decades of independence and planning.

India has followed the path of capitalist economic development with equity and justice. The central objective of planning in India is to raise the standard of living of the people and to open to them opportunities for richer and more varied life. Accordingly, removal of poverty has remained one of the chief concerns of the state. Various measures have been taken by the state to attack poverty. These measures include structural transformation in the form of land reforms and distribution of surplus land. They also include some remedial and protective measures with the enactment of laws with respect to minimum wages, contract labour, inter-state migrant workmen, child labour, bonded labour, and equal remuneration. Laws have indeed been enacted, but whether they also delivered where it mattered the most is the moot point. Then there are welfare measures by way of providing employment for which special thrust is given on area or group development, self-employment, and wage employment.

The question that should concern us today is—what should be our response to the new market oriented economic policy that the country has adopted for itself? What will happen to the poor? Even those who **espouse** the cause of economic liberalisation concede that disparity of wages, income and wealth is a 'necessary part of the transition'. They also concede that increased inequality may give rise to poverty 'in the short run' (World Bank Report 1996). But the question is—how 'short' will be the 'short run' and for how long will the transition period be in the state of transition or what will be its duration? 'Amidst the **euphoria** over growth and globalisation, poverty alleviation has been displaced from the priority agenda. Safety nets, though talked about, are yet to be worked out effectively.

In this situation, can the political system contend with the widespread dissatisfaction and rising aspirations of the masses?'

Vocabulary

Strive–(v) to attempt by employing effort, to exert much effort or energy. **Adequate**–(adj) enough. **Robust**–(adj) sturdy and strong in form, constitution or construction. **Resilient**–(adj) recovering readily from adversity, bouncy, elastic or springy. **Chunk**–(n) a substantial amount, a compact mass. **Unanimity**–(n) full agreement between a large number of people, consensus. **Limbs**–(n) arms, branches. **Pasture**–(n) a field covered with grass or herbage suitable for grazing by livestock. **Stipulate**–(v) to specify as a condition. **Vulnerable**–(adj) susceptible to attack, criticism, persuasion or temptation, or capable of being wounded or hurt. **Deplorable**–(adj) bad, unfortunate or of very poor quality or condition. **Euphoria**–(n) a feeling of great elation. **Espouse**–(v) to choose and follow, as of theories, ideas, policies, strategies or plans; adopt, embrace, follow, marry.

□

71

Bharat Ratna—The Highest Civilian Award

Bharat Ratna is the highest civilian award or honour given for exceptional service towards the advancement of Art, Literature and Science, and in recognition of public service of the highest order. It is generally conferred on 23rd January each year. The award was instituted by the President of India on 2nd January, 1954 with the conferring of this honour on Dr. Chandrashekhar Venkat Raman for his contribution to science and engineering, Chakravarthy Rajagopalachari and Dr. S. Radhakrishnan for their contribution to public affairs. Coincidentally, all three are from Tamil Nadu. There are in all forty-three Bharat Ratna recipients, with Sachin Tendulkar and Dr. C.N.R. Rao being the latest entrants. While Sachin has been honoured for his contribution to sports of cricket, Dr. Rao has been honoured for his contribution to science. Sports did not figure in the list of those who could be honoured with this highest civilian award as his contribution did not fall within the ambit of public service of the highest order. The medallion is made of bronze and shaped like a peepal (banyan) leaf. The ribbon is white. A replica with the sun with radiating rays can be seen on the **obverse** of the medallion with the words 'Bharat Ratna' inscribed beneath it. The national emblem is embossed on the reverse with the national motto 'Satyameva Jayate'.

Until not long ago, Bharat Ratna came as a surprise to its recipients and a joy to the nation. It's clearly not the same now. People these days **canvass** for their icons. They petition, they lobby for their cause, whereupon the state responds, sometimes with favour and sometimes with disfavour. Besides, the state takes its own time, weighs its options, pros and cons and the possible political mileage that can be derived from such honours. Since the government has its own calculations, it chooses its hour.

If we analyse the forty-three Bharat Ratnas given since its introduction in 1954, it can easily be demonstrated that those in the era of Nehru were obvious choices. They were all nationally respected and nationally acclaimed as true Bharat Ratnas: the statesman C. Rajagopalachari, the philosopher Sarvapalli Radhakrishnan, the physicist Dr. C.V. Raman, the visionary engineer M. Visvesvaraya, the social reformer D.K. Karve, the educationist Dr. Zakir Hussain, the Sanskrit scholar P.V. Kane, the sagacious chief minister of UP, G.B. Pant, the medical legend and chief minister of West Bengal, Dr. B.C. Roy, the saintly patriot, Purushottam Das Tandon. If Sardar Patel had not died before the institution of this award and if Maulana Azad had not declined to accept the award in his life time, both of them would have been honoured in the inaugural year itself. They were awarded posthumously. The happiness is for the giver, not for the receiver, when posthumously awarded. Why Dr. B.R. Ambedkar was not given the award in his life time is difficult to understand and why this was not conferred on JP in his life time is equally **baffling**, though it must be said JP would have declined it anyway. Belated attempts were made to posthumously award Netaji Subhash Chandra Bose. Taking it as an **affront**, this was declined by his near ones. Why J.P. Kriplani and Narendra Deva were left out is difficult to understand. They should have been some of the earliest recipients of Bharat Ratna, for Ratnas they are, award or no award.

There was then no system of awarding Bharat Ratna posthumously. This practice began in 1966 to confer this honour on Lal Bahadur Shastri. In fact, it was decided in his life time to confer this highest civilian award on him and the President Dr. Radhakrishnan was merely waiting for his return from

Tashkent where he breathed his last. His was not a conventional posthumous award. It was decided in his life time. But as the fate would have it, it was conferred posthumously.

After **conferment** of Bharat Ratna on Satyajit Ray in 1992 immediately after his death, the matter was taken to the Supreme Court as it was thought that this highest civilian Padma award had gone **astray**. In pursuance of the Supreme Court's judgement, the government constituted a High Level Review Committee chaired by the Vice-President of India, to go into the guidelines for Padma Awards and certain other aspects. The institution of these awards was revived in 1997 after the Review Committee submitted its report in November 1996 which the government accepted.

The recipients of Bharat Ratna are offered a **pendent** in the shape of banyan leaf. Banyan symbolises **renunciation**. In today's world the principle of the Great Renunciate may not apply, but those rollicking in **pelf** can certainly not be even remotely associated with renunciation of any kind. Imagine the kind of money Sachin Tendulkar has made by playing cricket! Sheer size of his wealth should have put him aside, but the government chose to rework the eligibility criteria to 'accommodate' him as Bharat Ratna. This was uncalled for. He would still be regarded as jewel of India. Making him Bharat Ratna to be placed alongside the peers who received this award simply does not go down well. This shows design and that is not good. This took away some of the **glitter** from Tendulkar's achievement. Not his fault, it is the government of the day that is to blame for the mess it created.

The list contains forty-three names in all. There can never be any unanimity about the choices made. Some heart burning can never be ruled out and we must learn to live with it. But then, there are a few names that do raise questions, some very disturbing ones. Viewed with a degree of neutrality, it would really be difficult to place Rajiv Gandhi in the list, his contribution being what it was. His assassination seems to have greatly influenced a decision in his favour.

Every Bodhi tree and every leaf of pipal reminds us of the Tathagat's teaching; it stands for a certain detachment, a certain freedom from worldliness, of renunciation. A true Bharat Ratna cannot be seen running for money. The highest civilian award must set the highest standard for others to emulate.

Vocabulary

Obverse—(n) the more conspicuous of two alternatives, cases or sides. **Canvass**—(v) to get the opinion of others, to solicit support for a cause or for vote. **Baffling**—(adj) making great mental demands, hard to comprehend, solve or believe. **Affront**—(n) a deliberately offensive act or something producing the effect of deliberate disrespect. **Conferment**—(n) the act of conferring an honour or present a gift, bestowal, bestowment, conferral. **Astray**—(adv) away from the right path or direction, far from the intended target, wide. **Pendent**—(adj) held from above, (n) an adornment that hangs from a piece of jewellery, chandelier, pendant. **Renunciation**—(n) rejecting, disowning or disclaiming as invalid. **Pelf**—(n) inform term for money. **Glitter**—(n) the quality of shining with a bright reflected light, the occurrence of a small flash or spark; (v) be shiny, as if wet.

□

72

Human Rights

The United Nation's Charter re-affirmed its faith in 'fundamental human rights, in the dignity and worth of the human person, in the equal rights and of men and women'. The purpose is to promote respect for human rights and fundamental freedoms for all without any distinction. The promotion of human rights has to be seen as an end to be pursued in its own right and not as incidental to the promotion of any other purpose. Human rights are inherent in our nature and without which we cannot live as human beings. This means there are some rights of men and women that cannot be violated even by the state. This puts limits on the powers of the state over the individual. Human rights are those minimal rights that every individual must have by virtue of being a member of the human family irrespective of other considerations. They are 'inalienable rights of men', and a state that violates them in its laws and its actions breaches one of the basic **prerequisites** of civil co-existence between states and, thus, it can be made accountable.

A number of international instruments have come up that not only codify human rights but also draw up measures for their implementation. Some of such instruments are International Covenant on Economic, Social and Cultural Rights, International Covenant on Civil and Political Rights and Optional Protocol to the Civil Covenant. India has played an important role in the drafting of the Universal Declaration of Human Rights and many of the articles are incorporated in the Constitution in the form of fundamental rights and directive principles. But while it ratified the **covenants** on civil and political rights, India had reservations on Optional Protocol which aimed at abolishing death penalty and chose not to **ratify** the convention on the Rights of Migrant Workers.

While human rights are classified into various categories traditionally the distinction has been between civil and political rights on the one hand and economic, social and cultural rights on the other. States may prioritise them according to what suits them the best, all categories are interdependent and indivisible. Poverty is one of the most important causes of the violation of human rights, especially in the developing countries such as India. In one of the landmark judgements, the Supreme Court expanded the scope of Article 21 of the Constitution by incorporating the right to food, clothing and shelter in the term of 'life'. Right to life is not limited only to bodily life. It goes well beyond that to include the right to live with dignity and that all that goes with it.

Solidarity right is another human right which includes the right to economic, political, social and cultural self-determination, the right to economic and social development, right to participate in and benefit from the common **heritage** of mankind, right to peace, to a healthy and balanced environment and the right to human disaster relief. These rights are basically collective in nature and can be realized through international cooperation as these rights are the consequence of globalisation.

Human rights can transform the functioning of a democracy to make it more participative in nature by constantly challenging the vested interests who have divided the society between 'haves' and 'have-nots'. In a country as populous as India with a large number of illiterates, it is always difficult to enforce human rights. The problem is further compounded because of plural and feudal nature of society. Severe discrimination and exploitation of those belonging to the lower **strata** of society still prevail.

Some of the most vulnerable sections of Indian society are women and children. Protecting their human rights is of dire necessity. Violations of human rights also arise out of political problems and the proactive role the states play. The Central Government brought forth the Protection of Human Rights Act, 1993 and established National Human Rights Commission (NHRC) as a statutory body. The Commission has taken up programmes that range from civil rights protection, the police, prisons and a host of statutes impinging on civil rights to the spread of primary education, abolition of child labour, child prostitution, and arsenic contamination of water and nutritional problems of children. The issue of **appalling** conditions in Indian jails has been seriously addressed by NHRC. It has prepared a Model Prison Bill to address this problem, but inhuman conditions continue to prevail in most jails of the country as the government has chosen not to bring in legislation. Instances of arbitrary arrests and detention are frequent in various states of India despite assurances of safeguards to protect detainees during arrest and detention.

But, it is the child-related abuses and violations that are a **blot** on the record of human rights in the country. This is **intrinsic** in our society. Child labour is one of the pressing issues in India. Allied to this is the problem of bonded child labour. This refers to the phenomenon of children working in conditions of servitude to pay off debts of their parents and according to an estimate there are not less than fifteen million children forced to work in appalling and inhuman conditions. The government has **abjectly** failed to enforce the Child Labour Act and the Bonded Labour Act. Child prostitution is a huge problem in India.

Education, most believe, is the solution to many of the problems of human rights. UN has assigned a special role to education and has formulated guidelines for human rights education. Such education must aim at **fostering** an attitude of tolerance, respect and solidarity inherent in human rights, provide knowledge of its national and international dimensions and develop awareness among individuals of the ways of translating them into social and political realities. In India where illiteracy abounds, education on human rights will be possible only after the literacy level is raised. The Supreme Court drew the attention of the state to the Article 45 of the Constitution which confers an enforceable fundamental right to education on all children up to the age of 14. The government has put in place the Right to Education Act. But infrastructure to meet this challenge is yet to be put in place.

Human rights teaching will have to be based on the values and **ethos** of society so that it is effective. We need to **allay** the **fallacious** impression that it is a Western concept. Since time immemorial, this has been familiar in India's civilisation centuries before the west had come to life. Human rights in various forms have been the cultural heritage of mankind. Human rights are about human dignity that needs to be upheld at all costs.

Vocabulary

Prerequisite – (n) an incidental benefit awarded for certain types of employment, exclusive rights, fringe benefits, perks, prerogatives. **Covenants** – (n) a formal agreement between two or more parties to perform or to not perform certain acts, a solemn agreement. **Ratify** – (v) approve and express assent, responsibility or obligation. **Heritage** – (n) practices that are handed down from the past by tradition, an attribute or immaterial possession that is inherited from ancestors. **Strata** – (n) plural form of 'stratum' which means one of several layers of material arranged one on top of another. it also refers to people of the same social, economic or education status. **Appalling** – (adj) causing consternation, something alarming and shocking or dismaying. **Blot** – (n) a blemish made by dirt. **Intrinsic** – (adj) belonging to a thing by its very nature. **Abjectly** – (adv) in a hopeless resigned manner. **Foster** – (v) promote the growth of, help develop, help grow. **Ethos** – (n) the distinctive spirit of a culture or of an era. **Allay** – (v) to calm or to lessen the intensity of, satisfy (thirst). **Fallacious** – (adj) intended to deceive, deceitful, fraudulent or unsound.

□

73
Sexual Harassment

The immediate provocation for highlighting the issue is invariably the incident wherein a junior level journalist was sexually assaulted at Tehelka, which is now in public domain. Even without this coming to light, sexual harassment has been a matter of concern. What exactly is this sexual harassment? The introduction to the Sexual Harassment of Women at the Workplace Act, 2013 says "sexual harassment results in violation of the fundamental rights of a woman to equality under articles 14 and 15 of the Constitution of India and her right to live with dignity under article 21 of the Constitution and right to practise any profession or to carry on any occupation, trade or business which includes a right to a safe environment free from sexual harassment". The protection against harassment and right to work with dignity are recognised human rights by international conventions and instruments such as Convention on the Elimination of all Forms of Discrimination against Women, which has been ratified by the Government of India in 1993.

There have been legal **luminaries** who have done **pioneering** work in establishing the prevention of sexual harassment at all workplaces. Naina Kapur is one such lawyer who helped frame and act as lead instructing counsel before the Supreme Court in 1997 in the famous Vishaka case. Accordingly, sexual harassment is a subjective experience. The point is, the behaviour is prohibited and therefore unacceptable. It is any kid of behaviour of a sexual nature that is inappropriate at the workplace. This can include **ogling**, objectionable gestures,

lewd jokes, showing offensive pictures or visuals, intruding into one's private space, personal comments on one's appearance or private life, stalking or even hitting on a woman at an office party. Personal questions or comments on one's marital status or private life, within a professional set-up can also be seen as sexual harassment. Sexual harassment at the workplace is often not **overt**. The offender often counts on getting away with inappropriate conduct and it is about the use and abuse of power. Circumstances described under the Act which would amount to sexual harassment include 'implied threat' or 'implied promise of preferential treatment'. Any kind of enticement or allurement can be implied threat or promise of preferential treatment. These can also be interpreted as an indirect comment with sexual undertones. If one says, 'you have a great **prospect** here...if only you keep me humoured....' This could well be called an implied threat or promise. All this could lead to a **hostile** workplace where one has no chance of progressing on the strength of one's merit or ability or where one may not get the right of equal opportunity at the workplace. Often, when such sexually implied overtures are unanswered with favour, a woman employee may well be excluded from important meetings and assignments or may be left to feel unwanted and unimportant. Persistent behaviour which isolates a woman employee creates a hostile place which can result in mental and emotional breakdown leading to adversely affecting her performance. If she is a good worker, this could cause a mental **trauma**. The case of the young journalist who recently quit Tehelka is a classic example of what sexual harassment could lead to.

It was argued in the Supreme Court in the Vishaka case that "it is the sexual part of harassment that creates the most discomfort, an unnecessary socially-conditioned **hurdle** when we are actually talking about women's constitutional equality at the workplace". Those espousing the cause of women's rights are clear in their mind that it is the responsibility of the organization to ensure that. According to the Act, every employer is required to constitute an internal Complaints Commission at each office or branch with 10 or more employees. The District Officer is required to constitute a Local Complaints Committee at each district, and if required at the block. Employers who fail to comply are liable to be punished with a fine up to ₹ 50,000. The US law is far more stringent. The US law stipulates that in **quid pro quo** cases of sexual harassment, an employer is always liable for a supervisor's or manager's harassment, if it results in a tangible employment action. The Tehelka case would certainly fall in this category.

The employer, courts aver, in order to defend itself must show that it exercised reasonable care to prevent and correct promptly any harassing behaviour, and that the employee unreasonably failed to take advantage of such opportunities provided by the employer. India's long awaited legislation against sexual harassment at the workplace, many argue, raises more questions than answers. The United Nations has recognised sexual harassment as a form of discrimination and violence against women. Under Vishaka judgement too, the need for a law against sexual harassment at the workplace was felt to ensure proper interpretation of the guarantee of gender equality. It is, however, not clear yet whether gender-based discrimination or sexist remarks are covered under this Act. Lawyers too are divided. Some say "sexual harassment is a form of gender-based discrimination, but all gender-based discrimination is not sexual harassment"; and yet some others say that "any other unwelcome physical, verbal or non-verbal conduct of sexual nature can be used to include sexist or gender-based comments" as more often than not they lead towards more serious offence. However, gender-based discrimination is not **explicit** in this Act, various interpretations notwithstanding. Internationally, workplace harassment includes both gender-based discrimination as well as sexual harassment for men and women. Therefore, while gender-based discrimination finds explicit mention in the US or European laws. And, perhaps rightly so! The cases of men being sexually harassed at workplace have never surfaced in India.

But having law in place is one thing and implementing it is quite the other as we saw in the Tehelka episode. One fondly hopes, men will shed some of their self-acquired importance and concede that women have an equal and inalienable right to live with dignity and honour and they are not subjected to sexual harassment off and on.

Vocabulary

Luminary – (n) a celebrity who is an inspiration to others. **Pioneer** – (n) someone who opens up a new line of research. (v) open up an area or prepare a way. **Ogle** – (v) to look at with amorous intentions. **Overt** – (adj) observable, not secret or hidden, open. **Prospect** – (n) the possibility of future success. **Hostile** – (adj) characterised by enmity or ill will. **Trauma** – (n) any physical damage caused to the body due to violence, an emotional wound or shock often having long-lasting effects. **Hurdle** – (n) an obstacle one is expected to overcome. **Quid Pro Quo** – (n) something for something, that which a person receives as return for something that person does or promises to do. **Explicit** – (adj) expressed, denotative.

□

74

Science Scenario in India

Immediately after receiving his Bharat Ratna, Prof. C.N.R. Rao, Scientific Advisor to the Prime Minister, issued a press statement that drew immediate attention of the whole country. He called politicians idiots who had persistently failed to attach due importance to science. Clarifying the statement later, he said that even though he had used the word, he did not quite mean that. His limited purpose was to show politician's indifference towards science-related matters, especially matters relating to providing funds for scientific activities that are, according to him and many others, crucial for India if India has to take its rightful place in the comity of nations. Prof. Rao himself provides the reason why. He said, "India has to change as a knowledge power particularly in science in the next few years. We do not find sufficient number of young leaders in science. Science must figure in our value system and medicinity must be avoided".

India has no choice as that is the only way, he says, India can become a great centre for technological innovation. And there is reason to believe India will become a major economic power in a few decades. Dr. Kalam had earmarked 2020 as the year by which time India would become a super power. Maybe it was this frustration Prof. Rao was giving air to when he **lambasted** the politicians for having ignored science.

What must have also frustrated him is the fact that we do not have educational institution in the top 50 or 100 in the world. The universities have decayed due to neglect, he believes.

Even the leading institutions are failing to deliver quality. In science and technology wings, there are just a few experts. There is a clear case of leadership crisis as we have failed to groom young leaders who could take the baton forward. The situation is alarming and calls for immediate repairs. Not only we have to take steps to **refurbish** our educational institutions, we have to **gird up** our loins to compete with the best in the world, particularly with our Asian competitors such as China and South Korea, who have taken tremendous strides. These neighbours of ours have outclassed us insofar as their output in the fields of scientific research, Ph.D etc. are concerned.

What we need to immediately aim at is not the quantity but the quality and that can be achieved only through elimination of mediocrity from educational and scientific institutions. Our contribution to world science at present is a mere 2.5% and only 0.5% or thereabout to the top 1% of scientific research. Our endeavour should be reach a level of 10% of the top 1% of the scientific research in the next few years. Needless to say, this can be achieved only if we drastically improve the quality and output of our scientific research. Towards that end, we must have large number of schools and colleges that are true fountain heads of knowledge capable of producing future leaders in science. Teachers and teaching should be the national mission of the nation in this decade. The leading institutions must take a lead in providing quality in schools and colleges.

The important thing is to encourage small science in the school and college laboratories. Big things emerge from small things. Small centres of excellence are vital for big leap forward. In our preoccupation with big agencies, small science has often been **relegated** to backyard. Outstanding individuals or groups can be groomed in small centres of excellence and they can be provided opportunities to work in important areas of science in the leading laboratories of the world. These young scientists could meet the **acute** manpower crisis that India faces today.

It is not that funding alone is an inhibiting factor. The absence of enabling and overall environment for innovation and creative work is a major factor stalling our movement upward. It is imperative to create congenial climate for the young minds to blossom. No doubt, the government has to play its part. But the private sector too has an important role to play to achieve this objective. It is absolutely necessary that the entire society works in **tandem** to eliminate mediocrity from every sphere of life to create an **ambience** where scholarship and science get their due share of recognition and respect. Bureaucracy too needs to be reined in as bureaucrats more often than the politicians play spoil sports. Prof. Rao would have bureaucracy altogether eliminated from the scheme of things. Why bureaucracy is considered a hindrance rather than as a facilitator is for the bureaucracy to **ponder** over, but there is no denying the fact that new ways of administering science have to be found. This may require changing the structures of our existing institutions as well as administrative and auditing practices. Anything that hinders the development of scientific temper must be done away with.

There are indeed many challenges and warning signals, there is no reason to believe why these cannot be successfully **surmounted**. There is distinct cause for hope that India will soon emerge to become a scientific hub in a not very distant future. All we need to do is to adopt the right strategies and provide necessary wherewithal for the pursuit of excellence in education and science. In order that science gets integrated with our value system, politicians, administrators and the society must develop love for science and take interest in its **propagation**.

India must prioritise scientific efforts to address the most pressing issues of the society. We must aim at making India a great knowledge power global leader in science, technology and innovate through judicious investment in education and science. And to top it all, India must not promote mediocrity in performance in any walk of life and must liberate science from the bureaucratic clutches.

Vocabulary:

Lambast – (v) beat with a cane, censure severely or angrily.

Refurbish – (v) to renovate, to freshen up or to make brighter and prettier. **Gird up** – (v) to prepare for a military adventure, to build up, to encircle, to fortify. **Relegate** – (v) assign to a lower position, to reduce in rank. **Acute** – (adj) extremely strong or sharply felt. **Tandem** – (n) an arrangement of two or more objects or persons behind one another. **Ambience** – (n) a particular environment or particular influence, atmosphere. **Ponder** – (v) to think deeply about a question or a subject over a period of time. **Surmount** – (v) to get over, to be on top of. **Propagation** – (n) the spreading of something into a new region.

□

75
A Growing Environmental Challenge

There is no contesting the fact that rapid urbanisation has stretched scarce resources. If cities, the concerned people believe, are to grow in a sustainable manner, urban governance systems will have to be streamlined and strengthened. The urgency is unmistakable as the urban share in India's population has steadily gone up from 17% in 1951 to 31% in 2011. There were only five cities in 1951 with more than a million people. Today we have more than 56 cities with more than ten million people each.

There is nothing unusual when there is transition from a rural-agrarian to an urban-industrial, urban-services led economy. This is an inevitable outcome of a growing economy. Urban settlements with high population density appropriate less land, facilitate a more efficient use of resources such as water and energy. They ensure greater **sustainability** and enhance the quality of life of people by offering better healthcare, education and other amenities that improve the quality of life. This results in greater productivity. Improved literacy and greater political awareness expectedly weaken the caste and other social barriers that tend to inhibit deepening of the roots of democracy.

Is it any wonder then that the top 100 Indian cities with 16% of the country's population consume a mere 0.26% of its geographical area while contributing a **whopping** 43% of its economic output! There is no denying that urban centres offer and provide better educational and healthcare facilities. But it is not all **hunky-dory** on this front because the way urban growth is planned and regulated in our country it raises **pertinent** and disturbing questions on its sustainability and its baneful effects on environment and the overall quality of life of its people.

Our cities are fast turning into concrete jungles. They are literally exploding with massive building construction activities attracting thousands of migrant workers from adjacent or even distant rural areas. The rich city dwellers hugely depend on domestic workers, small vendors, carpenters, electricians and so on. Strangely enough, the master plans that have been prepared for cities have no place for this auxiliary workforce. This has led to mushrooming of slums. One in every six city dwellers is a slum dweller in India today. He has no proper shelter, no food security, no access to potable water, no sanitation and toilet facilities. Needless to say, he often does not have the voting rights too. While poverty is not area specific, it is the urban poverty which is more ugly and demeaning. It is usually the urban poor who bears the brunt of environmental degradation.

However, instead of meeting this challenge head-on, the government seems shy of countenancing urban poverty. Thousands of beggars lining up the pavements were vainly tried to be shifted out of the city boundaries to present a glorious picture to the foreign delegates during the 2010 Commonwealth Games. This proved to be counterproductive.

Rapid urbanisation has taken a heavy toll on the dwindling resources. There is no city in the country today that can boast of having uninterrupted water supply. In most of such cities, water availability ranges from 1-6 hours a day. With the rising population, the least one could expect from the government is greater efficiency in water use and rehabilitation of local water bodies including ground water **aquifers**. Instead, the ever-expanding population is **obliterating** local water bodies and polluting water sources thus exerting enormous pressure on scarce water resources in the surrounding rural areas. At this rate, most cities in India are going to face a serious crisis in the coming days. According to an estimate, only 30% of the used water and most of the solid wastes in the cities are treated and the rest of it is allowed to spread out to ground and surface water sources.

It is not just that potable water has become scarce in cities. Clean air is equally scarce. Delhi is one of the most polluted cities of our country. Despite the court ordered use of CNG as a transport fuel, Delhi witnessed a thick envelop of smog last November. Experts described this smog as a 'toxic cocktail of poisonous gases'. Delhi thus enveloped reminded one of Beijing which too has become known from its smog and pollution. This seriously impairs the mental and physical health of people. A large number of cities of the world are afflicted with this problem caused by rapid urbanization and it is posing a serious environmental challenge.

If our urban centres have to grow in an environmentally **benign** and sustainable manner, the urban governance system will have to be streamlined and strengthened. We have to shed **myopic** approach for short-term solution and should instead aim for long-term solutions. We must re-orient ourselves to scientifically tackle urban waste disposal issues and must upgrade it without any further loss of time. The urban populace too needs to be encouraged to take part in government initiatives through empowered wings of local self-governments. The needs of the poor must no longer be overlooked; they should be accorded top priority.

Vocabulary

Sustainability—(n) the property of being sustainable. **Whopping**—(adj) very large. **Hunky-dory**—(adj) being satisfactory or in satisfactory condition. **Pertinent**—(adj) apposite, apt, to the point. **Aquifers**—(n) underground bed or layer yielding ground water for wells and springs, etc. **Obliterate**—(v) remove completely from memory or record, to do away completely without leaving a trace. **Benign**—(adj) kindness of disposition or manner, pleasant and beneficial in nature or influence. **Myopic**—(adj) short-sighted, lacking foresight or scope.

□

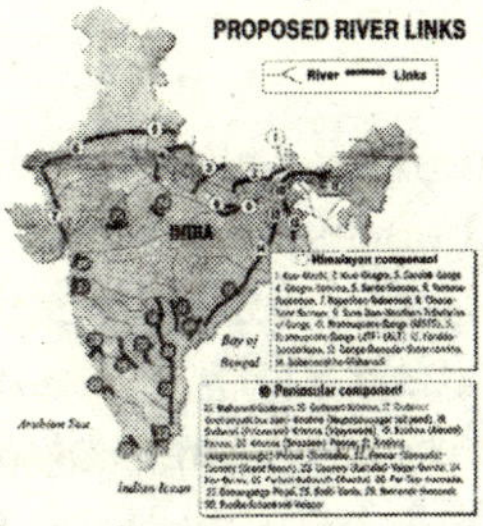

76

Interlinking of Rivers

The National Council of Applied Economic Research reported in 2008 that though India is a vast landmass, its large water resources are exhausting rapidly. Most of the water is from the perennial rivers such as from the Ganges, the Yamuna and the Brahmaputra, while the remainder comes from rainfall in the June-September period, most of which flows into the sea. Even as there are a series of large and small reservoirs and dams to **impound** much of this water, a rapidly-growing population and increasing urbanisation and industrialisation are eating into these resulting in a shortage of fresh water. Very few states have also had the vision to insist on rainwater harvesting mechanism to cater to the needs of the growing urban areas.

Monsoons are a time when those in the agriculture industry and in the political establishment look forward to renewed activities. Whether or not the water bodies will fill up is the question that is uppermost in their minds. This is particularly so in the southern parts of India. The climatic changes that have come about all over the globe have made it an annual event. This is **fraught** with uncertainty primarily because there are variations in rainfall patterns. The after-effects such as drought and flood have forced the policymakers to increasingly think about the necessity of inter-linking of rivers to ensure an equitable distribution of water throughout the year. The matter of inter-linking river (ILR) programme surfaced when the Supreme Court of India directed the Centre to constitute a special committee to oversee its implementation. There is not much progress on the matter as the policymakers are still not sure about the consequences.

National Commission for Integrated Water Resources Development Plan (NCIWRDP) estimated that India's water requirement will be in the range of 973-1180 billion cubic million (BCM) by 2050 when the population is likely to be in the range of 1.5 billion. The population is expected to stabilise by then. Though the country is richly endowed with land and water resources, shortage has begun to pinch. The large water resources are depleting fast and the impact is being felt all over the country and is, in some cases, rather critical. This calls for immediate steps to either replenish the depleting stock of water or find and an alternative solution. This is where the need for interlinking of rivers is felt.

The interlinking of rivers is aimed at linking different water-surplus rivers with water-deficient rivers so that the excess water from the surplus region is tapped. The benefits, in short, will be in the form of increased irrigation intensity, water availability for drinking and industrial purposes and for tackling drought and flood situations that keep recurring year after year.

According to the present estimate, annual food grain production is 200 million tones. The increasing population has pushed the need for more production. The average annual surface water flow available against this is 1,869 BCM. But due to topographical, hydrological, and other constraints, only about 690 BCM could be put to profitable use. The utilisable water resource of the country stands at 1,122 BCM. The average rainfall is estimated at 4,000 BCM out of which the average flow into the river system is 1,953 MCM. But the major part of it (80%) of the annual run off into rivers is during the rain months of June to September. Consequently, much of it remains unutilised apart from causing damage. Dams and tanks manage to store about 174 BCM while the on-going projects could store up 76 BCM in addition to 132 BCM identified as potential capacity.

The ILR programme has been planned at the intra- and inter-basin levels and it is expected to provide additional irrigation facility to about 35 million hectares of land which could **boost** power generation to 30,000 megawatt. Incidentally, the long-distance inter-basin transfer of water in not unknown to India. It has been in practice for quite some time. For example, we already have the Parambikulam Aliyar Project, the Kurnool-Cudappah Canal, and the Telugu-Ganga project in the southern states of India besides the Beas-Sutlej link and the Rajasthan canal in the northern parts of the country. Interlinking of rivers is a global phenomenon with the US, China and Australia heavily banking on this system.

The concept of inter-basin transfer of water was thought of as early as 1926 by Sir C.P. Ramaswamy Aiyar. The idea was to create a national water grid, transferring water from the Ganga and the Brahmaputra to central and southern India. Surveys were carried out by the National Water Development Agency (NWDA) set up in 1982 which identified 30 water links as it prepared feasibility reports for the links under National Perspective Plan (NPP). There were 14 Himalayan and 16 peninsular links. The objective was to contain floods and droughts, to **augment** income in rural areas with a special thrust on agriculture. The expectation was that the canals thus built would also boost waterways for navigation to reduce pressure on road/rail transport as also be cost-effective. It requires huge investment over a long period of time. The investment is thought to be necessary because a study by the World Health Organization (WHO) revealed that economic losses in India due to floods and droughts stood at $4,604 million during 1990-2001. The ILR programme is expected to help increase access to safe drinking water. At present, according to WHO, 92 per cent of urban and 86 per cent of rural population have access to safe drinking water. The programme is also expected to improve the life of women in rural areas as it is women who spend much of their time collecting safe drinking water.

Well, if there are perceptible benefits, there are also areas of concern. Several experts have raised objections to the programme. A forum of such experts said that instead of starting with identification of the needs of water scarce areas and finding area-specific solutions, the project starts by looking at the map of India and then decides that rivers should be interlinked. This, the forum says, is a reckless method of 'recasting geography'. Other objections include the fact that in unsuitable, **arid** or semi-arid, agro-climatic regions, excessive water transfer and usage could cause irreversible land **degradation**. The forum is of the view that linking of rivers violates natural laws and natural dynamics. The loss of flood plains and spill basins by human interference causes flooding. River linking would aggravate this further. The forum fears that as river linking leads to alteration of the seasonal water availability pattern, it would lead to an inevitable change in the cropping pattern from excessively irrigated lands. River linking would cause major increase in methane and other gases that contribute to global warming. The chief argument of the forum is that rivers will be in danger of dying especially as they are a major source of sustenance, and centre around social, cultural and religious traditions.

The politically important consideration was, many fear, the emergence of major national and transnational industries and rapid urbanisation in many of the 'low water availability' regions. It was supposed to help the commercial farming lobby for sugarcane. Many see ILR as an attempt to mortgage the nation's future for a **miniscule** affluent population. With the Supreme Court having stepped in, one hopes the matter will be settled in such a manner that it satisfies all and helps India as a nation.

Vocabulary:

Impound—(v) to attach or to confiscate. **Fraught**—(adj) marked by distress, pregnant. **Boost**—(v) encourage, promote. **Augment**—(v) to enlarge or increase. **Arid**—(adj) lacking sufficient water or rainfall. **Degradation**—(n) changing to a lower state, a low or downcast state. **Miniscule**—(adj) very small.

□

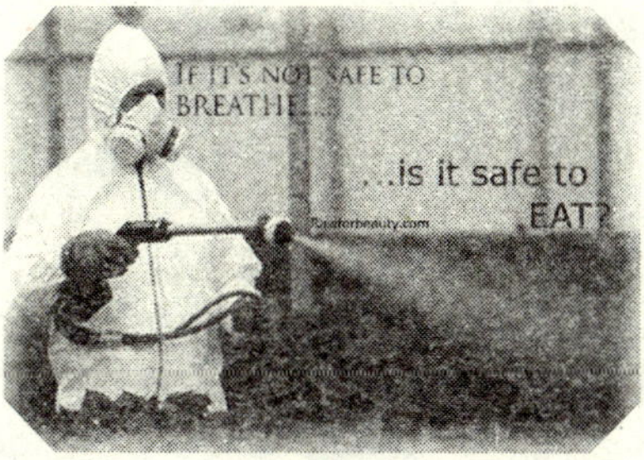

77

Pesticides in Food—The Silent Killers

Agriculture is the core of Indian economy. Reaching food to 1.21 billion people with diminishing cultivable land resource is an **arduous** task. This underlines the need for high-yielding variety of seeds, regular use of fertilisers, and judicious use of quality pesticides. It is believed that India loses about 18% of the crop yield each year due to pest attacks. The use of pesticides aims at reducing the crop loss to thus **obviate** the miseries of the farmers and augment their income. Besides, it also helps reduce soil erosion which, in turn, helps in ensuring food-safety and security for the nation.

But the farm-fresh vegetable that one picks up from the market everyday may in fact be highly deceptive and they may be quite toxic. Vegetables, fruits, staple cereals and pulses, meat, milk, eggs and poultry, drinking water and processed foods/ beverages in India, according to the experts, are contaminated with poisonous residues to various degrees. Studies have revealed that pesticide exposure is correlated with serious health risks, including cancers, endocrine disruption causing reproductive health disorders, organ damage, and immune system **impairment**. There are problems with the regulatory system that is related to chemical pesticides in the country.

According to a report, Surveillance of Food Calamities in India, 1993, found a high proportion of samples of milk products—bovine, human and others—had residues of HCH and DDT, above tolerance limits. Likewise, pesticide content was found to be higher than norms in all popular cola brands. Toxics like phosphoric acid and **ethyl glycol** were added in these brands for the Apex Court of the land had to serve notice on the cola companies. Pesticides have also been traced in bottled waters.

The Indian pesticide industry is the second largest producer of pesticides in Asia after China and globally it ranks twelfth. In terms of value, the size of the industry was estimated at ₹ 180 billion for 2010 and its export was worth ₹ 100 billion. The industry has grown at a Compounded Annual Growth Rate (CAGR) of 37.59%. According to a report, the world consumed 2.6 billion kg of pesticides with herbicides constituting the biggest part during the period. Currently, there are more than 1,055 active ingredients registered as pesticides in the United States, and they produce over 20,000 pesticide products that are being marketed.

There are no universally accepted standards. Most countries have imposed regulatory limits in the form of standards that are enforceable and guidelines that are desirable for different pesticides. The maximum contaminant's levels (MCLs) in the US take into account taste and odour, treatment feasibility, cost of treatment, and analytical detection. In India, as per the requirements of the Food Adulteration Act, pesticide residues ought to be 'below the detectable level'.

Misuse, abuse and overuse of pesticides are the root cause of the problem. Risks are mostly associated with chemicals irrespective of whether they are industrial chemicals, pesticides, household products or even stray chemicals found in the environment; and they, more often than not, raise environmental concerns and issues. Rice is the highest pesticide consuming crop in India followed by cotton. Andhra Pradesh is the highest pesticide consuming state followed by Maharashtra and Punjab. According to the Chairman of Punjab Farmers' Commission, Dr. Kalkat, the **catastrophic** dimensions of pollutants has wreaked havoc on the natural resources of Punjab, its rivers and soil health. Over 98% of spread insecticides and 95% of **herbicides** reach a destination other than their target species including air, water and soil. Sprays and vapour during application usually drift away and cause severe damage to the standing crops, livestock, waterways and the general environment. Widespread spraying of Endosulfan on cashew plantations in north Kerala has devastated many lives, causing extreme physical deformities.

Pesticides are one of the prime causes of groundwater pollution because of what is known as '**leeching**'. Some of the pesticides are persistent organic pollutants and contribute to soil contamination. Excessive use of pesticides also reduces biodiversity, reduces nitrogen fixation, contributes to **pollinator** decline, destroys habitats of birds, wildlife and fish, and threatens endangered species. Also, targeted pests develop immunity forcing development of a new and stronger pesticide. This keeps recurring. The handlers of these pesticides also develop risks depending on dose, toxicity, duration of exposure and sensitivity to it.

According to WHO and UNEP estimate, every year three million people engaged in agriculture in the developing countries experience severe poisoning from pesticides. Of these nearly 18,000 die. Yet another estimate shows that as many as 25 million people suffer mild pesticide poisoning every year. Indian diet contains vegetables as important component in food. Majority of Indians are vegetarian and consumption of vegetables is approximately 135 gm per day. It is, therefore, important to know about the pesticide residue in vegetables. Pesticides can create serious health problems like neurotoxicity, immunological effects, reproduction effects, developmental effects, carcinogenicity, etc. These factors are taken into account before registration of the pesticides. The problem, however, depends on the quantum of toxicity in the pesticides. It also depends on the way they enter the human body: by inhalation, ingestion or absorption through skin and on the frequency of exposure to them. There are thirty different **endocrine** disrupting pesticides that are found in fruits and vegetables. They are tomato, cucumber, cabbage, cauliflower, brinjal, gourd and apples, guava, mango and pineapple. These contain the highest dose of **endocrine** disrupting pesticide residues.

What should then be the way out? Doctors say 'eat organic'. Organic product is generally free of synthetic pesticides. Food items are grown under a very strict regime of rules. Harmful chemicals are not used and therefore it is strongly recommended that one should eat organic to the maximum extent possible. If it is not possible to eat organic, then one should at least set one's priorities right. One should avoid eating non-organic products which often contain pesticide residues such as lettuce, tomato, cucumber and apple. Children and pregnant women must avoid these. Also, children should be discouraged to put unpeeled citrus fruits like orange into their mouth as pesticide residues are mostly concentrated in the skin of the products. Washing of agri-products before consumption is strongly recommended and it would be a great idea to grow organic products to keep the silent killers at bay.

Vocabulary

Arduous—(adj) taxing to the utmost, testing powers of endurance. **Obviate**—(v) to do away with, to avoid. **Impairment**—(n) a system of reduced quality or strength. **Ethyl**—(n) the univalent hydrocarbon radical C2H5 derived from ethane by the removal of one hydrogen atom. **Glycol**—(n) a sweet but poisonous syrupy liquid used as an antifreeze and solvent, dihydric alcohol. **Catastrophic**—(adj) extremely harmful, ruinous. **Herbicide**—(n) weed killer, a chemical agent that destroys plants or inhibits their growth. **Leeching**—(v) drawing blood. **Pollinator**—(n) an insect that carries pollen from one flower to another.

□

78

Trends in Higher Education

The saplings of modern education in India were planted by the British in 1857. It was initiated with the setting up of four universities in what were then Madras, Calcutta, Bombay and Lahore (now part of Pakistan). These together with other universities that came up in post-independent India will unfailingly take the credit for the fact that when the winds of liberalisation and globalisation blew across the world in the eighties and nineties, India was able to reap benefits of modern education. There is no denying the fact that European ideas of 19th century had shaped the higher education in India. In the last two to three decades, higher education has witnessed tremendous and **bewildering** changes. The future promises to bring about more rapid and momentous changes.

Pure science and liberal arts were certainly the most prestigious and sought-after subjects in the past. Market forces have dealt a severe blow to this. In terms of attracting funding and student preferences, these have slid down to the bottom of the heap. Market forces and potential money-making capacity appears to have become the most important factor in determining student choice. Students today seek job-oriented courses. The government too has responded favourably to this alarming decline of interest in arts and pure literature by setting up a chain of institutes of science education and research. In every part of the world, the new mantra is STEM subjects. They are science, technology, engineering and mathematics.

There was a time when a large section of students chose one of a set of core courses in arts and science and a select few opted for professional courses like engineering, medicine, law and commerce. The range that they now have is mind-boggling. One could now opt for just anything under the sun from such **arcane** areas as nuclear physics to catering or fashion design. The old courses were generalist in nature and component. But the present trend is to opt for more specialised subjects from very early stage. A first year student today can well opt for **genetic** engineering.

From a mere 20 universities and 500 colleges in 1947, India has moved to almost 600 universities and over 20,000 colleges. This is quite impressive by any standard. India is the third highest in the world in student enrolment just behind the US and China. And yet, India has not been able to meet the ever-growing demand of the admission seekers. If things on this front have shown some improvement, it is largely because of the private universities and almost the similar number of deemed universities that have come up. But even these impressive gains cannot **obfuscate** the grim reality of the falling quality and the lurking fear that the system will not able to cope with the challenges the future holds.

There is no gainsaying the fact that academic standards have registered a perceptible fall. The malaise as engulfed the entire country barring a few elite institutions in the national capital and some other places. They are too few for anyone's comfort. The pressure of numbers, the shortage of quality teachers, the crass commercialization of education and the disastrous impact of linguistic and regional **chauvinism** are eating into the system of education. Institutions that are responsible for evaluating and maintaining standard often fail to do so because they can use only quantitative factors while doing so and in the process quality goes unfiltered. There is so much hue and cry over quality that some of the institutions are being forced to shut down, especially some of the institutions that imparted education on engineering and management. Mushroom growth of some of such institutions has dealt a death blow to the quality of higher education in India. A large number of students are running away to foreign countries for pursuing higher studies.

In the process, some of them are getting duped as well.

A few of the changes that are likely to sweep aside the present system of education are attributable to technological changes. Some foreign institutions in the US have begun to offer free online courses, often handled by celebrity professionals. Some of such institutions have grown so confident that they are promoting net and mobile-enabled technology to shape the future of higher education. A Stanford professor went to the extent of stating that by 2030 there will only be 10 universities left in the world. Even if this sounds like **bravado**, we in India will do well to pay attention to some of the assumptions supporting this line of thinking. Quite a few companies in India are already offering institution, specific mobile apps; the class-room of the future may be in our pocket. For instance, Indian Railways have enlisted the support of IIT Kharagpur for providing technological knowhow to achieve a speed of 200 kmph. Centre for Environment Education is established as a Centre of Excellence supported by the Ministry of Environment and Forests, Government of India.

Demographic pressure, together with the free play of market forces in a globalised and increasingly technology-driven world, will determine the shape and size of the university of the future. It is difficult to say if this change will be able to do away with the need of 'deep learning' that can take place only through mental process and not through screen-based inputs which the changed technology envisages. But there is a growing realisation that increased student mobility, internationalisation, use of emerging technologies like 'augmented reality', 'game-based learning', 'learning analytics', and such other futuristic features will transform higher education beyond recognition shortly, and those who fail to **adapt** to this change may be left high and dry. In this new emerging world there may be little or no inclination and time for disinterested pursuit of knowledge that was once the prime mover in the **realm** of higher education. These then are the trends that are shaping the higher education the world over, India not being an exception. While these trends may disturb some, they present as only hope for those who wish to fly on the wings of liberalisation and globalisation.

But there is also a new phenomenon called 'global education'. According to Dr. Mamdouh Shoukri, the President and Vice Chancellor of New York University, it is necessary for the next generation leaders to become part of the multicultural student community studying liberal arts and professional studies, science and law. There are universities that have introduced engineer courses in which students are taught humanities. They contend that in order to be innovative, engineers will have to have appreciation of knowledge beyond their technical forte, for an engineer with business acumen can be a better entrepreneur. A great supporter of global education, Dr. Shoukri believes Internet would not work. This is in complete contrast to what many believe that Internet was going to squeeze the number of universities in the world. He says, "no matter what the advanced technology does for us it cannot compensate for the human touch". That touch would come from an international university, he would have us believe. He goes on to encourage young students to do their master's degrees overseas because "the full experience, the settings, interacting with people from across the globe, helps you understand different cultures". So, even if trends in higher education are palpable, there is no last word yet as the higher education continues to be in a state of **fluidity**.

Vocabulary:

Bewildering—(v) baffling, confusing. **Genetic**—(adj) familial, hereditary, transmissible. **Obfuscate**—(v) to make obscure or unclear. **Chauvinism**—(n) fanatical patriotism. **Demographic**—(adj) of or relating to demography, statistic. **Adapt**—(v) accommodate, adjust or conform. **Realm**—(n) a domain in which something is dominant. **Fluidity**—(n) the property of flowing easily.

□

79

Digital Evidence and Cyber Crime

The **digital** world has made life easy but, at the same time, it has attracted many crooked minds who disrupt the life of others. Even without Dr. P. Vinod Bhattathiripad, the Cyber Forensic Consultant, having to say this, we would have known this because so rampantly some of these crooked minds are disrupting the life of others. This is cyber crime. But it does not mean that it is only for cyber crime that digital evidence is reliable. Whether the case is digital related or not, modern investigators across the world often look for digital evidence. For example, a young man was convicted for the murder of his mother on the basis of digital evidence, though the crime was cyber-unrelated. A deleted story was **retrieved** from his computer that showed the same circumstances in which he had killed his mother.

This is precisely because cyber space and digital technology form an integral part of our life today. Criminals often use digital technology while committing crimes. Evidences that help resolve such crimes are often found in digital equipment. All digital equipments—well, almost—have an in-built capacity to automatically create and store details when they are used or abused. Even in the case of a mobile phone, besides the details of calls and messages, it also digitally records the movement of the person carrying the mobile. This digital evidence not only helps establish a crime but also confirms the involvement of the criminal in the crime. Most investigators these days depend on the suspects' mobile phone details. Mobile phone's unique codes such as the mobile phone number, IMEI, IMEISV, and the IMSI help trace back calls and messages and lead to the suspect. All these codes are indexes to the call and message details, with date and time stamps stored in the data bases kept in the computer server of the mobile service provider.

It is important to fully understand what constitutes digital evidence and also to **encounter** a few essential questions regarding the implications of the use of digital instruments and their outcomes because they have become vital for an average person in today's working world. An example will best illustrate the whole thing. Gobind, a government employee having no family of his own, receives an unsolicited SMS text message from Kanta, professedly a single female looking for a companion. They keep exchanging messages and soon it **blossoms** into friendship. They choose to meet in a neutral city. Gobind checks himself into a hotel at the chosen centre at the agreed time and date. He is received by two men who charge him for having murdered their sister Kanta and blackmail him into coughing up a large sum of money. They have enough evidence against him as he and Kanta had exchanged quite a few text messages. Blackmailing stories like this are **rampant** today in every part of the world. This goes to show the power of mobile phones to leave digital footprints of their uses and abuses.

Not just mobile phone but any digital equipment is open to widespread abuse by criminals in a variety of ways and most of these abuses give rise to criminal charges. Digital evidence is the **datum** or information of **probative** value stored or transmitted in digital form. Experts define digital evidence as a string of **binary** data stored in the digital equipment. They call it 'bitstring' and this can serve as evidence in a certain context.

Digital evidence lies in the memory of the digital equipment or of the connecting computer server. No matter in which form it lies or is stored, it is useful for litigation purpose only if it is properly preserved till the completion of the court cases. This is not easy as it is often very volatile. If a digital memory device is exposed to excessive sunlight, water, or heat, it could lead to loss or destruction of the precious information or datum stored in it. Its poor handling during transmitting, archiving, searching, and accessing too could lead to loss of vital information. Therefore, it is important to take utmost care in preserving digital evidence to counteract the inherently **fragile** nature of digital devices causing a shadow of doubt on the integrity and fidelity (hi-fi) of digital evidence stored in such digital devices.

It is precisely because of the fragile nature of digital evidence that courts have suggested that evidences should possess the requisite scientific validity. The International High Tech Crime Conference in 1999 laid down a few guidelines to achieve and preserve judicial admissibility of digital evidence. Digital evidence has also been incorporated in the traditional acts of the Indian judiciary. The Indian Penal Code, The Indian Evidence Act, 1872, The Bankers' Books Evidence Act, 1891 and The Reserve Bank of India Act, 1934 have all been suitably amended in 2000 to legally recognize digital evidence. This also forms the basis for booking criminals under various sections of Indian IT Act, 2000. For sending an offensive message, a person can be imprisoned up to three years or fined up to ₹ 5 lakhs or both under Section 66A of the Act. Sections 66B (theft of digital equipments), 66C (identity theft), 66D (impersonation), 66E (voyeurism), 66F (cyber terrorism), 67A (sexually explicit content) 67B (child pornography), and 67C (concealment of criminals) are all aimed at tackling cyber crime variously.

Digital evidence plays a crucial role in modern crime investigation. It often helps to unequivocally establish not just the abuses of digital equipment but also various other traditional crimes. But in order that it is reliable, it must be collected scientifically and should be based on observed, provable/ disprovable empirical data. Cyber forensic investigators unearth and preserve data with high degree of integrity and precision by using scientific methods which could help legal professionals in establishing crimes. The digital evidence is already recognised and it is being extensively used by the investigating agencies and the judiciary has been making judicial pronouncements on the basis of the same with greater degree of infallibility.

Vocabulary

Digital—(adj) displaying numbers rather than scale positions. **Retrieve**—(v) get or get back, recover the use of. **Encounter**—(v) to come upon as if by accident. **Blossom**—(n) the period of greatest prosperity or productivity. (v) produce or yield flowers, develop or come to a promising stage. **Rampant**—(adj) unrestrained and violent. **Datum**—(n) an item of factual information derived from measurement or research (its plural form is 'data'). **Probative**—(adj) tending to prove a particular proposition. **Binary**—(adj) of or pertaining to a number system which has 2 as its base. **Fragile**—(adj) easily broken, damaged or destroyed.

□

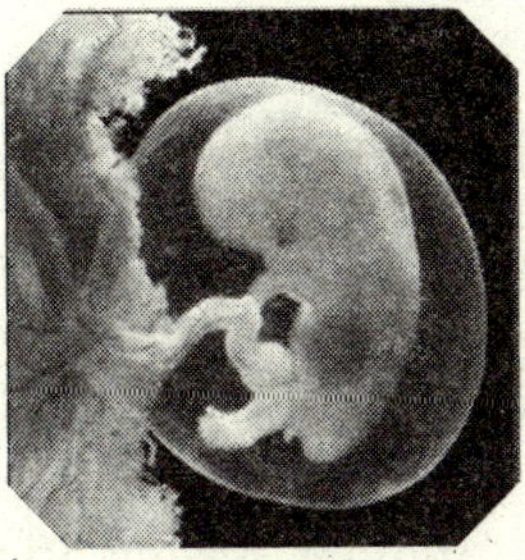

80

Human Reproduction

Human sexuality does not **emanate** from instinct or stereotypical conducts. It happens with animals. In human, it is influenced by superior mental activity as also by social, cultural, educational and normative characteristics of the places where the subjects grew up and their personalities developed. Sex, as we all know, is a phenomenon of life and it sustains life forms on the earth. The sexual population or the life cycle of every living being spreads the advantageous traits of humans in such a way that the generation next is more competent to meet the challenges of survival, whatever the clime and condition. This is so because sexual reproduction involves combining of specialised cells called **gametes** to form offspring that inherit genetic traits of both parents with each cell having half the **chromosomes** of the father and half of the mother. Human sexuality has many aspects some of which involve building up of personal identity in a social evolution of individuals in a society. Experts say "socio-cultural aspect casts human sexuality as a social norm under moral, ethical, philosophical and religious or spiritual framework. Medically, it deals with the physiological or even psychological aspects. Sexuality is also now viewed in the cultural, political, and legal context in a society".

Sexuality, at least in India, is seen within the framework of the institution of marriage that also involves home. Home is an environment that provides nourishment for the growth of young ones, guaranteeing mutual care and safety. Consequently, it instils a moral obligation and responsibility for the sexual behaviour of the partners.

Reproduction cycle begins with the merging of female gamete with the male gamete in a process that is called 'fertilisation' or 'conception'. This occurs through the acts of sexual intercourse, which ultimately leads to pregnancy. The embryonic development begins after pregnancy. Human pregnancy averages 266 days or 40 weeks from the start of the last menstrual period.

Fertilisation happens in the first week and it is a period when more than 100 cells are created. Implantation happens after 6-9 days from fertilisation. Three basic layers of embryo develop during the second week. Backbones begin to happen during the third week. The first sign of pregnancy is noticed in this week as the pregnant woman would not have period hereon. Formation of heart, blood vessels and umbilical cord happen during this week. Brain develops in the fifth week. Eyes and ears start to form in the sixth week and in the seventh week, all major organs of a human body begin to take final shape. By the twelfth week, the foetus is fully formed and acquires mobility. Sex organ is also formed during this period. By twentieth week, hair begins to grow as also eyebrows, eyelashes and eyelids. It is during this period that finger-prints develop and so are fingernails and toenails. The first movement of the baby is felt in 16 to 20 weeks. Eyelids open in the twenty-fourth week. This is also the legal limit for abortion. By twenty-sixth week, the chances of survival are almost settled. By twenty-eighth week, the baby begins to move vigorously and usually responds to touch and loud noises and swallows **amniotic** fluid and urinates too. By the thirtieth week, the baby is seen lying head down, ready to be ejected out, to be born. Its size is 240 mm from head to foot. The baby is delivered in the fortieth week or in the ninth month.

The symptoms of pregnancy include nausea and vomiting, excessive tiredness and fatigue. There is a craving for certain foods that are not normally regarded as favourite. There is also frequent urination, especially during night. Pregnancy tests detect hormones that are generated in this process. Clinical blood